DUST
TO
DUST

DUST

TO

DUST

A MEMOIR

23 April 2012

For Jake,

 We are stars and oceans and earth. May
my journey lead you to your own.
    Live forever,

BENJAMIN BUSCH

ecco

An Imprint of HarperCollinsPublishers

Small portions of this book appeared in very different form in *Harper's Magazine* and the *Michigan Quarterly Review,* the editors of which are gratefully acknowledged.

Grateful acknowledgment is also made to the following for permission to reprint copyrighted material:

W.W. Norton & Company, Inc., for excerpts from *Rescue Missions* by Frederick Busch, copyright © 2006 by Frederick Busch. Reprinted by permission of W.W. Norton & Company.

New Directions Publishing Corporation, for an excerpt from *Collected Poems* by Stevie Smith, copyright © 1957 by Stevie Smith. Reprinted by permission of the New Directions Publishing Corporation.

Harper's Magazine, for an excerpt from "Don't Watch the News," copyright © 2005 by Frederick Busch. Reprinted by permission of *Harper's Magazine*.

HarperCollins books may be purchased for educational, business, or sales promotional use. For information please write: Special Markets Department, HarperCollins Publishers, 10 East 53rd Street, New York, NY 10022.

FIRST EDITION

Designed by Suet Yee Chong

Library of Congress Cataloging-in-Publication Data has been applied for.

ISBN 978-0-06-201484-9

12 13 14 15 16   OV/RRD   10 9 8 7 6 5 4 3 2

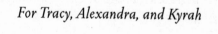

For Tracy, Alexandra, and Kyrah

Stories are . . . in a sense, about ending and about endings, and of course they are also the heartfelt prayer, the valiant promise, that what we have loved might live forever.

—FREDERICK BUSCH, "DEATHS"

CONTENTS

PROLOGUE   1

CHAPTER 1   ARMS   5

CHAPTER 2   WATER   37

CHAPTER 3   METAL   77

CHAPTER 4   SOIL   109

CHAPTER 5   BONE   143

CHAPTER 6   WOOD   173

CHAPTER 7   STONE   203

CHAPTER 8   BLOOD   231

CHAPTER 9   ASH   263

EPILOGUE   295

ACKNOWLEDGMENTS   307

PROLOGUE

I knew very early that I was a solitary being. I longed for the elemental. As a child I was drawn into the wilderness, the reckless water of oceans, rivers, and rain, the snow and ice floes, the mountains of rock, stones, and sand, the forests, and the ruins left vacant by human decline, neglect, and tragedy. The places we had given up or could not take were what attracted me. I wandered the woods and brooks with unsubstantiated confidence, and I declared myself daring with unseasoned conviction.

It was beyond me to realize that I borrowed much of that invulnerability from the protection of my parents. They worried and were vigilant. Though they did not follow me on my adventures between breakfast and dinner, they assembled a story of where I had been when I returned hungry. They encouraged my delusions because childhood is the time for magical possibilities. I did not consider the possibility of rejection or betrayal. My ambitions imagined no losses. What could be lost?

I believed, once, that I could predetermine my journey. I wanted to create something that could not be destroyed, and to do that I had to disbelieve the evidence of destruction. I had to look at the bone and ash around me as the yield of errors, not of dreams. But I grew up and found damage, and death, and the friction of incalculable consequences. I had mapped a path through the wild with wishful premonition in my youth, but I had come to find my way by mishap and deviation. War was wilderness, and I went there, too.

The soldier arrives home to discover that the war he has returned from has already been forgotten, and because he has survived as a witness to it, neither he nor his country are innocent. Both try to dream again, the soldier by remembering himself before the war, and the country by forgetting the soldier it sent away. The legionnaire returns to find Rome in ruins, its roads still straight, leading out the way he had once marched. It is, perhaps, better that his home is deserted. It can never be what it was before, and the people who can forgive us cannot know what we have done. But the arch at the entrance to Rome still stands, its carved letters clear in the marble. It recounts only victory. The paved roads are also there, leading to conquered lands where free people dig for the buried empire, its value being in that it is now lost.

My father, a novelist, experienced the world through language. It was an intellectual relationship to the physical universe. My mother was a librarian and understood. He could write with authenticity about experiences he hadn't had, could breathe life into people he hadn't been. He found a way to live outside of books—but not without some degree of astonishment that the things described in them often actually existed. I was different. I gained comprehension of my environment by throwing myself against it. Digging, cutting, climbing, stacking. What my father built with words, I built with pieces of the earth, stones, and wood. He wrote most about loss and failure because he feared mistakes and departures so much. Tragedy was inevitable to him, whereas I believed that the inevitable could be fought. I thought that with enough defiance, mortality could be made at least improbable.

Trilobites were unconcerned with legacy, yet we find them fossilized, their stone portraits preserved in the rock. These remains are merely impressions, their tissue and shell replaced with gray minerals, death masks rising back to the surface. I have felt the sun and wind on my face, and though I remember the sensations imperfectly, there is an imprint I carry.

Childhood is still present in me. I can hear my own echoes now, elliptical, my voice changed but not the wonder I had. In seeking to disinter my childhood, I have found it unburied.

CHAPTER 1

ARMS

I WAS NOT ALLOWED TO HAVE A GUN. MY PARENTS were fresh from Vietnam War protests, and they had no intention of raising a soldier. My mother was against the idea of toy weapons, and my father quietly supported the embargo. He had been a boy once, though, and was a war baby. His father, Benjamin Busch, had been a sergeant in the Tenth Mountain Division, fighting German troops in the Italian Alps. My mother's father, Allan Burroughs, had been a Marine in the Guadalcanal campaign against the Japanese. He called me "Little Son of a Gun," but I continued to have no guns at all.

I spent much of my childhood constructing forts in our backyard and gathering local boys for epic battles. Each spring the cornfield nearby was plowed and flat river stones rose in the rows for me to harvest. I spent the cool mornings walking the furrows and hauling pieces of lost sea ledges and mountains back to my fort site. The afternoons I spent laying them in place. I built thick stone walls and dug in, preparing for siege. No contingencies were made for escape or surrender. I played an officer wielding a maple-stick sword and falling early under withering fire. As I had no sidearm or rifle, I could not reasonably hope to survive a gunfight, and I honored those odds. No one ever came within stabbing distance, and I could never reach the enemy's line. Not realistically. Everyone else had something with a trigger. But casualties in war games came without consequence. There was no death in dying.

My father watched through the kitchen window, but I could never tell his mood as an observer of my recurring death. It was a small window and he was far away. One day in 1974, after I fashioned myself a rifle out of a length of old pipe, wire, and a board, my father turned to my mother and said, "Well, fair's fair," and for Christmas that year he bought me a toy M1 Garand, the same kind of rifle carried by my grandfathers in the war. It had a solid wooden stock, a metal barrel, and a wooden bullet painted gold and glued to the bolt inside. It could not fire, of course, but it was perpetually loaded. I went out into the vocal battle of children at war and sometimes, with my rifle, didn't die.

The fort grew from a simple stone barricade to a two-story wooden eyesore cloaked with bedsheets and ringed by a trench. Boards were hard to come by, so the structure evolved unevenly with what I could find discarded from projects around town. There wasn't enough wood to sheath the walls, so I used the old sheets my mother had draped over tomato plants in the garden during frosts. The rusting nails that held the cloth bled long orange stains from rains, and the fort always smelled damp. It became my focus of effort, and I continued to patch and expand the building for years, manning it every day. It had in it more nails than any house in town, and it would never be finished. My grandparents each visited once a year, and I would eagerly invite my grandfathers to inspect the fort. I knew they had both been in a war and would have good advice. My father's father would stand at a distance smiling at the complexity of the ideas at work, but I could tell he was disappointed by my craftsmanship. I explained the temporary use of the cloth as an excuse for what was still poor construction without it. My mother's father saw it differently. He would stroll out to the trench beside me with a cigarette and a glass of bourbon, and we would sit there for a few minutes. I crouched down in my trench and he sat on the edge with his feet inside, the ditch only as deep as his knees.

"Son of a gun," he'd say. "You stay low and let 'em get close."

He would sit and drink as smoke curled around his head. I thought, with him there, that I had done well.

A FEW YEARS LATER my father, a writer and professor of literature, took about a dozen students to London as a study group. My mother, my brother, and I went with him to live in a flat on the edge of Hampstead Heath. Britain had not yet fully recovered from World War II. There were sections of London that had not been rebuilt since the German aerial bombardment, and construction crews would still occasionally pull unexploded ordnance from the ground. Thirty-eight years had somehow not been long for the generation that had survived the random falling of bombs. It seemed impossible to find a British family that had not lost a member in The War. While my mother stood in line at a pastry shop with my brother and me, an old woman noted that my mother had two sons. She looked at my mother with a kind of sweet admiration and said, "How wonderful. One for your country and one for you." My mother was haunted by that immeasurable expectation of sacrifice, and years later she would repeat the old woman's words to me as if they had been a curse.

We took day trips to castles. It established stone as the material required for legacy, and I began to draw detailed pictures of battlements. I penciled every individual stone. They were designs for my own castle, a structure I would construct later, when I was old enough. I remember the staircase built inside the walls of Rochester Castle, and how the solid blocks of stone were worn into deep, smooth dips in their centers. I asked my father how feet could do that much damage to rock, and he explained that knights wore metal shoes. That made sense. I wanted metal shoes. I had seen some in the Tower of London, which was full of metal armor and handheld weapons, and the idea of knighthood weighed heavily on me. War became smaller, closer, and, in the artful stone of castles and sculptured steel of armor, beautiful. The savagery of medieval battle had left nothing behind it but alluring artifacts and mystique.

I attended school there and my class spent the year studying Roman Britain. The teachers organized a play about Queen Boadicea, an early Celtic leader of the Iceni tribe who fought heroically against Roman control in Britain. We could either be legionnaries or Celts. I wanted to be in the legion, but I was cast as one of Boadicea's warriors. We were referred to as barbarians, not Celts, taking on the name given to unruly peoples north of Rome, and we were considered a horde instead of an army. It seemed yet another step down. We were sent home with a list of things to make and instructions on how to dress for the play.

I showed the requirements to my father, who looked at them as if he couldn't read and handed them to my mother. Shield, sword, belt, dark cloak. To make a shield she gave me a large piece of cardboard from a grocery box, and we covered up the tomatoes printed on it with glue and brown butcher's paper. I said a warrior, barbarian or not, would never emblazon his shield with vegetables. I drew undersized dragons on it, which looked like smudges at a distance, and lightning stabbing out from the center, actually a common Roman shield design rather than Celtic. My mother had found some black material, which she wrapped over one shoulder and fastened around my waist on the opposite side with a safety pin. I wore brown shorts, no shirt, and one of my father's belts wrapped almost twice around my hips. Last was my sword. My mother was at a loss for how to make a sword. We finally just cut up strips of the cardboard, glued them together, and then wrapped them in black plastic from a garbage bag. It looked terrible. I was very disappointed and my father was happy to be free of blame for the errors I found in wardrobe and armaments. My costume might have done well in America, where expectations were low, but when I arrived at school I was immediately ashamed.

Some of the children came in elaborate armor that looked like accurate replicas of Roman uniforms. Their parents had spent weeks working on them, and the children were afraid to move much for fear of tearing something that had been carefully glued. The barbarians ranged in their interpretation, and we looked somewhat like a horde. The teachers had built an impressive wooden chariot as well as two matching horse costumes with papier-mâché heads and brown-cloth bodies each worn over two men. Half-blind, they pulled the chariot around the room with the girl who played the queen standing in it, and we followed. We rehearsed for days.

My part consisted of nothing more than following Boadicea's chariot into the room chanting angry nonsense, waving my embarrassing sword, lining up against the Romans, and then charging to my dramatic death. On the day of the performance for a hundred parents, the staff, and several hundred students, we dressed in our classroom and the Romans marched into the auditorium. The legion stood shoulder to shoulder at the edge of the stage. They looked wonderfully imperial, but I was relieved not to have been chosen for Rome. I could imagine how my armor would have looked if I had been left to craft it from a tomato box.

We assembled in the hall outside while speeches were made inside. At some point we were given a signal and made our entrance. My parents said that as we came in yelling, I was the barbarian most noticeably smiling. Boadicea gave her speech about liberty, and then we were to attack the Roman ranks, failing to achieve our freedom. I rushed up the steps at a boy wearing imposing leather Roman armor, and he made an uncomfortable slash at me. This was my cue to perish. In rehearsals, I had gone through the motions, pretending slowly to pretend. But this was the performance. I threw myself backward with a scream, my feet coming off the stage, sword and shield tossed into the air, and I struck the oak floor on my back with a smack that sounded loud even to me. I was told afterward that half of the parents stood up and the play went silent with a gasp. I lay unmoving, arms extended, eyes closed, laboring to control my breath. A teacher hurried to my side and stooped, trying very hard not to let her voice sound hysterical.

"Can you hear me, dear?" she asked. She had her hand on my chest. It was cold.

"Yes," I hissed, trying not to move my lips.

"Are you hurt, sweetie? Can you move?"

"I've been killed," I whispered, keeping my eyes closed.

The teacher withdrew, I heard my mother's voice in consultation with her, and the play went on, more boys falling carefully on the floor at the foot of the stage to the constrained sword strokes of boys dressed too well for fighting. Queen Boadicea, seeing all of her men killed, made another speech, drank poison, slumped in her chariot, and was pulled out of the room by the teachers dressed as horses. I had pretended at war again and had, again, been killed in front of my parents. It was my first memorable public performance and a blend of the two professions I would go on to pursue most seriously.

→ ←

I BROUGHT THE PROFESSION at arms home to Poolville, the village in Upstate New York where we lived. It had once been a prospering mill town on the Sangerfield River, with taverns, hotels, and a newspaper, but it had declined into a quiet hamlet of fifty homes. Its industrial history had been reduced to a few stone ruins along the water, collapsed remains of gristmills, woolen mills, and sawmills. Beside the railroad tracks were the foundations of the train station and creamery. The town was still surrounded by working dairy farms, and the field behind our house was used for crops. The farmer had planted corn the year we returned from England, and when it had grown even with my head, I treated it as ranks in a host. I took a steel lid from our galvanized garbage pail, its small central handle ideal to wrap my entire hand into, and dashed between the lines of stalks with a long straight sapling that was sharpened at one end. Hacking at the crop was forbidden, so I just ran through the claustrophobia of green leaves, fast enough to feel like I was cutting my way into their mass, surrounded, my shield pushing the arced leaves aside and my spear extended. I roared with what voice I had then and fought my way an eighth of a mile to the river. There I could look back, breathless, at the undisturbed field. My charging through it had left no gash that I had imagined rending in the ranks. The water was still a boundary, and I stood at its edge, slicing at its surface with my spear. Nothing to do but turn and walk back the way I had come, my shield glossy with dew. I passed through

again without making an impression, and my path closed in behind me.

It bothered me that I had to stop at the river's edge. I traced
the river all summer, using bridges to get to the other shore. The
far side was a wild tangle of vines and underbrush and took hours
to walk a mile through, but it left me alone on the riverbank, and
that made it mine. The river had been named, of course, but I
considered that to be its name in general, not the name here. This
part was unknown, like Antarctica, which had been named and
left almost entirely untraveled. One day that year, as the corn grew
to almost twice my height, I was able to advance quickly upriver
because I had decided to cross in the water. It was the day I had
risked what it could mean to be utterly wrong, slipping on the
slick rocks, the water depth difficult to judge by eye, the power of
the current inestimable. I had been given swimming lessons, and
in the blind chlorine burn of instruction I had learned little more
than to be worried about deep water. But this was a river, where,
even distorted, the bottom appeared more real than the abyssal
blue floor of the pool.

I stepped in with my spear. It was colder than I had expected
it to be in late summer, the water from rain finding its way out of
the hills. I arrived on the other shore, my jeans wet to the waist
and suddenly bound tight to my legs, my socks spongy and shoes
loose. The pebbles on the bank slid as I stepped on them, and my
soaked shoes bled water onto the dry stones. I did not like being
wet, but once I was soaked with my clothes on, I lost the hesitation
to be wet that way again. I could cross rivers. It changed my view

of boundaries instantly, and the absolutism of my parents' warnings about water. I had challenged the laws of men and nature, and
I was unharmed.

I slipped back through the field, leaned my spear against the
barn beside the asparagus patch, returned the lid to the garbage
pail, and went into the house. My pants had not dried, and my
sneakers squeaked and foamed bubbles through their ventilation
holes from my soaked socks.

My father was at the kitchen table reading. He was already
balding in the middle of his head, and he allowed an explosion of
beard to conceal his neck. He was overweight, which made him
self-conscious, and he always looked swollen in his khaki pants
and penny loafers. He took on the look of a Jewish intellectual gone
native in the frontier, haunted with secret knowledge of the wilderness. He had, in fact, been made afraid of nature. His Brooklyn
childhood had been filled with an overbearing mother who had
been an imperious naturalist and, by her constant examination of
plants and warnings about them, she had made exploration of the
outdoors into resentful labor. He couldn't remember the names of
the plants or birds that were repeated to him, and he avoided the
garden, watered no houseplants, and grew nothing but stories of
nature hunting us down. He had his hackles permanently up, and
protected my mother, brother, and me ferociously. We called him
"the Bear" and he enjoyed the title. Nobody fucks with a bear and,
like most bears, he took everything seriously.

My mother was the opposite in everything but our defense.
She was happy to walk in the woods and dig in her garden. My fa-

ther would watch her from the back porch amazed that she could make life from dirt, that earth was a comfort to her, and that she had an understanding with nature. They were madly in love. He would head up to his workroom and she to her garden and they would meet in the kitchen—always the kitchen. We could not get anywhere in the house without going through the kitchen, and one of my parents was sure to be in it.

I thought he might not notice me as I sloshed past.

"So," he said. "Are we safe from the river now?"

"River?" I tried to ask with surprise.

"I would think it difficult to get that wet without one," he added. "Well, there are lakes, too, I suppose."

No lies came to me.

"You'll pass swimming lessons before you go wading again," he said.

I went to my room to wonder, for the rest of my life, how he knew.

WE HAD NOT HAD A MEDIEVAL AGE in America. It was explained to me that with the invention of the rifle, swords had become merely decorative. I did not like to hear it, and it vexed my obsession with true chivalry. But rifles returned, slowly turning me toward the illusory romance of our Civil War. I bought by mail a bullet from a southern battlefield. There was no damage to it from impact. It was heavy, a .58-caliber minié ball, almost white, caked with oxidized lead, fired into soft dirt or dropped by the Union. That Christmas my parents gave me a bullet mold. It would have been from around the same time as my minié ball but used for a small hunting rifle. It was a simple brass clamp that closed two empty halves of a bullet together, leaving a small hole in the top to pour molten metal into. You had to make one at a time, keep the lead at a boil while you waited for each bullet to cool in the mold or dipped the clamp in cold water. I had no hunting rifle, no shells with primers, no gunpowder, no lead . . . but I wanted to make bullets.

I began by aiming the drip of candles into the hole. They were white candles and there was enough delay between the drops of hot wax for them to harden in the mold in layers, each drip visible in the soft bullets. They looked like they had been cut from quartz-colored seashells. I had one gray crayon and I melted it on our woodstove in a Coke can that I had cut in half. This way I could fill the mold in one pour, and I made one solid gray bullet. It looked real.

The large box of sixty-four crayons I got that year had copper, silver, and gold colors, made with fine metallic flakes, and I immediately melted them and poured them into the mold. After those, I had no more gray or precious-metal crayons, so I began to use other colors. I produced the projectiles carefully, as if they could explode in the process of their creation. I made handfuls of them, gave some away as gifts I can't remember explaining. "Burnt orange" and "turquoise blue" bullets. "Goldenrod" ones for imaginary guns.

When the school safety patrol went on a trip to Washington,

D.C., we stopped for an afternoon at Gettysburg. I was excited to visit Devil's Den and the field where Pickett lost his division. Standing on Cemetery Ridge, I tried to picture the charge against it by more than twelve thousand men, an effort that saw so many killed it exhausted Lee's army into a retreat from which it would never recover. During our last year in Poolville, my parents had gone to a dealer and found an 1860 noncommissioned officer's sword for me. It was a magnificent Christmas gift. I knew it had cost too much, but more than that, it signified my parents' admission that I was a martial creature, and that their prolonged effort to dissuade me from my natural tendencies had failed. My father looked wonderfully pleased as I held the sword in our living room beside the glittering tree, but I could tell by the tight smile on my mother's face that the gift had survived a great deal of discussion. The sword was said to have come from the battlefield at Gettysburg, but there was no proof that it had. I examined the straight steel blood-grooved blade, which had some nicks, and the brass hilt, handle, and pommel. Even in the Civil War, this sword would have been little more than symbolic. Its scabbard had been lost, and in my mind, that left it forever drawn. My parents would not allow me to run with it, for very good reasons, but I could march, raising it and swinging at the head of invisible ranks. I was careful not to strike anything solid, preserving the damage to the blade that I believed to have been done in battle.

Poolville was my hometown. I circulated through it as if the village were pumping me around. I did the hand mowing on the lawn circuit with Mr. Macgregor, who spent so much time on his

riding mower that he began to walk as if he were still seated. I
raked leaves for everyone who did not have children still at home,
and I weeded gardens in backyards. By the end of the summer, my
hands were stained green and there was a crescent of dirt under
my nails that took a month to grow out. I stacked firewood and
threw bales onto hay wagons, packed them in the lofts of barns
as they tumbled off elevators. I walked the railroad tracks and the
river, fished, and dug in old ash dumps for artifacts from the turn
of the century. On my rounds I would stop in to see Mr. Tuttle,
one of the last of the original families to settle the village, and ask
him for another story about the dam, which lay ruined behind his
house. He was always in his immaculate yard inspecting a flower,
picking up a stick, or watching the river pass. The elders were
never more pleased than on Halloween when we would all dress
up and go to every house. We did not understand the importance
of our annual visits to them, presenting ourselves in costume, excited for their offerings. I would always dress as a combatant of
one kind or another. I went from cowboy, to knight, to soldier,
to Star Wars stormtrooper wearing a deformed papier-mâché mask
I had made. It was a village that raised children and saw them
always in motion, gathering in the town square for baseball, hide-
and-seek, war games, and snowball fights. It watched us arrive and
move away.

My parents decided to sell our house in the village and relo-
cate to the rural landscape fourteen miles away. Before we moved
from Poolville, we mowed the lawn one last time, disassembled
the rusting swing set, and hammered the sandbox apart. It sat in

the shade of a pine tree and had been ignored for a few years. It split into pulpy strands of wood, and we found that we could have broken it by hand. The boards had rotted out on the bottom, and because it had never been lined, worms had worked dirt up into the lower inches of sand. When it was built, my father had bought bags of smooth play sand, which looked bright when first poured into the box, and it drained rain immediately. It was a dark tan now, stained by leaves, mined with pinecones, and held the water that fell on it. The odd square of beach seemed to have aged away from the sea. The sand also sat lower in the box, much of it lost by years of traffic. It had continued to migrate, finding its way back down rivers, along beaches, and into dunes.

For a moment the sand held the edges of the box, the long settled corners looking carefully built, defining the walled outline of an ancient citadel destroyed and filled with desert. My father began to cut into it with a pointed shovel. He threw it far into the yard to spread it out, and it disappeared into the grass as I raked it. A shovelful sliced from a corner had in it four plastic army men buried when their position had been bombarded years earlier. As the sand thinned in flight, showering in an arc across the grass, the soldiers bounced and rolled on the surface again. They were unchanged. I wiped them off and returned them to the bag in my room with the other soldiers that had not been dead as long but had been killed many more times.

Next, the stone walls of my fort were thrown into a pile behind the garage, the trench around it filled in and raked flat, my wooden fort dismantled and driven to the town dump. It was not in any way my parents' intention to destroy this monument, but there was, for me, a certain loss of history. As we abandoned our post with the last load of furniture, a small green square of perennial ryegrass lay where, for eight years, my fort had guarded the house from the fields.

The Sangerfield merged into the Chenango River south of Poolville and continued down the valley to the larger town of Sherburne, running along the railroad tracks, swelling with tributaries until it became the Susquehanna and emptied into the Chesapeake Bay hundreds of miles away. We moved in the direction of the water, finding a house in the shale hills above Sherburne in country large enough that we could not see any neighbors. It was like a colonial outpost, and I set to work as if it were. I cut several miles of pathways through brush and swamps, constructing small shelters on the high ground and in the sapling tree lines along the way. My new fortress was built beside a stream next to an old spill of discarded fieldstones that served as my quarry. Thirteen years old and isolated in the countryside, I began a long period of mostly solitary play. I went down the hill to Sherburne for school, sports, and work, but it was not my hometown and I remained emotionally distant from it. Instead I bonded immediately with our land.

My parents mostly contributed books to my interest in warfighting. Birthdays and Christmas brought David Macaulay's *Castle*, *Harper's Pictorial History of the Civil War*, and *Tim Page's Nam*. I patrolled the land each day with a hatchet, a machete, and a pair of Japanese military binoculars captured by my mother's father in World War II.

I was allowed as many blades as I could carry but no firearms of any kind. Without neighbors for war games, or the emergence of any true adversaries in the surrounding hay fields, I couldn't call a rifle a pressing requirement, though with what was left of my youth I continued to practice at territorial defense and pretend at survival. Each afternoon as the sun set, my father would stand by the porch of the house and call out toward the distant darkening woods for me to return from the frontier for dinner.

IN 1987, I LEFT HOME for Vassar College to study studio art. I drew political cartoons for various campus papers and ran for student offices. I began serious drawings with charcoal, blackening my fingers with burnt wood sticks to mark images onto newsprint, then rubbing the ash back off with erasers. I made meticulous intaglio prints, engraving lines into zinc and copper plates, inking them, and pressing them onto paper. I worked clay into nudes, cut metal, carved wood, and painted oil colors onto canvas with rabbit-hair brushes. My thinking was expanded by work like Frank Stella's 1959 painting *Tomlinson Court Park*, Malevich's *White on White* from 1918, and Robert Mangold's 1973 *Imperfect Circle #2*. I shifted from realism to abstractionism. But I also made bottle-rocket launchers out of copper tubing and pine when the sculpture studios were empty. They looked like advanced versions of the first rifle I had made for myself out of a pipe and a board. At night I worked on campus patrol circling parking lots and unlit paths with a radio and heavy flashlight. Despite discouragement of military recruiting on campus, I found my way to the Marine Corps Officer Candidates School in the summer after my junior year.

I sat with several hundred other young officer candidates from colleges around the country in a hot metal classroom in Quantico, Virginia, as the staff filed in to be introduced. The commanding officer of the school was to make a speech. It was to be the last moment of wondering if we had made terrible mistakes coming here. Colonel Fox stepped to the podium, his officers and senior enlisted Marines in a line before him, and gave his speech. It was one line:

"Attrition is the mission."

There was silence as we waited for him to say more, perhaps something lauding our interest in service to the nation, or something inspiring to encourage us through the next ten weeks. There was no more, and he stepped away. We glanced at one another. He was not referring to an enemy. Within six weeks we would lose 40 percent of the young men in the room to unsatisfactory leadership evaluations, injuries, and integrity violations. The door slammed behind him and the instructors began to scream at us. We went into complete disarray. As I was pressed out of a door, called a "hatch" from that moment forth, I turned to see an instructor hurl a chair. We were re-formed into platoons outside on the parade deck—the ground was called "the deck" from then on—and we remained ill at ease for the rest of the summer in a land we had the wrong names for.

I had arrived after an undistinguished year as president of my class, and the recruiter had made much comedy of a President

Busch from Vassar joining the Marines. George H. W. Bush was president then. There was a certain delight in the persecution I received due to being a Vassar student, and once I made the mistake of taking pride in it. We rarely saw an officer. This was by design. The officers were in command, but the senior enlisted Marines were in charge. There was a difference, and the appearance of an officer, a rank we hoped one day to achieve, was built to be an event, an almost spiritual witness to something near perfect. It was on such an occasion that my sense of humor reflected poorly on me.

We were to be inspected by the Captain, and we had been polishing brass belt buckles and black leather boots all morning. We had ironed for hours the night before and had burned every loose green thread back into the cotton camouflage uniforms with lighters. We lined up and the officer made his way around the squad bay, one officer candidate at a time. He was preceded by a gunnery sergeant and followed by a staff sergeant. They were immaculate, and we were all found, individually and collectively, to be a mess. We were to make no eye contact, even if we were eye-to-eye, and we were also not to look away. I stood at attention, seeing nothing, as doom converged on me. We were to greet the officer with our college and contract. I said, "Vassar." There were only two types of contract, air and ground, but I said "infantry" instead of ground. I was nervous and said both school and contract without a pause in between so it sounded like "Vassar Infantry." Few words were less likely to appear together. The Captain paused as he looked at my uniform. He continued to not look at my face. His brow bent slightly, and I could tell that something I had said was wrong. I thought that it was "infantry."

"Not to be rude, Candidate Busch," he said, "but isn't Vassar a girls' school?"

He meant it as a serious question—not everyone knew that Vassar had been coed for twenty years—but I thought that this was my moment to prove that I was unafraid. Someone with pride in his school able to stand up to what was unintended as a joke. I said, and said too loudly, "Women's college, sir!"

The women at Vassar had already trained me to correct the term "girls' school" when I heard it. The staff sergeant's head spun, and he looked at me as if an octopus had come out of my face. The Captain nodded, looked straight into my eyes, and stepped away to the next candidate. I stood in a hush, the other candidates waiting for me to be killed as the staff sergeant stepped in front of me and turned, one pace behind his commander. He was shorter than I, and though I stared just over the top of his head, I could sense his wrath. He was almost trembling. That night, after a day spent crawling in a swamp, wearing the uniforms we had cleaned with such care for the inspection, I was told to push on the floor until the building sank. I thought that I would have a heart attack from doing push-ups. My suffering was eventually ended, and I was sent to my rack by a bemused instructor who said, "I got a joke for you." I stood waiting, my arms dead at my sides, for him to tell me, but he turned and walked away.

I carried an M16-A2 service rifle there, but we never fired live ammunition. Mostly, I cleaned it. For ten weeks I cleaned it, carried it, aimed it, and cleaned it again. It sweated carbon from years of shooting blank training rounds in the humid July of Quantico, Virginia, and I was surprised to discover how porous oiled steel can be. We marched endlessly and incorrectly, and my rifle slowly formed a bruise on my shoulder from drill practice. There was something pleasing about its weight, and it became what it was supposed to be—an extension of me. Every Marine is a rifleman. Every Marine recites the Marine Rifle Creed:

This is my rifle. There are many like it, but this one is mine.

My rifle is my best friend. It is my life. I must master it as I must master my life.

My rifle, without me, is useless. Without my rifle, I am useless. I must fire my rifle true. I must shoot straighter than my enemy who is trying to kill me. I must shoot him before he shoots me. I WILL . . .

My rifle and myself know that what counts in this war is not the rounds we fire, the noise of our burst, nor the smoke we make. We know that it is the hits that count. WE WILL HIT . . .

My rifle is human, even as I, because it is my life. Thus, I will learn it as a brother. I will learn its weaknesses, its strength, its parts, its accessories, its sights and its barrel. I will ever guard it against the ravages of weather and damage as I will ever guard my legs, my arms, my eyes, and my heart against damage. I will keep my rifle clean and ready. We will become part of each other. WE WILL . . .

Before God, I swear this creed. My rifle and myself are
the defenders of my country. We are the masters of our
enemy. WE ARE THE SAVIORS OF MY LIFE.

So be it, until victory is America's and there is no
enemy, but peace!

I wondered about the final line. It sounded like the final enemy
would be peace itself. It still made sense that way. Peace would destroy everything we were preparing for. The staff sergeant instructor at OCS had said, "If you can see it, you can shoot it, and if you
can shoot it, you had better only need one bullet to kill it. We don't
shoot to wound in the Corps . . . and we don't miss." I thought of
my toy rifle with its perpetual single golden bullet.

I graduated from OCS and went back to Vassar for my senior
year as a studio art major. My Quantico rifle was recycled to be
cleaned for another ten weeks by another officer candidate who
would never get to shoot it at anything. I felt diminished without
it, and so in December of that year, I bought myself a rifle at a
Kmart in Poughkeepsie, New York. It was a Marlin .22-caliber long
rifle with an artful hickory stock, and I thought it an appropriate gift to myself on my twenty-second birthday. My roommate
seemed suspicious of my new possession but allowed it to lie, un-
loaded, in its box in my closet. Two months later, on February 23,
1991, I watched on television as the United States–led ground war
was launched against Iraq. It lasted nine days. Within twenty-four
days combat troops began to return home. I had missed my generation's war.

→ ←

THE DILAPIDATED TRAILER that I lived in after college had
been abandoned for years and was filled with the damp, uncircu-
lated smell of an empty home. It was positioned on top of a small
hill behind a hay barn, its back window overlooking an isolation
of young forest that blocked a view of the river beyond the pasture
below. The trailer looked out of place on the old farm, its top half
painted a fading mint green that looked powdery with wear, and
the bottom half white, its doors and windows wrapped with dull
extruded aluminum trim.

I worked most days as an assistant for the artists Harry Roseman
and Catherine Murphy in Poughkeepsie. Catherine was going to
begin a representational painting of a target on a tree and wanted
real bullet holes in it. She didn't want all the impacts to be in the
center. That was the difference between art and war. I brought my
rifle, and Harry and I fired it for the first time. The rounds tore
through the paper with an aimed randomness that violated the
perfection of its numbered circles. Then I cleaned the rifle, and
Catherine spent a year painting the target.

The trailer sat on what was left of an old estate. There was a
large, noble home, an in-ground concrete swimming pool, a carriage house with a workshop, servants' quarters with a garage, a
greenhouse, a chicken coop, a small cabin, a barn with a paddock,
and the trailer. The original proprietor had dammed the river as if
he had owned it in order to raise the water level so that he could
run his boat and pull water-skiers. It was an extravagance that the

new owners could not restore, and the boathouse, built on the raised shore of Fishkill Creek, had collapsed. I gathered the posts and boards of the boathouse and burned them, leaving nothing but an earthen depression that had once been filled with water, a motorboat held suspended above it. The morning after the fire, I sifted the ash to pick out the warm nails so that the horses and sheep wouldn't get any stuck in their hooves.

The oaks and maples near the river had been protected with rock wells several feet deep, but most of the trees had since died and rotted down into the stone-lined holes in the pasture. Everything was in decline, the original owners long gone and the new owners living beyond their means and station. They did not want anyone to know how little they truly had. A strange collection of renters stayed in the various buildings. Above the carriage bays lived a sign maker and his wife. He was a bitter army veteran of the war in Vietnam, and I would stop in to visit him as he made signs and ranted politics. There seemed to be no one he could not list reasons to despise. But he had a soft spot for the horses that roamed the pasture and fed them oats that he bought. Beside the trailer was a long chicken coop that had been cleaned out and inhabited by a man who rarely left its dark interior. He always appeared at the door in the same black T-shirt that had a skull and crossed salmons and said SPAWN AND DIE on it. Inside, the space looked dim and soft with discarded couches he had found. A woman rented the cabin, but I saw her only three or four times in the year that I lived there.

The trailer was surrounded by debris. Everything that had

broken on the estate was laid around it in a staged disorder of perpetual abandonment. The family had the hoarder's thought that objects retained a value, even in ruin, and should be coveted. Disregarded items depreciating in storage were still in inventory. Fence posts and extra shingles, cans of half-empty roof sealant, bricks, tires, heaps of rotting firewood, lawn mowers, propane grills, and an old Ford Bronco. Because these objects were being stored, they were often covered by plastic tarps. The bright blue tarps partially concealed the newer deposits, but the older tarps were either green or were bleached gray and looked solidified, as if they had been cast in plaster. They had been pressed down by weather for so many years that what they protected could be seen like bones through thin skin. Nothing was ever removed once it had been dumped near the trailer. The collection was cumulative. Tall grass grew between the junk, and the yard in front of the trailer had turned into little more than a path, large enough to drive a truck through with something else to leave there.

Inside, the space was glossy with polyurethaned veneer. The walls and ceiling were both covered with smooth, thin birch panels stained a golden pine, but water had found its way in. The veneer cracked and the shiny finish curled as if it had been burned. The ceiling sagged and split open at the panel joints, revealing the pink fiberglass insulation. It looked like whale flesh being sliced. It was a frail capsule. In the small back bedroom, the ceiling had fallen in and there was just swollen insulation overhead. I would seal off that room and live in what was left. The trailer had electricity, and water came to it from the barn through a garden hose that lay stretched across the lawn like a striped snake sunning itself. During summer days the water baked in the hose, came to the faucet hot, and smelled of rubber. At night it came in cool. If the mobile home had ever been inspected, it would have been immediately condemned and destroyed, but it wasn't that kind of deal. I wasn't going home, I had no money, and I needed a place to live where I could trade labor for rent.

I cleared away all of the refuse in front of the trailer and planted a small garden where I grew tomatoes, corn, green beans, and herbs. A woodchuck began to grow large grazing in it. On a day off, I lay on the roof of the trailer with my rifle, waiting for him. It was hours before he ambled up to the corner of my plot; I held my breath and shot him through the head. There was no hunter's celebration, no trophy to mount, but I took a picture of the rifle and the woodchuck lying beside each other and sent it home. I had a rifle—and I could use it.

At night I worked at a Kay-Bee Toys store in a worn-down mall nearby and offered advice to parents buying plastic rifles as Christmas presents that year. Some made realistic sounds, some had red lights in their muzzles, some cocked. There were very few for the serious boy at war, and I was always disappointed when someone selected a purple rifle with pointless buttons and accessories. I would get back late after restocking the shelves and work hunched over on exacting ink drawings, an easel propped on a table in the miniature kitchen. The year went by quickly, and fall felt early when it came. My grape tomatoes littered the ground under the plants after the first frost, and the vines dangled from strings and stakes as if they had been boiled. At night I could hear the black walnuts drop through the glass of the empty greenhouse.

I had no phone and my fiancée, studying in Russia, would have to call a pay phone in front of a nearby grocery store once a month. We would arrange the next call each time we spoke. What money I made I put toward a small diamond ring for when she returned.

In the winter, everything in the trailer froze. I used hay and manure to cover the garden hose that brought water from the horse barn to the trailer but not the pipes underneath the bathroom. In the morning, the water in the toilet bowl was frozen solid and I had to crawl under the trailer with a hair dryer to heat the drain and the feed lines. I packed the space with hay and flushed the system with boiling water every night. The shower still froze in the wall, and I tired of trying to defrost it. I joined a local gym and took showers there. My parents came to visit once. They entered the trailer as if it might fall on them and were at a loss for where to sit. They stood feeling too large and awkward in the space. My mother brought me some purple irises from a local store. They left and my father told me that she cried on the way home.

Sometimes, in the winter, I would go inside the greenhouse and watch the snow fall through the holes in its roof. I could see exactly where the stark branches of the black walnut tree extended over the building by where the panes had been smashed in. It was quiet. The light in the room was tinted almost blue by the thick snow on the glass that had not yet been struck by walnuts. It was like looking up from underneath a frozen pond that had been drained of its water, strange slats cut in the shell of surface ice, and

I felt more like I had fallen in from above than like I had entered by the door below. The air was still, the winter wind kept from the space by the glass walls, the cold coming in from above with the snow. I could hear the snowflakes tapping lightly on the side windows and the edges of empty pots.

IN THE SPRING of 1992, I accepted my commission as a second lieutenant in the United States Marine Corps and returned to Quantico for nine months of training to lead infantry platoons for the next three years. I left my .22 with my father for protection (from the KKK and local lunatics) and for pest control on their rural tract in central New York. I was sent to Okinawa, South Korea, Australia, Ukraine, and the swamps and deserts of America to carry a rifle for the Marines. My father shot a rabid raccoon one day, while I shot nothing but targets. He had been a rifle marksmanship instructor as a Boy Scout in his late teens. I had become deadly accurate, but our only enemy then was peace. One night my father heard wild dogs or coyotes in the field behind their house and went forth into the night with my rifle to defend his old dog. He fired a number of rounds out into the darkness, toward the sounds of the pack. He was moved by the urge to defend his home, his family, against invasion and the invisible enemies that encircled us. Years passed, and the rifle leaned against a bookcase in my father's writing workroom with what bullets were left in it.

→ ←

IN APRIL OF 2003, I entered Iraq as the commanding officer of a light armored reconnaissance unit. There seemed to be at least one AK-47 assault rifle in every Iraqi home, used mostly for communication. Three to seven rounds would be fired into the air and, often, answered in kind from somewhere nearby. These sometimes sounded like delayed conversations in code. Warnings and acknowledgments. We knew enough to tell when the shooting did not involve us. Celebratory fire was common, too. I watched the sky over Iraq every night as tracers rose into the darkness like sparks, getting slower as gravity caught them and pulled the tiring lead back toward the ground. The phosphorus ignited on the rear of the bullet would betray the origin of the shot, but after the tracer burned out, the projectile would continue on its invisible trajectory, falling into other people's lives. It was estimated that hundreds of Iraqis were killed each year by stray rounds fired in celebration from personal rifles. I found it odd that celebration and mourning were coupled in so many single, detached acts. All bullets land somewhere.

I did not fire a weapon during the entirety of my first seven months at war, but I was responsible for every bullet in my unit. We had killed people, and they would remain dead despite my condolences. Defensible actions still produced inexpiable grief. As I was leaving Iraq, intelligence reports noted that sniper rifles were a much sought-after item on the Iraqi black market. A war against our occupation was beginning.

At home, my war was not popular. It was deemed, by the evidence, to be unjustified. An unjust war. Despite injustice, it was not

ended and seemed, by various costs, to be expanding instead. Marines sent to kick in the door during the invasion were being sent
back to deal with increasing regional violence in places like Fallujah
and the Syrian border. The insurgency had begun, and foreign terrorists were using entire Iraqi neighborhoods against us.

An Iraqi boy, surrounded by war, could not play war. He could
not build a fort and pretend, even, at its impossible defense. Our
enemies had blended with the local populations, sometimes *were*
local populations, and we were necessarily forced to regard everyone with almost equal suspicion. To avoid accidents, we made it
illegal to sell toy weapons in stores, and toy guns were confiscated
and destroyed whenever found in homes; a child playing with a
toy rifle might be mistaken for the enemy and shot by a soldier
on patrol. In Iraq, there were consequences for children acting on
their imagination.

I returned home at the beginning of October, and my unit
began a hurried demobilization. I cleaned my rifle and pistol one
last time and turned them in to the armory to be reissued to a new
mobilized reservist and carried back to Iraq. The war would go
on, and the rifle would stay in it. I went home and auditioned for
a small role as a police officer on HBO's *The Wire*, where I carried
an empty plastic prop pistol. It had no weight to it, and I was pretending, again, to be armed. One day in Baltimore, while walking from the dressing room through an alley to a film location, I
heard a production assistant relay the call, "Rolling!" and I thought
I might be in the shot, so I quickly stepped behind a building.
On both sides of the alley were row houses. A man slid out from

under a car, saw me, and began to step backward to his house, loudly defending himself from charges I hadn't made. A heavy man stood silently by the engine. I watched him while I spoke to the other. I looked like a cop, had a badge on a chain around my neck, and he was looking at my plastic pistol, real enough to scare him. I explained myself—*only an actor*—and he smiled, not believing a word, until I continued down the alley. It had been this way for me in Iraq.

Sometimes when I was not filming, while walking along the street or standing in line at a store, I would be gripped by the sudden feeling that my pistol was missing. My *real* pistol. I would instinctively reach for the spot where my drop holster had hung on my leg in Iraq before I could catch up with myself. Rituals are slow to leave the blood. And blood, I had learned, was important.

I have been welcomed home many times, but I have never come all the way back from the places I have been. As I walk now, I am still balancing myself on the smooth beach stones in Maine, my face rough with salt and grit, looking for seashells and bombs in the wrack, the smell of dry cut hay, smoke, and gunpowder in the wind. My childhood is here with my war, home now, and I remain scouting ahead with my dusty rifle and fishing rod, my parents following behind worried about where my errantry will take me.

CHAPTER 2

WATER

My father thought that everything could be repaired with duct tape. He used so much of it to cover rust holes on our station wagon that on the days when he picked me up from school I would jump into the car and immediately slide down out of sight. I had a Seattle Seahawks coat from the Sears catalog with glossy silver arms that tore with wear, and my father couldn't have been more pleased that his duct tape matched. He used it to patch my silver moon boots, too. I was horrified by the amount of duct tape I sported in winter. I looked like a ragged astronaut as I slowly forged my way through the snow to the ruins of the old Poolville dam. I had been warned to stay away from it, but I wandered there anyway. The town was a different place in winter, and I felt different in it. It was the time of year when you were conscious of the act of dressing for the weather. You had to wear protection. I understood that the elements were against me, but I was not old enough to be afraid of what that meant.

Clumps of slush passed as the river moved toward the oceans. It was during cold like this that snow fell into the river and became pasty, the motion of water creating a temperature that kept its volume from freezing but did not allow the snow traveling on it to melt. There were no individual flakes visible, just like ice and water betrayed nothing divisible from their sum, and there was no marking of time in the passing of water. The river took on a deadly hue and an opacity that hid its rocky bed from view. I wondered how the color of water could change, disguise its depth like paint. I understood when it browned with mud during floods, but this seemed to be a color without particles or pigments. It could secretly be as deep as the center of the sea.

The cement walls still stood on either side of the river with an empty lock on the far shore. The dam itself had collapsed decades earlier. Its large fallen slabs lay in the river, upsetting the now unrestrained flow of water. Fragments of ice, broken away from sheets upstream, bumped and rubbed their way over the sunken pieces of concrete as awkward tectonic events. Their scraping made a sound like thick glass being dragged across a hollow wooden box. Glass plates would sink but ice did not. The lighter weight of ice to water never made sense to me, the heavy solid substance being able to float, somehow not as dense as the liquid that it was made of. Near the shore the splayed shards of dam were covered by a white glaze of ice. I was not allowed to go near it, and I usually didn't. If I slipped, my layers of clothing would sponge the cold water and I would be gone like all things that entered rivers but did not live in them.

A deep pit still remained where the water had once poured over the wall. It was wide and seemed to have chambers like a heart circulating portions of the river within it. The current pushed through the center, leaving pools of trapped water on either side. Most of the floating ice would continue downstream, but some would be pulled into circling masses in the pools. On the edges of the gyres, a few pieces would reenter the course of the stream and be taken away, but what spun in the center would stay there until it was flushed out by a flood.

A young deer had fallen into the pool farthest from the edge that I stood on. It was unable to swim out of the revolving current. I remember seeing its head turning with the ice, its eyes open, in the morning. It stayed that way for the entire day, dead, looking at the orbiting shore passing by, over and over again, out of reach, its body held underwater and in place by the whirling ice floe. It turned on its side that night and remained that way for over a month, young, spinning in the middle of a circle of broken ice, counterclockwise, frost gathering on its coat. I stood on the dam and watched the water move by, throwing stones onto the ice to be carried out to sea.

This was the beginning of the melt, and spring would bring the floods that washed soil and death downstream. Parents forbid children to go to the river for fear of their consumption by the current. My parents were aware of my attraction to water and had rehearsed their warning about drowning.

"That river has taken children all the way to the ocean," my father would begin.

"Even the ones who could swim," my mother would add.

"Their parents searched for them for years and years," he would say, beginning to believe himself. My father believed all stories about human worry, even the ones he made up.

"I won't go in," I would say.

"You could slip. You can't even be close to the water," my mother would demand. "Do you understand?" She would become firm as my father drifted into his story, his warnings always confessions of his nightmares.

"Yes," I would say. There was nothing else I could say. I hoped it was the answer that would free me from further examination.

"Good." My mother would lean back as if a judgment had been pronounced.

"Those children never came home, and no one could save them," my father would say.

I believed him, but I went down the railroad to the river. The raised bed of the tracks and bridge works channeled the water in an absolute way that the open fields could not, and the floodwater rose up to just beneath the I beams. The heavy steel bridges appeared to float, suddenly fragile and exciting. It was especially so on the railroad trellises where I could see the water through the widely spaced wooden ties. Standing in the center above the violent, inscrutable passing of winter, I felt like I was losing my balance.

It was as if the flood had come from somewhere far away, spilling into our town. I still could see no evidence that the vanishing snow had done this. I would watch the water and deracinated trees press under the bridges. It felt good to be so close to this much trouble. I secretly hoped that the bridge would collapse and I would have to survive the flood. I wouldn't have. The water was cold and convulsing with violence. It churned as if driven by propellers below its surface. Anyone falling into it would be spun by braids of current, pulled under, and exhausted. I wondered if rock was being tumbled along the bottom. I wondered how the fish, blind in the turbid spate, would survive. I wondered if any of this mud would make it up the coast to Maine.

I BUILT FORTS to accompany every family trip that we took. I called them "outposts," and their architecture varied by the materials and terrain available. We spent a few weeks in Cutler, Maine, during each summer in the 1970s, and I would begin building as soon as we arrived. We stayed near a small cobblestone beach pushed up between two large outcroppings of broken rock. All of the littoral stones were gray and rounded to a dull polish. When the tide came in, they looked like glazed pottery. They clacked together like marbles when they were dry but made heavy, hollow sounds when they struck one another in the waves. I could not stack them, so to build a fort I piled them like eggs on wide bases. The walls had to stay low because of the inclination of the rocks to roll apart and settle back into the equilibrium of the beach. There was no way to tell how deep down the stones went. I tried to dig a shaft to find out, but the rocks kept falling into the hole where I had upset their balance. They lay like a pile of fallen moons, quietly and imperceptibly still rotating, all of their edges spun smooth, and they felt held together as a larger heap by the lunar pressures of the ocean. The entire beach seemed to adjust to my intrusion like platelets sealing a wound. A hole could not endure, much as a pile could not. The rocks were just sand of a greater scale.

To build a roof, I gathered driftwood and tied it together with nylon strands of rope from lobster traps that had washed ashore. Sand fleas leapt around in the shade as I cleared the seaweed from between rocks on the floor. From my fort, I could watch the tide rise and eye the lobster boats as they did their rounds in the cove. The salt breeze swept in from the sea through the holes in the piled cobble walls. Despite my contention that it was a shelter, the fog made the inside as wet as the outside.

During one of the last years that we summered in Maine, in the cove, the entire wall of a small house bumped against the beach at high tide. At low tide it rested on the seaweed, touching the edge of the retired water two hundred feet away, unable to return to sea. I wondered how the wall had come to the cove and where the other three sides of the building had gone. I did not know if a flood carried them all to the ocean in separate pieces or if waves had taken away the land underneath and pulled the structure in to be torn apart. I knew that it had once been whole, and now it was not. It had been standing architecture, but its verticals had been made horizontal, and its window no longer regarded a horizon. The portal that had probably looked out over the sea now looked into it, a dangerous hatch hopelessly open to a cellar of water.

I watched it do this for a week. One day, having seen that its pattern was predictable, I decided to ride it in on the tidewater. It was a rectangular wall made of studs and clapboard with a single missing window in the center. I walked out to it and stood on the boards, testing their strength. There was still some evidence of white paint caught in the rough, weathered grain of the siding, but the wood looked old, unpainted, and gray. It had been built with square nails. The tide began to come in, and as the wall lifted and drifted, I looked through its window at the ocean floor. It was the same ground that I had walked on hours before when the seaweed was matted to the rocks, but it was submerged now, and wild with the violence of surging water. Waves slapped against the edges of the raft, but the ocean framed by the window at my feet was rarely disturbed and allowed a glassy view of the deepening water.

I had brought a long stick with me to serve as a guide pole, and I had my fishing rod. For some time the wall hovered above where it had rested at low tide and did not move toward the shore as I had expected. The ocean beneath me began to darken with depth, and the unconsumed beach got farther away as the water rose. It was the first time that I had really been on the ocean alone, and I felt the panic of a poor decision made in defiance of large forces. As the wooden rectangle tipped slightly with the swell of incoming waves and turned, it finally occurred to me that I might be swept out to sea instead of delivered back to shore. The seven-foot stick that I had brought as my only maritime tool was now much too short to reach the seabed, and I was at the mercy of the ocean. Children lost at sea would never come home, and no one could save them. My father had warned me.

The sun was over the trees, and I could see the black line of seaweed left by high tides on the rocky shore. Within an hour or two, the sea would stop rising, pause, and then begin to recede. If the raft had not moved inland by then, it would surely head out of the cove with me standing on it. Soon my parents would be coming down from the house to sit on the rocks and read, and I would be grounded if I ever stepped on the ground again. Being grounded and dying at sea were almost equally bad, and I worried about both as I paced on the wall. I thought that my weight might have changed the pattern of the raft. I looked for sharks. I was told that it was too cold for them this far north, but I had also been told that there was a tooth fairy, so I watched the water for fins. Larger swells arrived from somewhere far away, and the wall began to inch inland. The rectangle floated uncomfortably on the humps and rolls of water and showed itself to have been constructed for another purpose. Its long wet wood bent slightly over waves and made me uneasy as I rode on its doomed deck. A few of the clapboards in one corner were loose and slapped against the studs as the wall tipped and pitched. I had not noticed that they had pulled off of their nails until the tide broiled beneath me. I considered that the wall might come apart, the waves peeling boards away until I was left suspended in the water by the frame of the window. It would be like an ice raft, melting one board at a time and leaving nothing but the hole in its center.

Within an hour, though, I was mere feet from the slosh and gurgle of waves stumbling into cobblestones. The wall swayed back and forth, held away from the rocks as if by magnetic opposition. Through the window I could see the clean rounded stones in the shallow water. I took a running jump, fell short, slipped on the wet stones, and came down on my shins and hands. I had been carried on the ocean unharmed until I was confident in my safe return to the land. But I had not drowned or been eaten; nor had I been caught amiss. Just shaken, bruised, and awarded a lesson in insignificance. My parents arrived, and I walked up to greet them, trying not to limp.

The wall would be further divided until it washed ashore as smooth gray splinters spread along countless miles of coastline, unrecognizable and confused with pieces of broken ships and shattered trees. Nothing sent to sea returned as the thing that it had been. Everything washed up as wrack.

During the coastal winter storms, the immense swells of water would churn the rocks on the beach and my outposts would be ground back into the deep bed of round stones pressed against the land. The driftwood would be drawn again into the sea and set back adrift. Despite the rearrangement of every single stone, the cove would appear unchanged. The docks in Cutler would sag more, but they did not age perceptibly. The only thing that I noticed to be missing from the beach was what I had labored to build on it the year before, my architecture restored to its components and reabsorbed. I would return to the coast and toil again against impermanence. The shore and waves had never noticed that I had come or that I had gone. They had no memory of me.

IN POOLVILLE, I WOULD LEAVE the house early, giving my parents a general destination, the screen door slapping closed behind me as I ran out. There were not many places for me to go, and if I went from one to another, I would stop at home and report my next location.

"Be home by five," they would always say.

I would agree, and head out on foot or on my bike without a watch. One day, standing on the bridge at the edge of town, I watched an old man cast into the rapids. I didn't know how long he had already been there. A spoon lure flashed as it returned to him through the water. He repeated the act, throwing the ornament in an arc toward the far shore of the river and drawing it back flickering over the brown rocks. It was a gray day and there were no shadows to catch, the current dark, and the hooked metal pulled by its invisible thread kept spinning back to the fisherman untouched. He moved ritually, his eyes fixed on the water, his hand turning the miniature handle on his reel with the consistency of factory labor, his feet absolutely still. I waited, watching the simple mechanics of religion, and finally descended the rocked path to the landing below. I stood beside him. Seeing the river from the brink exaggerated its mystery. From above, I had seen the transparent current, the fragile depth of water over the stones, and the large curled pool turning beside it to the left, circling as if it were separate from the river's flow but powered by its passing. From the height of the bridge it looked small and exposed, but from the finger of gravel on shore it became large again, its depth incomprehensible. The man nodded to me as if I had joined him for a voyage. He continued to cast the lure and call it back.

"It's a shame," he said. "Used to be there were good trout here."

"They all get caught?" I asked, having fished this spot myself for years with little result.

"Naw. I reckon they moved. The river changed. Used to be there were deep rapids here at the bend."

"What happened to them?"

"Well, it's hard to say. The river shifted. I guess the floods pushed the rock away and the water slowed down. That pool there was never here. Trout need fast water. You'd need to build a dam to bring 'em back."

"A whole dam?"

"Well, enough for the river to drop off it. Only really needs to fall a foot or so to make the trout happy. This spot was a good pinch point for a dam because of the bridge, but it's washed out now."

I was upset to hear that the river could shift. The river had always been here. I had understood its bed to lay with the constancy of mountains. It was a vein from the hills and a measurable boundary to men. Immutable boundaries were important. I had watched it flood, its waters rise and change colors, but that it could change its form was a revelation. I was young. I resolved to build a dam below the bridge and restore the river to what it had once been. I could, at ten years old, alter the depth and speed of a river at this spot, at this pinch point, exerting the influence of an old man's memory on a force of nature.

I told him that I was going to dam the river for him so that the trout would return. I remember that he awarded me a smile as he strung his lure into an eye on his rod.

"Anything can be tried," he said, and made his way back up the path, picking where to step more carefully than I had done in descending. I did not know that I would never see him again, but I took my promise seriously and stepped into the water.

The pool was deep, turning counterclockwise, and I could not reach the stones at the bottom without putting my head underwater. I went to the shallows instead and began to pick rocks from the rippling water, stacking them from the shore into the river. I built the dam as a wall, fitting the stones together and then laying them like scales on the upriver side so that the water would curl over without pushing the barrier down. I figured that over time, more rock, pebbles, and silt would gather, strengthening the dam, and that I could keep improving it. I built from both shores toward the middle, and the current in the center began to quicken as it was channeled. I focused on reinforcing the completed sections as the river hurried through the gap, and the dam grew thick and level on both sides. I worked through lunch, then into the afternoon, not stepping out of the water. My socks were pasty and sneakers slick, my T-shirt hanging limp into the water, soaked heavy and stretched. The opening in the dam was now about six feet wide, and the river made the inscrutable sound of adult voices through a wall, the uneven rocks carving tubes of air into the compressed surge. It moved without a pulse, a torrent of colored glass. Whatever I placed in the void was torn up and thrown downstream. I kept trying, using larger flat stones.

At dusk my father appeared on the bridge above me. I had told my parents that I was going to the bridge in the morning, and they knew it to be the first place to look if I ran late. I often ran late. I didn't notice him watching as I struggled stones into the racing water, trying to make them stay as the channeled current flushed them downstream. He stumbled down the path and stood on the landing, watched me for a few more minutes, and then told me it was time to go home for dinner. I looked up at him from the gap in my dam, soaked, losing, and defiant with a plate of slate in my hand. I could feel the water tearing fragments of stone away under my feet, the river digging to make more space.

"I just need one huge rock, Dad. Just one to fill this hole. I can't hold the water back and fill this gap in time."

He looked on as I was swept through, holding my stone, the river collapsing the edge of my dam as the base was eroded. I dropped the stone and stood in the rapids watching the world pour through my obstacle. My father, standing on shore, watched too. It was almost a ceremonial moment, both of us silently observing my failure and regarding my attempt. It was getting dim, the low sunlight passing over the depressed river, leaving it in shadow. My instinct was to fight the river all night. I could block the breach with logs and quickly fill in behind them with rock. I was still planning against circumstance as I stood beside a current so strong that I could no longer even stand up in it. I watched the smaller stones being peeled away, weightless, as the river ripped into its bed.

"I just need one huge stone," I said.

"I think it's time to stop."

Had my father not spoken of endings, I may have never stopped. I smelled like river, dull and old, my skin soaked with fish, algae, leaves, and stone.

I stepped out of the water on the other side, and my father and I climbed back up to the bridge on different paths. He did not ask me why I had undertaken to build the dam. He seemed to understand that it was instinctual, part of a natural progression of acts that he could do no more than observe. He got into the station wagon, its duct tape bandages filthy after a long, muddy spring, and headed back to our house a little less than a mile away. I stood beside my bike on the bridge, as I had that morning, looking down at the dam. It looked not incomplete but as if it had been finished and had then ruptured. The water rushed through the weakening rift into the pool, the rapids now deepened and redirected. The course of the river, in that small space and for the moment, had shifted. I had moved it.

AT SOME POINT, I had allowed that my model-battleship collection was no longer precious. The ships had been more interesting in their assembly than in their later possession. With our move away from Poolville months away, and objects beginning to find their way into boxes, I decided to scuttle my fleet in the Sangerfield River.

I had built the models over five years, keeping them moored in a diagonal row on a bookshelf. My father marveled at my understanding of their sum from their estranged parts when I opened the boxes. I discarded the directions immediately, began building from the picture on the cover. Following the directions seemed like doing a textbook assignment. Working from a single image made more sense to me, engaging in a visual reconstruction instead. The ships were not fictional, nor were their wars, but photographs were never used to depict them. They were always presented as paintings instead, rich with fantastical struggle on the high seas. Somehow I finished the models with very few extra parts, usually produced not by missing their place but rather by not putting them together in the proper assembly sequence, their later addition being impossible after certain pieces had been glued in, a consequence, of course, of ignoring the directions. I deployed the fleet down to the rug for slow circular battles from time to time, but not often. I had collected American vessels and had only one German ship. The narrative of play required too much willing suspense of disbelief with those odds. I always pretended that there was heavy fog.

When I got a hollow plastic Iwo Jima mountain for Christmas one year, I could not use the ships because they were the wrong scale for the plastic Marines and Japanese soldiers. I tried to pretend that the flotilla was in the distance, but it didn't work. My room was too small to separate foreground from background. The entire war was restricted to one oval rag-weave rug that had, along a stained edge, the musty scent of dog vomit left by our old Lab, Gus. It was the one time when I could apply a relevant naval aspect to my war games, but scales could not be mixed in play. The Matchbox cars matched the HO-scale train set and its miniature buildings (1:32); Britains knights had to remain alone, as did the *Star Wars* action figures, but each was in a time and place of its own for me anyway. Plastic army men all came in roughly the same size and could be used together, but the ships were so miniaturized that people could not even be seen on them. In the stamped sheets of tiny parts, there was nothing small enough to be a person. They varied from 1:426 to 1:720. How could anyone possibly combine models of that scale with troops on the beach large enough for me to see the expressions on their faces? Perhaps because there was so little visible connection to the human drama of war, I had less attachment to the ships. They were machines. In play, I was drawn instead to the things that bled. I could hear the soldiers yell to one another, suffer, express fury . . . but the ships were only intriguing at the moment of their assembly or destruction. I had assembled them, and now, moving away, I could only destroy them. I placed them carefully in a wine-bottle box and walked to the bridge by the cemetery.

The river straightened for a few hundred feet as it met the road from the northeast and ran parallel to it before crossing under the bridge to continue west. It had been here that I had tried to dam the river, beside the cemetery I passed through to fish, where my parents owned two plots. This was the edge of town and might as well have been the shore of an ocean. I went through the phlox and wild roses to the riverbank and placed the ships in a row behind a large, smooth stone. They jostled as the water curled around the boulder and were slowly drawn out into the current like a string of leaves. I waited on the road with a pile of round stones the size of eggs, and as the ships separated into the stream, I aimed at their decks, tried to smash them open.

I hit and missed. The sharp, precision-molded deck turrets, antennas, conning towers, and antiaircraft guns sprinkled down, still moving with the current, the bright gray fragments clearly visible as they settled into the rippling dark bottom. The clean gray stones I had thrown also nested in the algae-covered river-bed as foreign to the river as pieces of battleships. The USS *Arizona* was sunk again as it had been at Pearl Harbor, and the USS *Saipan*, similar to amphibious assault ships I would later be stationed on as a Marine, went down with its helicopters and landing craft. My bombardment became less organized as I ran out of stones, and I strafed the water with handfuls of gravel from the shoulder of the road. The fleet floundered, its destroyers destroyed; the USS *Enterprise*, which had escaped battle damage in several wars, was finally lost with all her aircraft, the deck splitting from its hull and turning underwater in the current followed by a trail of tiny spinning planes. Despite the symbolism of destroying battle-ships in the water beside a cemetery, its veterans honored with numerous American Legion flags, I was still too young to regard

the loss as a human one. These were American warships. Our
men. But the clean decks were free of a human presence, and I
left it at that.

One ship, the USS Missouri, had run the gauntlet and was making the turn under the bridge. I had taken too much time shell-
ing the Enterprise to notice. It had taken on water from a strike to
its deck and several misses that had splashed over it. It leaned
to its starboard side. I knew this term from comic books. But
its raised leeward side trapped air, and the ship could not take
on any more water, nor could it sink. It languished, tilted like
a dead fish bloated with gases. I hurried over the rocks along
the shore to get up to the road above, carrying a flat stone the
size of a frying pan, and got to the bridge as the ship turned
underneath and sped up. It was pulled by the quickening water
slipping through the wide eroded gap in the dam I had failed
to finish the year before. I hurried to the downriver side of the
bridge and waited for the ship to appear. I held the stone above
my head. The ship arrived in view; I timed it and hurled the rock
down. There was a brief rifle pop under the stone, immediately
swallowed by the sound of its plunge. The hull splintered and its
thin shards were flushed away along with the crushed fragments
of plastic battlements. The rock held the rest beneath it. I looked
into the water at the pieces, walked the route back, stopping at
each site to peer at wreckage. I ended at the spot where the Arizona had been sunk. Its deck lay flat on the bottom, the shape of a
slim fish. It was late in the day and I turned away, heading home
with the empty box.

→ ←

I BOARDED THE USS *HARLAN COUNTY* in 1992 as a lieutenant, having only once before been on a ship. My parents had
told me the story of our family taking a small ocean liner to
England when I was a baby. It was cheap and they thought it would
be novel. There was a storm in the Atlantic en route, and all they
could do was hold me and brace themselves against the walls of
their tiny cabin as the ship rolled in high seas. They were terribly
sick and afraid that the ship would capsize and sink. My father said
that he was convinced they were being attacked by giant squid and
that the captain had sworn the crew to secrecy, confining passengers in their berths while they fought them with harpoons. "Happens all the time in books," he said. That was as much as they ever
said about the voyage. I had no memory of it myself. They used
this experience to judge that all ships were bad, and that all trips
on ships would likely end badly.

Belowdeck on the *Harlan County* the crowded berths were filled
with young Marine officers preparing for an amphibious assault
on a beach in the Chesapeake Bay. The rain and snow that drained
through Poolville and Sherburne ended up in this body of water,
the fragments of my battleships inching closer every year. It was
just a training exercise, and we were to conduct a landing against
a defended beachhead in daylight. It was essentially a reenactment
of D-Day under similar conditions and with few improvements
in equipment or tactics. I was not sure what the point was. We
were doomed to be massacred on the open sand, and we were

excited to die anyway. We spent the night passing between the tight, moist quarters and the open deck above. The bay was calm, the water black below us, and the flickering lights along the shore taking on the primitive appearance of torches and candles. The ship throbbed, idling in circles, and we pretended we were truly deployed, the sparkling shoreline not our own land. I felt far from home.

In the morning, we dressed in full combat gear, waterproofed our packs, loaded blanks into our magazines, and filed into a beach assault craft. These were much smaller open boats with a ramp in the front, built in the 1950s, and we stood in lines, shoulder to shoulder, facing the beach as we were piloted on a collision course with it. As we got close, the shore became vast and the expansive water became less impressive. The line of sand showed that water was not boundless when viewed from this direction. It was the first time I had considered this, as I had always stood on shore looking out at illimitable sea. I peered through the helmets, packs, and rifles in front of me as they swayed with a slight delay from that of the boat. The beach appeared empty, no defendants showing themselves in the dunes.

The boat's pace suddenly changed, as if it had driven into tar, and it stopped. We all stumbled forward and then back into place. We had run aground on a submerged sandbar a hundred feet from shore. I thought that they would back off and try another access point, but they dropped the ramp and gave the signal to disembark. The first rank leapt into the water and disappeared, their rifles held above their heads. The second rank paused, looking down off the edge of the ramp as if something inconceivable had just occurred. I took a breath, jumped, and ran underwater as far as I could. I felt like I was running in syrup, slowed to hardly walking in the gelid water. Our buoyant packs were lifting our backs and pushing our helmets over our eyes. Fortunately the water was only about seven feet deep, and within fifteen feet my head was above the surface. We had been trained for jumping out of sinking ships. As I struggled toward the beach, my boots slipping through the loose sand, I was happy that I wasn't in the open ocean splashing a hole in burning fuel. By the time I got out of the water, I could do little more than stagger. My cotton uniform was bonded to me, abrasive with sand, and it seemed, suddenly, like I was carrying immense weight. My legs were slow to respond and my bones were cold. I was stunned by my incapacity. I threw off my pack and dropped behind it to aim at the bluffs. The beach was being swept by imaginary bullets, and we returned fire in kind, exchanging nothing but sound. Evaluators walked immortal and would touch us on the shoulder with fate. Either you were assigned wounds and made "combat ineffective," or they would lean down and say, "You're fuckin' done." I was killed along with the three Marines around me after only a few minutes on land, and we were grateful to lie dead in the sand, the waves behind us, and the hopeless effort farther inland, men being touched on their shoulders to the sound of gunfire.

We took out dry uniforms that we had carefully packed in Ziploc bags and changed our clothes in the cold wind. I could see the impressions left by the dead, the bloodless traces where the wounded had been dragged, and the tracks where someone had made it all the way to the top of a dune. I looked out at the ship and at our footprints emerging from the sea, the moment of our evolution. The waves had already washed the sand smooth, and our first steps appeared as if we had fallen from the sky at the waterline and crawled inland.

SIX YEARS AFTER storming the Chesapeake Bay, we loaded our light armored vehicles onto the USS Fort McHenry at the navy pier White Beach, Okinawa. It was part of an amphibious assault fleet that would take us to an exercise in South Korea. We were to have a night of liberty in P'ohang, but there was a storm as we crossed the East China Sea and we were sent to quarters as the wave height increased. Pulling into port was ruled out; we would have to remain at sea until the storm passed. I went down to check on my Marines in the lower-deck billeting space. It was crowded but near the center level of the ship, so the swaying was only miserable. Back in my cabin in "officers' country," I found the flaw in naval hierarchy. The officers stayed high up in the ship, and although they were given more space and privacy, the privilege of rank backfired when there was a storm. The higher you were in the ship when it swayed, the more violent the motion. It can be best described using a clock. If you watch the hand swing back and forth between 10 and 2, the movement is rather little near the base of the hand and increases as you climb toward the tip.

The hatches remained closed and red lights illuminated the

metal gangways. I felt sealed inside an immense machine, pipes running up the walls with electrical wires, water, and ventilation, everything labeled. The interior was a labyrinth of welded metal plates. I stumbled up stairways holding on to chain banisters as the ship listed. The higher I climbed, the more I was thrown. Sailors were being tossed against the walls, back and forth, and I was staggering after them as whistles blared their coded messages over the intercom.

I made it to my door, a thick steel bulkhead, and waited for the ship to tip the right direction to open it. Once inside, I found that I had not prepared my belongings for high seas. The floor was covered with papers, pens, rolling cans of Coke, and clothing. The cabinet doors had not been secured, and they banged open and closed with the sway of the ship. I cleaned up, latched everything closed, and climbed onto my bunk to take Dramamine and wait for the ship to turn completely upside down. I watched as the two metal desk chairs slammed from one side of the room to the other and tried to think of anything but throwing up. I thought of my parents' story of their trip with me in the ocean liner, holding me in a tiny room as the ship pitched and rolled, the crew fighting giant squid. They were right about ships.

There was a low hum in the room and in the halls, like the metal was vibrating. Everything in the ship was metal—the bulkheads and decks, hatches and desks, pipes and weapons. I was in an entirely metallic environment, and it was both without sentiment and unforgiving. Its comforts were sparse—no rugs or wallpaper, nothing that could burn. The element that the navy feared the most was fire. And water. It was fire that drove the ship, tanks of fuel and massive engines that made the propellers churn and the hull shudder. But water took the ship down.

I asked a passing naval officer if I could go up to the bridge. I was escorted and allowed to stand out of the way for a few minutes as the crew fought the storm and charted their location. Like all pilots, they worried about where they were. The Captain was there. It was late and he looked tired. The bridge looked small with all the sailors at their stations. I held onto a handle welded to the bulkhead beside the hatch. Everyone was tense. Countless thousands of ships had gone down in storms over the years. Armadas had been sunk, treasures lost, sailors and passengers drowned. Few captains had survived the loss of their ships. I respected that.

The next day, as I looked out over the Sea of Japan, I could see no shore. The storm had passed and we were now barely swaying on sullen waves. The surface looked fatigued, its leaden whorls no longer throwing spray or disorganized. It rose and fell as if it were covered by a heavy gray tarp, weighed down by a recent rain, anchored at its distant edges, its great expanse stretched tight. Lead could be like this, molten but its color unchanged. It could move like this if there were enough of it, all the bullets from battlefields and armories draining into a pit. At the bottom lay all the ships.

FOR YEARS I TRAINED for war on land, aquatic activities limited to patrolling in rainstorms, crossing swamps and streams on foot. Our amphibious landings were mostly notional, assaults beginning after the moment we would have landed. I was sent with a detachment of Marines to Ukraine, and we were assigned to a former Soviet base north of Odessa to conduct a joint amphibious assault on a recreational beach with the Ukrainian Naval Infantry. Ukraine had only one ship after its independence. It reminded me of the USS *Harlan County* alone on the Chesapeake Bay. I was given a Soviet map with Russian names still printed on Ukrainian towns. Invaders name places. It was an unremarkable site aside from the history of the water. The Black Sea had been a lake and was somehow filled by a deluge of Mediterranean bilge that came in when the land between the lake and the sea collapsed during an earthquake or from the pressure of rising seas seven thousand years ago. The dense salt water of the flood was now trapped and dead beneath a layer of mostly rainwater catchment brought in by rivers. The different waters never blended, and the salted floodwater, kept below the fresh river water, became anaerobic, supporting no life. No plants or fish live below the two-hundred-meter shroud of low-salinity sea. This event is thought by many to be the source of the biblical flood story. The villages along the shores of the lake are still there; the stick homes and wooden boats still sit in the places where they had been drowned and now, without oxygen, cannot rot.

I stood on the beach looking out over the flood that was the Black Sea now and corrected my position to be on a hill high above the lake that had been poisoned with seawater. Below me in the dark brine, on the submerged shore, early people had pointed at the coming water. The story has been carried as both myth and truth, history. It is written in the Bible. It has been assigned language of record by writers who were not witnesses. But the story has survived. And the water is there. I have seen it.

I accompanied the Ukrainians out to their rusty ship while my vehicles stayed on shore. We couldn't afford to risk one of our LAVs sinking in the Black Sea during a brief deployment, and they were designed to cross little more than rivers, delivered all the way onto beaches by amphibious ships or LCAC hovercrafts. The exercise began and I rode in an old Ukrainian vehicle kept running by a wonderfully drunk maintenance chief and now painted bright yellow because they didn't have any green paint.

"The Russians keep the green paint so that they can see us come!" he shouted when I asked about the color. "But they are afraid of bees." I thought the interpreter had said it wrong, but all the mechanics made buzzing noises and laughed.

We rumbled toward the beach, where many locals lay on towels sunning themselves in bathing suits. Behind them, rigged cans of gasoline began to explode, symbolic of naval gunfire from battleships they didn't have, suppressing imaginary beach defenses. The people turned casually, watching the cloud of black smoke drift over them. We were getting very close to shore, and I looked over at the Ukrainian commander in the hatch beside me.

"People," I shouted over the engines.

"They will move," he yelled back.

We were almost ashore and they were not moving. The vehicles lumbered in the water, but as they emerged from the sea, they burst inland. The people suddenly dashed in all directions, vehicles running over their towels. I could only watch in amazement as mothers fled with their children, leaving toys to be crushed.

"See," the commander said as we passed the beach and I disembarked to rejoin my detachment. I turned to look back at the beach, expecting casualties and disorder, but the people were already back, shaking out their towels and laying them down in between the tread marks of our invasion.

We settled into defensive positions for the night, digging in. As the sun set, the mosquitoes rose in clouds and were maddening. Behind us, on the beach, loudspeakers blared "Take on Me" by A-ha as we scanned the tall grass for opposition forces. Young women in bikinis began to stroll through our perimeter back to their apartment buildings, waving to us in our dirt holes and vehicle turrets. I had to ask my gunner if I was hallucinating. *Apocalypse Now* suddenly seemed to be a realistic depiction of war. Under a bright moon, the Black Sea was still.

WHEN I WENT TO WAR it was not by ship. By 2003, I was a major in command of a Marine light armored reconnaissance company and we were running late for the invasion of Iraq. We flew over the oceans in C-5 cargo planes landing in Kuwait to drive into Iraq. My unit was at the Iranian border quickly, and we remained there for three months. Patrols were endless as we tried to project omnipresence throughout an immense piece of territory. We waited for our turn to catch "Saddam's Revenge," a miserable illness that was going around. It was transmitted through minor indiscretions with local food or a lapse in obsessive-compulsive use of hand sanitizer. Marines were quickly overcome within an hour or two and incapacitated with fever, dizziness, and dehydration. There was nothing to do for it but accept an IV and wait. It was my turn. I could feel nausea rising in me and went to lie down in my tent to sweat it out. It was at this moment that an emergency meeting was called by the town council of Jassan.

My section of light armored vehicles arrived in the village, and there were already a hundred men gathered in the street by the gate into the government building. I passed through them with several Marines to find the open courtyard inside the walled compound filled with more men. They were wearing headdresses of rank, one or two tightly woven black circlets, *agals*, pushed down over red or black checkered head scarves, *keffiyahs*—both a display of their tribal position and, I was told, evidence that some had made a pilgrimage to Mecca. There was more emotional energy than I had ever felt in Iraq. Even the surreptitious Sheik Hattam, senior tribal leader, who seemed to move by gliding, his feet invisible beneath his *dishdasha* and *aba* cloak, had changed his disposition. He seemed undisguised, set aside his urge to pull in too close to me and murmur acquisitive suggestions through an almost toothless smile. He welcomed me happily into the council room, which was packed tight with village elders.

"Let one man speak, so that all can hear," I said as I sat down beside the chairman. Everyone immediately began to speak. I turned to the chairman and asked that he choose one man to explain the situation, although I was familiar with the story. It was about water rights and old regime anger. The Diboni canal from the Tigris brought water seventy kilometers to the towns of Jassan and Badrah. A chain of criminal real estate deals had delivered a piece of land into the ownership of Saddam's first wife, Sajida, his first cousin, who mothered both his sons, Uday and Qusay. A large farm was built, and instead of digging wells, as they were required to do, they installed a pipe in the wall of the canal near the town of Ali Hassan and "stole water," lowering the flow to Jassan. The people wanted the pipe sealed. It was both a practical and a very symbolic act. I asked if there were any representatives from the farm to defend the use of the pipe, and the room burst into chaos.

"They do not come because they know they are wrong!" Hands were in the air. It was as if someone had tossed a beehive into the room. I calmed them and invited discussion, which led to an hour of heated exchanges between men who completely agreed with one another. I recorded the injustices and grew increasingly dizzy. A little boy, maybe six years old, delivered a note to a councilman and then vanished. It was unfolded and passed down the row, open, each man reading it and becoming visibly anxious as it got closer to me. Discussion stopped. It arrived at the teacher I had enlisted to interpret for me, and he looked back down the row of men. One man shook his head no. The teacher began to refold it, but I asked him to read it. He looked hard at the note as if it were suddenly not in Arabic.

"You will be unhappy," he said. "But please, it is not from Jassan."

"It seems to be a very short note on very large paper," I said.

"Yes," he said, and read it in a whisper. I could feel the men at the table lean in to hear. The fan in the concrete room didn't work, and the whisper sounded loud.

"By the lion of Iraq, Major Busch will die tonight."

The note was signed "Saddam Fedayeen." They were the elite paramilitary unit most loyal to Saddam, his praetorian guard, who had been fighting with the most commitment since our invasion. Only my name was written in English, very carefully, and it was obviously penned by another hand than the one that had written the Arabic. I was surprised that my name was spelled correctly. Iraqis always spelled my name wrong, convinced that I was directly related to President Bush. I smiled as if it were a joke, took the note, balled it in my hand, and threw it over my shoulder. It was an oversized sheet of lined military paper with the Iraqi coat of arms, the Eagle of Saladin, on top. Paper was rare in Iraq. There were no trees. I knew that the rest of our time in the region would be tested by how I responded. I had already convinced myself of what I was about to say.

"I cannot be killed by conventional means," I told the teacher. "Let us deal with troubles that are of real concern. Your water."

He was uneasy. I turned to the council, which had quickly whispered the contents of the note to those who had not seen it, and then the entire room had gone dead silent again, everyone at a loss as to where to look. Most of them stared at the teacher beside me, waiting for him to interpret my response. I took the moment to lie.

"Please understand that I cannot fear cowards who send their threats in the hands of children. They want you to be afraid again. Why should you be? You are free men. You now decide what is right in your village. Saddam Fedayeen? The bravest of them was the child who carried their note."

I was pleased with the language I had chosen, especially since I thought it might very well be the last thing I was ever to say— my defiant final words an affront to my murderers. I wrote them down on the back of an area map tucked in my notebook before continuing the meeting. The teacher relayed my words to the others in Arabic. I looked up and smiled again.

"I think it is time you decided this matter with a vote," I said to the chairman. I told him to have all those in favor of leaving the water access open raise their hands. None. All those in favor of sealing it. Unanimous. He looked to me for my endorsement, but I said that I was pleased to see the council rule with undisputed justice. America would be honored to provide security while they sealed the pipe. I suggested he announce that it was the decision of the Council of Jassan that the water access to Sajida's farm be sealed forever. I had to put the words in his mouth, and he had waited eagerly for them. The men in the room were instantly changed and my impending assassination forgotten. There was an excitement, and I used it to call in Staff Sergeant Shaffer, who was in charge of my security for the meeting. He had been guarding the entrance, but we had not thought to stop children with notes. An oversight. I relayed that there was likely going to be some drama when I left, and to have the Marines go on high alert, scan the rooftops and windows within view of the council building for rifles. He was all war business and hurried out into the crowd, the men opening to let him through and closing behind him. I urged the chairman to announce the decision to the people outside while I stayed out of view, hoping that he would gain recognition as a sovereign leader. The courtyard broke into wild celebration. I was so dizzy that I was losing my balance. I put the map with my last words into my notebook, picked up the balled note, and traced the wall to the door, my fingers guiding me along the plaster for balance.

When I emerged, it was to the chant of "Good Busch!" by several hundred men. I thought it a perfect time to be killed, and I walked into them as if it were inevitable, right hand on my heart in the gesture of greetings. It was late dusk and the village felt smaller in the dim light, the men cheering felt more numerous, and I was moving as quickly as possible to get to my vehicle and drive off, less to avoid being shot than to hide my illness, which had dramatically worsened in the hot room. I was worried that I would look weak, throw up, or pass out in public view. It would have been a night to stay in the celebration and enjoy the smallest victory of the war. I scaled the vehicle, sank into my commander's hatch in its turret, swung the machine gun out of the way, waved at the celebrants, and drove off.

The next day I had a high fever, stomach cramps, shallow breaths, and diarrhea to accompany the predatory sun. We had no cold water so I had to sip from a hot-water bottle and declared myself supernaturally miserable. I refused an IV. Shepherds and townsmen were in the canal filling a pipe with concrete, the water from the Tigris pumping past them into the desert, and I lay in my small nylon tent watching the sun passing from one side to the other through the tan fabric. I felt ignescent but I had not been killed. I did not want it to be because my assassination was an empty threat or because my Marines made a shot at me too difficult. I wanted to believe that I had lived because the village did not want me to die, and had protected me on my drive away from them into the desert and night.

WE HAD BEEN NORTH on the Iranian border for three months and were happy for a new mission when it came. We moved south, crossing the Tigris at Kut and then the Euphrates at Nasiriyah, staging there in the "Ace of Spades" house. An Italian unit was stationed there as well and had wine and fresh seafood flown in. We could barely get our mail. My unit was to reinforce the Twenty-fifth Marines to provide security during the first payment made to all former Iraqi soldiers in the region. We were paying the men that we had fought not to fight us again. The soldiers ranged from several generals to thousands of conscripted privates spread into the arms of armed discontent by Ambassador Paul Bremer's witless dissolution of the Iraqi Army. An abandoned stadium was chosen as the location to conduct the payment. As the site was organized for both efficient disbursement of funds and protection, I was drawn to athletic symbols painted on the walls. At some point earlier in Saddam's rule, athletes were colorfully painted competing in their sports. The paintings were crude but easily discerned. Later, the old paintings were covered with cheap water-based paint and internationally established sport symbols were painted over them in black. Near the ground the spring rains washed off the new paint and exposed portions of the original images, joining them in abstract combinations. One such disparate pairing looked like an ancient fresco and it stopped me in my tracks. The colorful legs of a runner were exposed below the black symbol of a swimmer stroking through waves. It brought to mind the lines from the poem by Stevie Smith:

> Nobody heard him, the dead man,
> But still he lay moaning:
> I was much further out than you thought
> And not waving but drowning.

At the time, the image symbolized Iraq for me. The juxtaposition of the visible and of what lay below the surface was captured in this unintentional collage. We were studying the simple surface while what mattered happened underneath it. For everything that we saw there was something more important that we couldn't see. Thousands of people walked past without so much as a glance before it was painted over again.

There is a Greek wall painting from 480 BC known as *The Tomb of the Diver*. An athlete is memorialized diving through the air toward the water. He has not yet struck the water and he never will, held suspended above it. It is as if the world under the surface was too much to imagine even with paint. It was the other side. Neither heavens nor hells should be painted.

Back at our base, I stood beside the Euphrates, its banks wrapped with razor wire, dry as if there were no water inches away. It looked opaque like the Tigris did, moving slowly through the channel it had cut in the ancient dust. There was nothing about this green river that made me want to go into it. It kept passing, heavy, slow as paint, heading for the sea. But it would not have surprised me to hear that the river vanished into the desert beyond Nasiriyah, creeping into the silt underneath the surface to fill wells and become oasis pools in places that could find no explanation for the appearance of water. This river moved without passion, wearing down the land and carrying it toward the coast. Both the Tigris and the Euphrates emptied into the Persian Gulf, which the Arab nations called the Arabian Gulf. Conflict in the region had extended to naming the sea.

FOUR YEARS AFTER our invasion of Iraq, I found myself on the southwestern coast of Africa working on a miniseries about the war. Combat was ongoing four thousand miles away. I had been out of uniform for two years and had moved to Michigan with my wife and daughter when I left them again to play a Marine. The show was based on an embedded journalist's book, *Generation Kill*, recounting the invasion, and my unit had operated in all of the towns that were depicted. It was surreal to stand in the re-creation of places I had really been, wearing a uniform as mere costume and pretending to be at war. I had been in the invasion and had slept in the ruins of Babylon, once the location of the hanging gardens. Mesopotamia is believed to have been the location of Eden. It is a desert now.

The waves curled and lunged at the Namibian coast. In the tangle of sea wrack were clam and mussel shells and the spider remains of tiny reddened crabs. Flights of seagulls and ducks moved past as if pulled by a thread from the north. Pelicans, too. Dolphins' fins rolled slowly like gray gears at the place in the ocean where waves seemed to anticipate the shore ahead and begin to gather volume. The dolphins also headed north, moving with a laborious grace. On the beach, the water withdrawing through the rounded pebbles made a cracking sound as rocks tapped against one another in momentary buoyancy. It was June and the beaches were empty. It was winter in Africa.

The dense mist had pushed far inland, and as the sun burned it off, I found it held dust. It was like fine glitter moving past, small and reflective. I realized, seeing it sparkle, that my lungs must be full of it. I had been breathing glass powder and had not known. It was the dust from the crack between the continents that had spread apart, and it gathered in massive coastal dunes, orange with rust from iron. When the lands were a single island, the space between Brazil and Namibia had been an inland sea, later ripped open and drained by tectonic-plate separation, the fault line probably looking like a thin river once, the fresh water surrendering out and the ocean moving in, with a tree lying across the rift.

In the Namib Desert, away from the coast, burnished purple rocks that clinked together with a metallic ring were the only dark specks on the ground, and the ground was all that was left of Pangaea's inland sea. The soil was coarse and granular, composed of the small, sharp pieces of immense granite formations. This was all water and forest before the continental drift. Now it was clouded quartz and bleached red pebbles embedded in an even tan of sand. It was like weathered concrete and barely allowed the impressions of footprints when I walked on it. The morning mist was dense and the desert disappeared into it, making its endlessness seem possibly greater. Low tufts of lichen covered the small surface stones exposed by winds and provided the only evidence of life. Springboks grazed on it, somehow surviving on the meager triumph of growth that drew moisture from the heavy morning mists. There was enough of it to tint the desert floor an uneven light green as I looked out. With the sand, the lichen seemed like a reef beginning to grow before the arrival of a sea, or one from an abandoned sea that had receded forever. A sea had receded forever. It felt like a place before language or what remained after language had failed.

BACK HOME IN MICHIGAN that December, the snow was thick on the fields, while summer returned to Africa. I borrowed a five-foot auger and walked out onto Lincoln Lake to drill a hole. I figured myself to be near the middle of the lake and put down my armful of gear. I set the blade and turned it in my hands, gouging through the ice to make a hole the width of an old coffee can. The ice was about twelve inches thick, and I had to pull the auger out every few inches to clear off the frozen peelings. In a few minutes, there was a perfect circle of dark water.

Beneath the ice that I kneeled on was a closed space. I imagined it as the gel in a medical cold pack, blue syrup pressed between bedrock and a thick slate of ice that gathered snows on its surface and froze its way down. I found it hard to believe that fish were alive inside this sealed compartment, and that they would happen upon my dangled bait in the lethargic subterrestrial cold. But people caught fish this way.

I lowered the small, baited hook into the water. Earthworms are no good for winter fishing, so stores sold bee larva, which locals called wax worms. It was 13 degrees F. outside, and I was chilled after I stopped moving. There were no clouds, and as I stood on the ice, the cold went all the way into space. The exposed water in the hole immediately began to freeze, and I had to continually break the thin, clear crust resealing it. I stacked the brittle pieces in a tiny pile like glass from a broken window. I jiggled the line and waited.

I had punctured the frozen lid, expecting the embryonic lake to burst up, relieving the pressure of the heavy ice cap. But the water stayed in its place. Water always knows the water level. I fell into monastic study of the hole, like staring at a painting, and felt far from other people. But there was no desperation in this act of survival. I was waiting, but maybe not for a fish. I was thinking of diving in, finally giving in and going under. The water circulated by temperature, the warmth of the bottom rising and pushing down the colder water near the ice. The slowly rotating water must have been like a slight breeze in this submerged cavity, brushing past dormant grasses and idle fish. There was less light for the plants and less oxygen for the other things down there. Everything was living slowly.

After about an hour I caught a bluegill. It was small, beautiful, and bewildered as I pulled it through the hole, its colored scales as elaborate as a Chinese parade costume. I held it and we looked at each other. It now knew more than I did. It had been on both sides. I let it go to take the story of above back below. I was wearing thin socks and my feet hurt with cold, so I gathered my gear and poured the remaining bait into the aperture. The larva disappeared quickly into the murk, falling toward the dirt at the bottom where they could never become bees. I thought I had seen this water before. It looked like the Sangerfield River in winter, the Sea of Japan after a storm, the Black Sea, and the Tigris at dusk. I walked off and could not see my hole from the shore. The ice was thinnest at the edge and would melt toward the middle, where I had been, as the days warmed up. It would form a shrinking ice raft with my hole in its center, and then it would all just be a lake again.

CHAPTER 3

METAL

IN 1976, WE LIVED IN EDGEWARE, ENGLAND, AND I quickly determined that I was not going to stay. My father was chaperoning students for a university study group, and I went to the local elementary school, where we sang "Onward Christian Soldiers" together in the gymnasium each morning and did not recite the Pledge of Allegiance. The boys in school called me "Yank," and I had the impression that they meant it not as a term of endearment. There was considerable laughing involved at my expense. I responded with "Brit," but they seemed proud to receive the title. I hadn't heard "Yank" before and had no idea what a Yankee was, shy of its appearance beside "Doodle Dandy," which I began to imagine was even worse.

I was the only American in the school. I began to exaggerate the cultural differences I was accused of having and spoke with a heavy Texas accent, like a cowboy from a western film. I decided that it was insulting to be labeled a Yank, cloaked myself in national pride, and asked my father for a retort he deemed to be of equal force. He pondered it for a while, probably weighing language, balancing acceptable words against my insistence that I be given something offensive. He finally said that sometimes British sailors were called limeys because they had eaten limes to avoid scurvy at sea. He didn't elaborate on what, exactly, scurvy was, but "limey" sounded rude enough to me. I went to school the next day enlivened by my secret reply and desperate to use it as soon as possible. I was shunned from a game of Thunderbirds, a British television show, being played with wooden blocks. My exclusion was due only to my race, Yank. I became gleeful with reproach, and I called them all limeys. There was a silence, and then someone threw a block. I have no memory of the struggle that followed, but I recall the aftermath: blocks everywhere, someone crying, me being pulled away by a man who had been called in by the teacher, and that he also called me a Yank. The fault for the disturbance was laid on me. The report from the teacher, upon which I was to be punished at home, was four words long:

"He was very naughty."

Back in the house we rented, I was told to think about what I had done. My father looked guilty, my mother looked at my father, and I did not think about what I had done. I thought, instead, that we had come to England on a plane and that I would go back home in one immediately.

I had thirty-five pence saved. My mother said that it was not enough money to buy a flight ticket. But I also had my father's 1944 pictorial book of airplanes. I announced that I would build one of my own and fly it over the ocean myself.

Beside the house on the right was an alley separated from the yard by a fence. The residents in our neighborhood lived in tight quarters and stored their old lumber and pieces of furniture neatly behind their homes in the narrow lane. I learned that most of a British Spitfire had been made of wood, which was very encouraging, given my supplies. I decided to piece together an airplane and fly to Maine, where we had friends on the coast. I would go back to America alone and wait for my parents to return. I explained my plan to them and asked for a box of nails.

I worked on my project every day after school. My knowledge of aircraft construction was thin, and my book of World War II fighters, *America's Fighting Planes*, only pictured them flying, frozen in dogfights with German Focke-Wulf 190's and Japanese Zeros. I had to start with something simple, and I guessed that the pilots must all be sitting inside boxes of various sizes. And why wouldn't they be? I began by building a square. This was to be my cockpit. Two long boards were fixed on either side as wings, and a warped piece of oak window trim was nailed to the front, as close to the center as possible, to serve as a propeller. This frame sat above the ground by six inches, the height of two bricks I borrowed from a pile left after a patio was torn up and replaced with a rose garden.

Neighbors gave me more wood and pieces of used aluminum foil that smelled of bacon, sausage, and fish. A British gentleman inspected my work with sincere curiosity every day. He would always say, "Rather think you'll give Fritz some trouble in that beast," after I had explained what it was. He said this in the same tone he might in addressing a colonel. I had no idea who he was referring to, but I always agreed that I would. I would tell him that I was to fly to America, and he would nod slowly.

"I see, I see. You'll want to be stopping in Greenland for fuel then," he would say, and continue on his way. It was always as if we had never spoken before, and he always said the same words.

I can't remember how long I actually worked on the plane. There was a tail projecting from the rear of the cockpit on the curved leg of a broken table; two wings, almost matched, glittering with aluminum foil; a propeller that could not spin in front; and a seat made from a wooden fruit box. Someone in the alley had promised me a broken lawn-mower engine. I was going to need time to repair it with my hammer, screwdriver, and imagination. After I got the engine, I expected to be able to leave within a few days. I began to make a list of things I would need for the trip. I asked my mother to make some soup.

It was at this point that my father decided to quell my ambition. Besides lunacy, there was impending disappointment that he wished to protect me from. It was unlikely that my plane would fly, even with a broken lawn-mower engine symbolically attached to an immobile propeller. My father came out to the alley as I hammered more nails into the boards. The excessive nails were pointless, but it was something that I could do. Every intersection of wood glistened with nail heads. He circled my craft. He paused occasionally as if to remark but he said nothing. He finally stopped and said, "I hate to tell you this." He couldn't look at me, afraid, maybe, that I might catch him conjuring a story. He kept staring down at the wings. I guessed that he was going to point out my missing engine, wheels, and windows, all of which I had imagined plans for, but it was something far more dangerous. He was drawing on his own youth, perhaps stories he had been told as a war baby by his father.

"You see," he said, "airplanes need special metal for their wings."

I looked at my fragile collage of aluminum foil donated in pieces by all the neighbors. I had nailed some of them down. The foil had been carefully flattened but still bore the creases of having been wrapped around dinner plates or balled up.

"It's a long flight over the Atlantic, Ben. You've built a good plane, but without the right kind of metal, the wings could fall off."

"Why?" I asked. I had used enough nails to stop bullets.

"Metal fatigue," he said.

He was very serious. He explained that heavy winds and the pressure of staying high in the air made wings move and that the joints weakened. Wings could fall off this way. He made no allusions to Icarus, and I would not have understood the reference had he done so, but I thought about plummeting into the ocean halfway to Maine. I studied the wings, and metal fatigue seemed possible now that I thought about it.

"I think that we should take it apart so that no one else flies it," he offered.

It was kind of him to pretend that there was any possibility of that. We dismantled the plane, which took about five minutes, and I returned the pieces to the places in the alley they had come from, riddled with nails. My father left me with the remaining wreckage and went back inside.

I stayed in the alley peeling the aluminum foil from the wing boards. The older gentleman appeared and stood watching as if he had forgotten something. I straddled a board and shrugged, picking at shreds of foil nailed to it.

"What's happened here, then?" he asked.

"Metal fatigue," I said.

I JOINED THE BOY SCOUTS almost as soon as I could. The lure of a uniform and adventure was an easy sell. We met in the basement of a Methodist church in the next town over from our home in Poolville. Meetings consisted of little more than a formation to recite the Pledge of Allegiance while wearing our tan shirts sewn with bright symbols, and then a period of instruction of some kind relating to rope tying or first aid from the handbook. I quickly became disenchanted. There were no martial skills being taught, the camping trips were uninspired, and I was not in great company. There was, however, one good reason to attend the meetings.

At the end, as the whistle blew at the nearby box factory for the afternoon shift change and we waited for our parents to pick us up, we played capture the flag around the church. One team hid its flag on the street side, and the other behind the building. As we could only play on church grounds and most of that ground was covered with church, the two teams were channeled into the slim spaces along either side to get to the front or the back. The game was necessarily forced to be one of feints, scouts in the front and rear of the church trying to draw enough opponents to protect one side while sending the few fastest to the other side in hopes of passing the church untouched and getting behind the defense to find the flag. It was worth tying knots to get to this.

We were also required to do community service, which, from what little I can remember, consisted of chores for the church. We stacked the pastor's firewood and cleaned out the crawlspace underneath the church. The crawlspace had in it an interesting discovery.

We removed old boards, faded curtains, and broken strings of Christmas lights. Why these things had been stored beneath the church in this space I do not know, but in the back, stacked in a pile, were the original organ pipes. The crawlspace was dark and dry, the floor composed of a blend of chalky powder and dirt. We passed the pipes to one another on our hands and knees, coughing as the dust brushed off the metal. The original church had burned to the ground in the great fire of 1886, and the current building had been immediately constructed on the same site in 1887. Some of the soil was likely ash from the first church. The 1887 organ was replaced in 1958, its pipes tossed underneath the new one.

It was as if we were deep inside a cave or a tomb, unearthing votives left in a burial. They were surprisingly heavy, and some of the longest ones had been bent in half to fit in the cavern. The oldest scout, a boy in his late teens, asked to take the pipes with him, and I was curious as to what purpose he could find for them. He said that they were made of solid lead, and that he would melt them down and make sinkers for fishing. I didn't ask him how he would do this. He seemed to know. We carried the pipes outside, and they looked different than they had in the dirt. Where our hands had rubbed them, the lead tubes showed a dull shine, as if our fingertips had been wet or had burnished them by touch. They were all different lengths, and we didn't lay them out in any particular order. Their flues were turned in different directions and had the look of thin sharks laid on their backs. A row of organ pipes is called a rank, the flue breathes through a mouth, their notes are called speech, and the first sound is called the attack. So many human and military terms were applied to an organ, and an organ is, of course, a part of the body. The pipes had been silent for years, no air rushing through them to the pitch of exact notes. All that music passed away into the air of the church, and now these pipes were to be melted and used to catch fish.

That evening, as the sun went down to the sound of trains passing, we played capture the flag in our uniforms, filthy with leaded dust and ash from beneath the church, searching for a flag and defending our own, knowing little more than how to tie a square knot and how to pledge allegiance.

WHEN THE TRAINS STILL RAN through Poolville, a friend and I would put pennies on the rails. We could hear the train blowing its horn miles away at a road crossing in Earlville, giving us enough warning to run down to the Willey Road crossing nearby. Far away, the sound was like a whale's song tuned for water and projected too loud for air. The notes were long and exhausted, drifting over low hills and filtering through trees in between the towns. The horn began again as the train rounded a bend and crossed a bridge over the Sangerfield River, closing on our intersection, but the pitch was different than it had been in the distance. It became violent when it was close. We placed the coins carefully on the shiny center of the rails as the train hurried toward us, unstoppable, its horn blasting sound that cracked the air and scared us back into the grass. It passed us as if it were not operated by people. The ground shook as the force of the machine pounded the earth and the sky with its engines and its moving weight. The clacking of steel wheels over the tiny gaps between rails, the clank of chains dangling between freight cars, the shrill rub of metal wearing against metal rushed by us and we watched our pennies vibrate off onto the tar-heavy ties and crushed pumice bed. When the last segment of the train had passed, howling away from us into the fields, we would rush up to the warm rails and search for our coins, no longer coins. They had been transformed back into metal worth only what it weighed.

Over a summer in 1980, I had flattened a small fortune of four dollars, four hundred pennies, on the tracks. The coins were pressed into stiff ovals, some with slight ghosts of Lincoln's profile still visible when I tilted them just right in the sunlight. They were not round because they were rolled flat from one side to the other, the wheels crushing the coins in one direction. Pennies were not yet copper-plated zinc. That didn't happen until 1982, the year we moved away from the trains, the year the trains all but stopped running.

We called them copper but they were actually brass, 95 percent copper and 5 percent zinc. I collected pennies and knew about their composition and production dates. From 1864 until 1962, pennies were made of bronze, 95 percent copper and 5 percent tin and zinc, with some interesting exceptions during World War II. In 1943, in order to make ships and ammunition, pennies were made from steel and coated with zinc to prevent rust. I had bought a handful of them when we lived in Iowa City not far from a coin shop. They were stronger than the copper alloys and, even an entire generation later, looked as if they had just been made. I could still find wheat pennies in circulation back then too. From 1944 to 1946, salvaged ammunition was used to make pennies and the brass used in shells had a higher zinc content, making it yellow. Steaks of lighter brass could be seen in some of those coins due to uneven mixing of expended brass shells in the melt. I kept the older coins in a small wooden box. I saved every penny dated before 1960, the wheat design ending in 1959, but I was not yet thinking that the coins of my day would be valuable, too. By 2010, the copper in a penny stamped before 1983 would be worth more than two cents.

We had "new" pennies from the 1970s, and all we knew was that they were worth one cent. I laid each one on the tracks several times to make them as large and thin as possible. When I had enough, I took them down into our cellar and punctured them, one small hole on the top of the oval, with a hammer and a nine-penny nail. I didn't want anyone to know that I had wasted four dollars.

I tried to sew them onto a shirt as armor, like Roman copper mail called *lorica squamata* that I had seen in a book, but the cotton was thin and the weight of the flattened coins stretched the fabric until it sagged. The neckline pulled low and I looked like I was wearing something made for someone much larger. The metal scales tapped against one another and tinkled, their number ringing. I cut the threads and put the scales into my sock drawer next to my cigar box of old coins. I still have one somewhere, smooth, its hole sharp in one side as if I had just struck a nail through it.

IT WASN'T JUST COINS that I collected. I had collections of HO-scale trains, Britains knights, plastic army men, *Star Wars* figures, Matchbox cars, antique bottles, swords, bayonets, helmets, antique postcards, stamps, wooden boxes, fortunes from cookies, model warships, wine-bottle corks, rocks, shells, sharks' teeth, tools, baseball cards, comic books, and curiosities. I have saved every piece of correspondence I have ever received, while my father burned every one of his. We were different that way.

In Poolville one year, I read in *National Geographic World* magazine that some kids had set a record by collecting one million pull caps from cans. It was to go in the *Guinness Book*. There was a photograph of them all smiling around the pile of aluminum tabs. I kept coming back to it; something about the immensity of the task and the commonplace items gave me a sense of achievability. I chose to accept the challenge that had in no way been made and began collecting bottle caps. Most soda still came in bottles then; beer, too. Poolville had no bar, nor a store that sold bottled soda, but Hamilton did, as did Earlville. I could get to Earlville in an hour on my bike, and so I went to find bottle caps.

Earlville also had no bar that I knew of, but it had a roller rink that served sodas and did a brisk business on the weekends. The rink stood at the edge of town, set back from the road behind a gas station. It was the only place to risk awkward public courtship or to self-consciously exhibit a truly useless skill as if it were being judged. Despite these attractions, after a year of mastering the art of rolling pointlessly in ovals, I was not allowed to go there anymore because my parents said it was a firetrap. They had it in their heads that a fire was inevitable and imminent. Whenever I brought it up, which was on Friday of every week for several years after the safety ban had begun, my father would describe his vision of the tragedy in detail.

"The whole place is made of lacquered wood with two doors," he would begin.

"Three," I would quickly interpose, knowing where the gap would be.

"And the entire building is surrounded by local criminals flicking cigarette butts."

To this I could not respond because it was somewhat true. I would wait instead as if the point were not worth responding to. He would look at me and then deliver the end of his nightmare, which, through expanding description, he had so horrified my mother with that she was beyond restoration. I couldn't even ask about roller-skating with my mother in the room anymore because she would look at me as if she were identifying my charred remains in the morgue.

"Imagine," he would say, "hundreds of kids trying to escape a fire sweeping across that combustible floor . . . through two doors . . . on wheels."

I could picture it, and it seemed a potentially comical disaster. Something meant to be funny instead of awful. Three piles of children wedged in the exits, all of them running in place, the skates just letting every step roll like cartoon characters stood still with legs spinning in circles as the flames approached.

"It's never happened," I said, though I wasn't sure it hadn't.

"That's exactly what everyone says before it does," he replied. It was a closing statement, and he delivered it as if nothing could possibly follow its perfect finality. He was right to use it as such, and although I knew that it would come, I never came up with a counterpoint until the roller rink fell out of fashion. When I was sixteen I recounted that I had asked to go to the rink about a hundred times, and it had not yet burned, meaning that I would have been safe all one hundred times, just like all my friends. After my long punishment for their prediction of calamity, my brother was allowed to go.

Despite the ban, I asked at the rink that they save all of their bottle caps for me in a shoe box, and a friend of mine or I would come get them every week. I did the same at all the gas stations that had soda machines. People always pulled the caps off on the dispenser immediately when they bought soda, and I had a box and a sign next to every machine. In Poolville, I collected the caps at Jim Pound's junkyard. The office stood next to the railroad crossing where I laid pennies. It had a machine serving bottled sodas for thirty-five cents, and Jim respected the urge to salvage metal objects.

I would wander his yard for hours, a few acres of hulks laid out in disorder like a storm-destroyed harbor. Dump trucks from the 1950s; long, heavy cars from the 1960s and '70s; piles of tires, engines, pieces of vehicles; and the wreckage of serious accidents. The derelicts in the area farthest from the road were almost inaccessible to tow trucks anymore. They were beginning their slow union with the earth, rusting into it and being consumed. Grass and small trees were returning to the lot, and the vehicles seemed to sink deeper, their colors fading and rust climbing up their sides and spreading from the bald hoods and roofs. Many were missing their windows from years of mischief, and all of the glove compartments hung open, ransacked for treasures. I could still find a penny or two under the seats. My arms were small and thin enough to search in the grimy spaces that were often filled with the chewed paper nests of mice. Mice were collectors. The junk dealer, too.

On the far edge of the lot was a small shed, and in it was a

trove of keys. The keys to every vehicle that had ever ended up in
the yard as well as crates of uncut keys and keys to locks. There
was no longer any order to them, if there had ever been, and they
lay in piles on shelves and spilled across the floor. I was fascinated
by this collection. It was like having access to every secret that
had ever been kept. The histories of all the vehicles were there
in those worn brass objects, carried in pockets for years before
ending here, buried in the secrets of others. They had traveled
to this place, been gathered, been forgotten, and were now lost
like the locks they had opened and the cars they had started, once
so familiar to someone. They lay around me like coins, the dull
gleam of oiled brass pressed and cut into similar shapes. I didn't
take any. Did not find them to be a collection I could comprehend,
these keys to nothing. But I remembered them when I poured my
boxes of bottle caps into wine-bottle boxes in the second story of
our garage. And I remembered them again when I dropped handfuls of brass from expended ammunition into metal boxes in the
Marines.

The caps began to add up, and I set to counting them. I had
been collecting for two years and had expanded to include a bar
in Hamilton and a tobacco shop that sold soda. The caps were
mostly Coca-Cola, Pepsi, Budweiser, 7-Up, Schlitz, Canada Dry,
Miller, Michelob, Orange Crush, Löwenbräu, Grape Crush, Pabst
Blue Ribbon, and A&W root beer. The smell of them was unfor-
gettable. It was a blend of musky grain and artificial fruits, and
bees would cluster by the sliding door, drawn by the sweet scent.
More memorable than the scent though was the sound they made

being poured. They fell together like tiny empty cans, their multitude ringing like shallow bells. I began to feel accomplishment, self-defined as it was, and to imagine celebration. National Geographic World would come and take my picture as I stood in front of a pile of one million and one bottle caps, a one-paragraph story about my effort.

But then we moved. My parents made decisions about what would be packed and what would be tossed. My boxes of bottle caps were now in a tight, orderly stack, and I watched as almost everything else in the second story of the garage was thrown out. All of the original doors to the old house, the window shutters, old wood boards, broken furniture, and storm windows crashed to the ground. I was shocked by the sudden intensity of these things being discarded. We had kept them all undisturbed for more than ten years, and now, just now, they were deemed useless. It was because we were moving. These things would have to be carried, and that changed their value as possessions. My father announced that we would not have the room to move my bottle caps; it was time to let them go. We were moving to a country farm that had twice as much storage space, so that was not the issue. We had a full-sized station wagon, and the entire collection could fit in one trip, but that would be something that I could not do on my own. I had carried almost all the caps in plastic bags for miles on my bike. They swung from the handlebars. As long as my strange compulsion had not imposed on my parents, they had allowed it to continue. But now its conclusion could be justified. I couldn't believe it. I made child's arguments but they lacked the gravity of adult sensibility. The collection would be driven to the dump—it could make that much of a trip, two miles in the opposite direction from our new home.

I was as sullen as I could be during the loading of the boxes into the car. They filled the rear compartment with the back seats down. I had counted over three hundred thousand a few months earlier. A long way to go from my goal, but quite a number considering my thin resources. The road went out of town and curved following the Sangerfield River upstream of the fallen dam. A new facility had been built on top of the old town dump, a landfill, the buried garbage still rotting below it and seeping household poisons into the river beside it. I had fished downstream for six years, never knowing that the water was contaminated.

New refuse was all placed on a concrete platform and then pushed into a trench, where it was compacted into a metal container for removal by truck to a landfill elsewhere. The bay was clean when we arrived in the morning. My father and I backed up to the platform and opened the trunk. He removed the boxes from the car and poured the caps in a pile on the floor. I refused to help. There was that sound. The sound of frail bells and their echo in the covered metal space. The man who pushed garbage into the trench watched with his head cocked to one side. He knew that he was witnessing something peculiar, but he didn't ask. Even my father poured them slowly, beginning to recognize the enormity of the effort to gather them. The pile rose in the center of the building until the last box was emptied. We stood looking at it. I could feel my father's regret. He apologized, finally, saying he never meant me disrespect in the decision to end, for me, my quest. We got back into the car and drove silently home.

At our new house in Sherburne there was a barn that had been built fairly recently by the previous owners. The upstairs was large and empty. There was ample space for one million bottle caps left over after our boxes of books and old dishes had been stacked, but that collection was gone now. My model battleships were gone. I still had my pennies in a box, small enough to fit into a locked wooden tool chest in my room. My parents divided the barn space in half, one side left unimproved for storage and the other for my father's workroom, which was built facing the house and field. It was filled with his collections, books and artifacts from trips. There were all of the typewriters he had ever used for his manuscripts, a sheep skull from England, stones from the coast of Maine, and gifts from my mother, my brother, and me. It was a sacred room and he went there to write every morning until noon. We stayed away with the strict guidance that during this time he was never to be disturbed for anything except fire or severe emergency.

Of all my collections, many of which continue, the one I remember with the most clarity is the bottle caps. I will never forget the sound of it being poured out onto the concrete floor, never forget staring at its mass glinting in the sun, never forget my father looking from the pile to me with an apologetic sense that by his hand a great endeavor had ended in tragedy.

➤ ◄

MY ATTRACTION TO METAL continued through high school,
where I kept active collections, and college, where I used it in
sculpture. I drew on found objects and changed their context, re-
thinking metal and its use. But it was always something I had to
seek out. I made it something I took the time to notice. When I
joined the military, metal just became the environment.

I had flown to Bridgeport, California, in 1993 to catch up with
my unit. The Second Battalion, Eighth Marines had deployed for
a month of mountain warfare training, and I had inexcusably
missed two days of it to get married. The base was high in the
Sierra Nevada mountain range, and the air was dry, empty of any
vitality. I brought my seabag into the canvas tent, and the other
lieutenants pointed at my empty cot. It was the broken one. They
were being as disrespectful as they could be, given that I had got-
ten out of hiking for two days. It stung most because I had come
directly from my wedding and forgone a honeymoon in order
to be with my platoon as quickly as possible. This sacrifice was
awarded no leniency. For two days I had not suffered equally.

The next day I was to take my platoon sergeant and three
squad leaders on an aerial reconnaissance with an insert into a
landing zone at a much higher altitude than our base camp. I
checked my compass and oriented my map. We were still using
compasses then, adjusting our location based on attraction to
magnetic fields caused by iron deposits near the surface and the
earth's metal core.

Normally we could fit fourteen Marines in a bird, but we could not take more than five here due to the low air density. The helicopters were old, CH-46es, Vietnam-vintage aircraft with two sets of blades interlocked above. I could not bring myself to trust them. The dueling blades spun in between one another in such perfect timing that I imagined they would inescapably experience some minor mechanical arrhythmia and collide, sending shards of glass fiber, epoxy, and metal skin into the air, the helicopter body dropping like a coffin filled with us.

The interior of the troop compartment was violent with the uninsulated sound of blades and engines. I couldn't hear the pilots yelling to me from seven feet away. I switched my combat helmet for a crew helmet so that I could speak with the pilots and tell them where to put us down. It looked like a football helmet with no face shield, the sides cut off and replaced by earphones. The crew chief ran a long curled cord into the cockpit and plugged me in. Suddenly I was in their discussion, the secrets of flight revealed to be little more than an endless conversation about position.

Pilots are known for the consistent calm in their voices. It is the nonchalance of incredible competence. They spoke altitudes and directions to one another, and I listened. Nothing they said had anything to do with the map that I carried folded into a small square in my hand. I had only a map of the ground. Everything they said was about avoidance of dirt and stone. They regarded the earth from different contours than I did and sounded slightly condescending when they spoke of what lay below them. They were only a few years older than me, the crew chief about my age, all of us young for what we were doing. We started up the valley past a rock peak that had a large wooden cross on it. I knew that it had been placed there in memory of a crew killed in a helicopter crash at that spot. The pilots told me again as if we were flying past their own graves.

We flew slowly. The engines were shrill, and the smack of the blades slapping the air filled my head. The vibration of the metal shell seemed excessive. Marines called them whistling shitcans of death. The crew chief laughed when I pointed out a slow drip from a hydraulic line. He said that I should be happy to see it drip because it meant there was still hydraulic fluid in it. The craft shook and I looked over my shoulder, out the small round window, at the terrain passing below. I tried to make sense of my flat map as I took in the sharp outcroppings of rock and deep ravines. As we rattled through the valley I could see little more than mountain slopes from the windows lining either side of the helicopter. We were pressing what little air there was against the stone beneath us in order to stay aloft, and we moved up like a cable car suspended between two ridges. The mountain on my side dropped away, and the helicopter tilted suddenly as if it had been swatted. We were struck by a crosswind, and with the air so thin already, the aircraft was driven toward the rock cliff on the other side. I was still, my helmet tight, map in my hand, a dangling wire placing me silently in between the pilots as their voices changed.

"Turn into it!"

"I got nothin' on the stick."

"Drop for some air."

"We're gonna clip the rock."

"Grid two-three-four six-two-nine."

I didn't realize it at the time, but the pilot had called out the grid as our last known position. He did it guessing that we were about to crash.

"Brace for it."

The crew chief and I exchanged a look. We could both hear the pilots, tethered to their voices by our spiraled rubber cords, unable to do anything. Bracing would not avert fate in this situation. I knew less than he did, but I guessed that if we hit the rock, the blades would splinter and we would roll down the side of the valley on fire. The weight of the engines would tear them away from the fuselage, ripping the troop compartment in half, and seat belts would be of little comfort as hydraulic fluid and burning fuel covered us. The aluminum ribs would buckle, and the thin skin would crumple as we tumbled, dead in our seats or wishing that we were. There is rarely a survivor from a helicopter crash.

"Flare the fucking blades!"

This meant that they were making a last-ditch effort to overpower the side wind and push away from the cliff.

I looked across the bay at my squad leaders. They were alert, though they could hear nothing said by the pilots. I could see the cliff approaching through the windows behind them. It was happening very quickly. The rocks and brush looked like they were being magnified, and I was able to see small details. I resolved to remain completely calm, knowing that the only part of oblivion my Marines could see was my face. I stopped hearing the pilots, though they continued to speak. I smiled. The engines screamed and we went weightless with rapid descent. The pilots banked and dropped low for less wind and thicker air. The helicopter stabilized and their voices became calm again.

We landed in a dusty space marked by a tiny black X on my map, and I took off the crew helmet and put my own back on. As the Marines carried their gear out the back, I stepped in between the pilots for a moment.

"Seriously," I said.

"Yeah," they both replied.

"We almost got a wooden cross out of that shit," said one pilot.

Their faces were shiny with sweat. I nodded to the crew chief and ran out the lowered gate in back with my pack. They lifted again, blowing sand, dust, and sharp segments of dry grass in a cloud over us, turned, and fell back down the valley, the pilots driving their empty metal shell through the invisible wind.

I LEFT ACTIVE DUTY in 1996 and joined a reserve light armored reconnaissance unit in Virginia. I began to pursue a career in acting and was cast as a Marine extra in the feature film *Rules of Engagement*, which was being made in the area. The production was to head to Morocco, and I went with it. I would play a Marine under fire. It was both make-believe and prophetic.

The first scene we filmed in Morocco involved aerial photography, and I dressed as a crew chief, a nonspeaking role, helmet wired to the pilots. The helicopters belonged to the Moroccan military, but the production had coated them in a gray removable wax paint to match Marine markings. We flew fast and low over the stony desert, one Moroccan and one American pilot in the cockpit, and there was all the feeling of a real mission. I held onto the .50-caliber door gun that had been strapped down to the floor on a makeshift mount. The cameras were late setting up on the roof of the Kasbah miles behind us, and we cut circles over the vast shattered world outside of town. We would do that all afternoon. The pilots were bored. They took the bird high and then did air stalls, the helicopter dropping weightless, my feet lifting from the floor in the sudden descent, the desert hungry for us to fall into it. At the last moment they would level off, halting the plunge to catch air and power the engines. But my body was still falling, my weight bearing down as the floor of the helicopter suddenly rose, and my legs buckled so quickly that I fell into a crouch. I pulled myself back up on the gun and looked out the open door. We were close to the ground, the pilots laughing, and I saw a man on a carpet in the center of an expanse of pebbles. He had a rifle and his head was pulled under a shelter of cloth held up by a thin stick. I asked the American to ask the Moroccan pilot what the man was doing there. He said that the family had sent him there to guard their property. I looked again as we circled the dead land, the dry, rusty terrain covered with worn-down rocks the size of fists, and the slumped figure in the middle of it more cloth than man.

"What would he do if someone walked out here?" I asked.

"He would shoot them."

"How would he know that it was an enemy?"

"It is understood," said the pilot. "No one walks out here that does not know they shouldn't."

"I wouldn't have known," I said.

"Then you would have been shot," he said.

This was southern Morocco, and beyond this crumbled wreckage of the Atlas Mountains lay the sands of the Sahara desert. The tribes and governments could not agree on the location of national borders, and so they warred over lines in shifting sand, Morocco and Algeria both vying to own more emptiness than the other. As the sun got low we flew back to Ouarzazate, and the man was still there, unmoved. I was told that he would be replaced at some point by another family member, who would know how to approach him without being killed.

I imagined him out there alone all day in the heat staring out at the shimmering stone horizon, huddled all night in the cold moonscape, a handful of bullets, reciting stories to himself to stay alive.

During my time off I would go to the souk. It was frequented by French tourists and the prices were high, but the merchants respected a long negotiation. I would look through the rugs quickly and then ask for prices on the few that interested me. They were hand-woven, made of hand-dyed, handspun wool, and they looked very old, though I had no sense of their true age. The merchants claimed that they were Touareg rugs and that they came in from the desert. Maybe they were. I would sit with these men for hours as they sipped small glasses of sweet tea. I politely refused it, pretending an allergy so as not to offend their hospitality, but I knew that the glasses were just rubbed clean and a debilitating stomach flu was passed around this way. I was initially using my per diem to purchase rugs, but by the time I left, I had traded my watch, sunglasses, and all but one set of my clothes for Moroccan goods. Tourists did not want to waste time haggling and usually paid the price asked, which disgusted the merchants. The first price was exorbitant, an insult to which the customer was to respond as if it had been said in jest. This was a formality, an invitation to counter with an equally absurd low offer. The merchant could then feign repulsion and usher the customer into the store for tea and hours of reconciliation. The stores all looked much the same, and inside they felt like shallow caves. The rugs stank of sheep, the leather of camel, and there was a dry odor of human grime mingled with the wet scent of tea. I liked that the rugs had not been made by machinery. Someone had woven them, chosen patterns and colors, tied the small knots along their edges. Someone, an artist, had looked at it finished and signed it with that last look. And maybe it was old, used on the floor of a tent for years, a familiar object, before it was sold to a man who knew that I would come for it one day. Someone would.

Ouarzazate was a post on the trade route from Africa to the northern cities of Fez, Marrakesh, and Casablanca. It sat at the crossing of the Drâa and Dades valleys south of the Atlas Mountains. Named by the Berbers to mean "without noise," it was not a formal town until the French imposed a garrison there after Morocco became a protectorate in 1912. Western tourists stopped on the way to see the sand drifts farther south in the desert, and a Club Med was built for them. Despite its dirt, Ouarzazate could not feel ancient anymore, and everyplace but the small souk was cleaned for European tolerances. I stayed in the carpet stalls as much as possible, and one of the merchants would thrill when I came by. We argued prices in broken French and shards of English, and I bought rugs, rings, and knives from him. He gave me a hint one day that he thought I would appreciate. There was another market outside of town, only open one day a month, and no tourists would be there. I thanked him and went.

The monthly market was a local affair, and I was regarded with suspicion as I walked through. Sheep and goats were being sold by the herd, and there was an entire dump truck loaded with tomatoes. People had come out of the mountains to trade, and few were using money. I bought a brass powder horn and then stopped at the blanket of an old man. No one was looking at his wares. They were all found objects, picked out of the trash and off the desert floor. The collection looked like that of a mystic chosen to represent a life on earth. A camel-bone-handled knife with a broken blade, a pair of bullets, a bottle opener, some seashells, a small tin of bent nails, and a handful of coins. He became almost breathless by my interest in the coins. He could not speak any English or French, and he scurried to a nearby merchant, who returned with him. The merchant was sullen and would not look directly at the old man. He gestured for me to look at his merchandise, while the old man watched my hands as if I were performing a trick. I picked up the coins. I did not recognize any of them except the aluminum lira from Italy. As I held each one up, the man would say something and look to the merchant, who would purse his lips and translate into French. That often did me little good, as my French was weak, but I got most of the names. Arabia, Tunisia, Egypt, Morocco, Italy, and Spain. None of them was much older than thirty years. One felt heavy, was worn smooth, and had a hole punched in it.

"*Halaka*," the old man said.

I looked to the merchant, who paused. "*Halaka!*" the old man said again, his hands in the air as if repeating the word made its meaning more obvious. "*Ait Benhaddou.*" The merchant thought, and the old man watched him waiting for the word. A taxi driver had stopped, along with several curious merchants and a pair of teenage boys. The merchant, slowly aware that he had gained an audience, stood straight and made a confident pronouncement.

"*Les conteurs*," he said.

The old man looked at me, eyes wide, mouth making the shape of "*les conteurs*" without a sound. I did not understand. The taxi driver translated the French to English.

"Storyteller, mister."

"*Je non comprend pas*," I said. "I don't understand."

"This a storyteller, uh, wear this. From the mountains, you see? *Ait Benhaddou. Bon chance.*"

I gathered that an itinerant narrator from the Atlas Mountains had worn the coin as he traveled, at some point stopping in the ancient town of Ait Benhaddou, now largely uninhabited, and had given it to the old man or traded it, perhaps as a good-luck charm. This was all a guess. The conversation was to produce no more detail in any language. I bought the coin for the effort of explaining its origin to me, and because I thought it would make a good gift for my father, who was a storyteller. It was in poor condition, but I could identify most of its markings. It was an 1852 bronze dix centimes coin from the first year of the Second French Empire under Emperor Napoléon III. Later I learned that 1852 was the first year it was circulated, and that it would continue to be accepted as French currency until 1935. It had been stamped in Paris and traveled into the Atlas Mountains, where it ceased to be a coin and became instead an embellishment. When I returned from Morocco, I gave it to my father. He slipped it onto the ring of his key chain beside the keys to his writing room, and I went back to train with my Marines, a veteran of fictitious combat.

MY RESERVE UNIT was mobilized to attack Saddam Hussein in 2003, and I knew that the war would be strange when we had to send a detachment from Kuwait into Iraq to get a supply of ammunition with which to invade Iraq. Our transportation to the war had delivered us late, and we were behind the assault by over a week. As we loaded our weapons and stowed boxes and bullets into every open space in the vehicles, I kept rechecking the list: .50-caliber rounds for the snipers' special application scoped rifles (SASRs); 5.56-ball ammunition with tracers for the scouts' M16-A2 rifles; 5.56 linked ball and tracer rounds for the squad automatic weapons (SAWs); 9-millimeter ball for the offi-

cers' and corpsmen's pistols; 25-millimeter high-explosive rounds
and 25-millimeter armor-piercing rounds for the chain gun; 81-
millimeter high-explosive, illumination, and red phosphorous
mortar rounds; 7.62 linked ball and tracer rounds for the vehicle
commanders' machine guns; AT-4 disposable shoulder-fired antitank missiles; TOW missiles for the antitank LAVs; grenades. All of
this metal to be fired in anger. I already knew that lead was bad,
jacketed in copper or not. I was surrounded by boxes of it. The
benefit of lead was its density, its weight, and, because of these
things, its capacity to maintain momentum through air resistance
once fired. It gave bullets more range and accuracy. The copper
jacket was only there to keep the bullet smooth and pointed. The
vulnerability of lead was its soft nature and the ease with which it
could be damaged, made inaccurate. Lead is also poisonous.

The other ordnance I understood. They exploded and the
concussion or fragments of steel killed you. Everything we were
packing was designed to puncture, burn, shatter, and kill. The
only metal that concerned me by its mere presence was that of
the 25-millimeter armor-piercing rounds. We usually used stan-
dard tungsten-core, discarding sabot-tracer rounds, but in the
scramble for ammo, it was thought that we had been given some
fin-stabilized rounds meant for use on aircraft. They were heavy
with death and composed of depleted uranium, a metal denser
than lead and meant to punch through thick steel armor plate.
Although I found comfort in its lethal design should I need to use
it, sitting beside a box of hundreds of these pieces of uranium
spoke more to short-term thinking. I could defeat the enemy be-

fore me and die of radiation damage years later to the medical denial of the military. There was already talk of trouble caused by antiarmor tank rounds that had been composed of the same metal in the Gulf War, this same ground. This type of uranium was a by-product of enriched uranium production for power plants and nuclear weapons. Thus "depleted," and emitting less alpha radiation, it was molded into bullets and sent to us. When uranium completes its decay, it is lead. The progression from one metal to the other must have seemed ideal for weaponry. The bullets sat between my gunner and me in a large box, linked together and fed into a chute to the chain gun, radioactive or otherwise, while we looked through our sights for someone to shoot them at. All the Iraqi armored vehicles we encountered had already been destroyed by air strikes or abandoned, and the need for armor-piercing rounds never presented itself. We were told that the radiation was minimal, not to worry about it. It was only dangerous if we breathed it. They had said the same thing to troops field testing the effects of nuclear bombs in New Mexico.

On the way from Kuwait to Nasiriyah we passed large lots beside the highway filled with the shells of cars and trucks. They were all completely rusted and frail. I did not at first realize that these gathered wrecks were all that remained of the Iraqi retreat from Kuwait in 1991. This was the highway of death where the routed army of Saddam Hussein was caught in their stolen cars and charred with bombs. Everything was beyond any kind of salvage, the fire baking off the paint and the metal rusting to a burnt orange.

We found Iraqi tanks, light armored scout vehicles, and troop transport trucks all along our route. They always seemed long abandoned even though they had been parked where they remained mere weeks before. All had been struck by missiles or tank rounds and burned, causing their rapid decay. In Iraq, metal was rare and noticeable. War was a contest of metals.

CHAPTER 4

SOIL

THERE IS A VASTNESS TO THE UNDERGROUND. WE tend to forget the mass and depth of the world as we stand on it staring at the horizon and wondering at the infinity of unsubstantial sky. We have seen the cuts in the earth where its secrecy was exposed. Beneath us, veins of water are moving in the deep, punctured by wells and the failures of dirt to know its place. We have built cellars, making a space in the underworld below our homes. I have always been a digger. I know the smell of unlit soil. There is a satisfaction in discovering the rocks and lifting them out, descending into the land. It is, to some, a calling similar to the one that drove Neanderthal artists to carry fire and pigments far into caves to leave their handprints. These people dared to go into the subterranean pitch to paint animals and, in that black cavern, to imagine the outside.

✦ ✦

AIR AND DIRT are different things. Dust is almost both. I was allergic to dust. "House dust" it was called, though I could not tell one dust from another at the time. It was said to be composed primarily of human dander. I was given allergy shots for a year when I was nine and declared safe from the skin I shed. It made me think about the fallout on top of bookshelves and the places that were rarely touched. I was leaving a thin snakeskin, coating my room as I grew out of the dead parts of me. But dust was different in different places. So was soil.

I learned to value dirt from my mother, who introduced me to the gardening life. I can still see her crouched as if in prayer between rows of bean plants. The frail, earnest shoots of seedlings made her happy, and she would spend the winter planning for spring. As she looked out the kitchen window at the snow behind the house, I knew that all she saw was the square trace of her garden. She taught me how to make black earth from a pile of orange peels, eggshells, pulled weeds, and raked leaves. In some ways, it was disappointing to see the compost pile dwindle after so much labor to build it up. There was something incalculable in the magic of decomposition, the fibers releasing their gathered volumes of water, the earthworms working through the damp mass inside, and the mysterious heat of decay. Disappointing to see how little dirt everything was reduced to in death.

It was the deconstruction of leaves that was the hardest to believe. Our house in Poolville was shaded on two sides by aged maple trees that sounded like rushing water when the wind blew. In the fall, they dropped a deep layer of bright red and orange foliage on the front lawn, and I was charged with raking it into piles. I would wait until the last leaves had all come down before I took out the bamboo rake. Beneath the buoyant curled leaves that had been last to fall was the damp flattened mat of leaves that had been pressed against the earth by rain. They had already lost most of their color and darkened, rolling up together when I raked them into a pile on an old white bedsheet. I would make a sack by lifting the corners of the sheet into the middle of the pile and gathering the four ends in one hand, then I would carry it over my back to the compost pile. There was a faint smell of stale tea in the air. Raking leaves and planting daffodil bulbs were the last acts before snow fell.

In the 1970s, winter brought deep snows to central New York. Games turned to short days outside with too much clothing on and long periods indoors looking out through windows. I could not work on my wooden fort in the winter. I would walk out to it, stepping over the raised ridge of snow that lay on my fieldstone barricade. I built snow forts, but the wooden fort would have to wait until the thaw.

The fort sat on four posts sunk about eighteen inches into the earth. The floor was a foot above the ground, leaving a low crawlspace underneath it. I could see the frozen dirt and decided that if I could not build, I would dig instead. I struggled under the fort with a flat-head screwdriver, a hammer, a small planting spade, and a little red bucket from the sandbox. I lay on a garbage bag, chipping at the dirt with the screwdriver. The earth shattered into crumbs and

I scooped them into my bucket with the tiny shovel. I went down a few inches a day, working invisibly until darkness. The ground remained frozen, its frost line staying ahead of me as I burrowed, and I came in for dinner with very little evidence of a day spent in soil. By winter's end, I had completed the bunker beneath my fort. Standing up in my dirt pillbox, I had dug too deep to see out.

The spring came and the melting snows filled my cellar with water. The walls weakened and my father suggested that I fill it in before the fort, its footings exposed, sank into it. My small spade handle had broken off in its labor against frozen earth, and I wrapped the pieces in plastic, dropping the package into the water before I began to fill in the bunker with my mother's garden shovel. Someone digging someday would uncover my spade and know that I had dug there long before they had. It may have been my first strange statement about the ownership of explored space, and of my leaving some signature there. I had gone down into the earth. I had dug a cellar, stood in it at the bottom of the known world, and then filled it in. I knew something small about the underground, and I left it buried where I'd found it.

Exploring, I found other places beneath the surface. I used to walk through the stone chutes and briar-tangled spaces in the ruins north of the river. They were what remained of the mills that had put Poolville on the map before the turn of the century. Water held by the dam was rushed through a causeway to a cast-iron turbine that powered textile machines. The concrete tunnel was still there, and I had discovered its entrance behind some brush. It was not a secret that the mills had been there, but few in the town knew about them. Almost no one even crossed onto the other side of the river where the ruins spread out in an arc, consumed by trees.

I went into the tunnel. It was square, or seemed square, as I could not tell how deep the sediment was. It felt soft and moist, unable to dry completely in its long rest away from sunlight. There were no human footprints inside. I liked the cool air. I moved forward cautiously, bent to make myself small. A shaft in the ceiling dropped light into the tunnel forty feet ahead. The light was encouraging, although spiderwebs gathered around it like mold. I stood in the hole and looked up at the trees high above. It was as if I had fallen into a well. The tunnel continued, changed direction, and I inched its length crouched in the dimming gray. It ended abruptly at a sealed metal grate, and I could see green growth through a narrow, rusted slit. I was disoriented by the underground and its lack of reference to the surface. There was just the shaft. I had been moving without a natural pace, and I could not guess the distance that I had traveled. I sat on a pile of trapped branches and looked back.

I walked the ground above, tracing the entrance to the shaft and then onward, underestimating the distance. It was like my measurements of the underground were abstract and, also, that the tunnel now went in an ambiguous direction through the earth. I felt like I could not walk, exactly, above the tunnel, even in a straight line aimed from its entrance to its end. I began circling until I ended in the stone cellar of a mill, finding the metal grate beside the base of a large, rust-frozen turbine. It is hard to accurately imagine the things that you can't see, even when they are real.

The stone walls had been well built, and I wondered how they had been allowed to fall into ruin. A grand old house stood nearby, still straight beside its massive derelict dairy barn, clapboard paintless and gray, the color of the wooden wall I had ridden on in the sea. They were the last structures standing on this side of the river, connected to the town by a steel-frame bridge with thick, loose wood planks that thunked like tribal drums when a car crossed it.

The ruins of the mill and dam are still there, more ruined maybe. The house and its great barn are gone, dismantled and burned by the owners for safety. The steel bridge has been removed and replaced by a new, soulless concrete span. No thick thumping boards as cars pass over, the river still channeling water past from somewhere higher to somewhere lower. The tunnel is unchanged, the fallen dam sending no water through it to the turbine that can never turn again.

ONE HOT AUGUST DAY, my Boy Scout troop went camping on the hill behind the box factory in Earlville. We hiked down the street from the church and up a dirt road on the hillside above the floodplain. We could see most of the town and the overgrown Chenango Canal that passed through it. It was the success of the canal that had inspired the village to name itself after the canal commissioner, Jonas Earl, in 1835. The canal was abandoned by the turn of the century in favor of the railroad that had come in 1868. We built lean-tos out of pine boughs on the slope across from a forest, and ate what we had packed. I had brought almost no food. My parents considered Tang an extravagance at home, but it had vitamin C and required no refrigeration so I was awarded a large can of it for my weekend in the wild. Although it tasted good mixed properly, I thought it would be like candy if I adjusted the proportions. I was camping and as free from household law and order as I could be. I mixed very little water with it, only enough to make an orange paste that was as luminous as nuclear waste. I proceeded to spoon it into my mouth until my tongue burned, my teeth hurt, and I got a headache from the dangerously high blood-sugar level. It was in this condition that I played hide-and-seek in the graveyard that night.

At the base of the hill spread over five acres was a cemetery that had been completely overgrown. I had not even known that it was there. The brush was especially thick along the edge of the trail, and the graves could not be seen. As the sun went down and the forest yellowed, the boys in the troop ran into the woods, leaving someone to count. I hurried down the hill around trees to the sound of ascending numbers and found a pit just deep enough to get belowground in. Another scout jumped into one not far from me. In between us was a depression with a smooth cut stone laid in it. It was a burial with its epitaph fallen facedown. I realized that I was surrounded by unmarked pits and forsaken graves. I was crouched in one. The Mount Pleasant cemetery had gone bankrupt after having sold perpetual-care plots in the 1890s for only twenty-five dollars each. It had been officially abandoned around 1928, and many of those buried there had been moved to a graveyard in the center of town. Vandals had knocked over almost all of the remaining headstones by the 1940s, the plot records were lost, and the people left here had been long forgotten. All I knew at the time was that I was hiding in an unmarked grave, and there was no explanation as to why it had sunk so deep. I leapt out, thinking myself mere inches from the dead.

The voices of boys calling out to one another filled the forest over the faint counting that came from across the trail. It was dusk and scout leaders rallied us back. We left our graves and returned to the shelters just as it began to rain. It was a haunted night of stories about the open burials and missing bodies.

The next morning we had our fire pit in a clearing above the abandoned cemetery. I learned that eggs explode when placed in hot coals, and that a brush saw with deep teeth used to cut wet branches would jump and bite the hand nearest to it. I still have two short scars on my knuckles. While I was field dressing my hand, two scouts found a stone sinker for a fishing net and a scraping tool while digging a latrine. The top of the hill had been a prehistoric native settlement, but it had never received any official designation as a protected site. In the forest on top were hundreds of test pits where diggers had searched. There was no order to them, holes of different sizes, all of them looking like graves that had either been dug up like the ones in the cemetery or been left empty and worn down by years of rain. The clay below the topsoil was always the last layer thrown on the piles, and it looked new and discolored on the forest floor. I wanted to dig, too, but I had brought no shovel and my hand was bandaged.

On the other side of the site was a gravel quarry that had scooped away acres of the hillside, revealing what the ridge was composed of. It was a glacial deposit, the stone stripped from bedrock and rolled by moving ice left to settle in piles, heaped beneath us. The smooth hills around us were all unrecognized as aftermath. I stood on the cliff worried about all that must have been lost. There was no way to know how many Indian graves and artifacts had been sifted in machines and hauled away in trucks to become roadbeds and drainage fill, wampum beads packed in with pea stones, and arrowheads spread out with gravel. Looking at the lip of the quarry, I could see that the topsoil was not very deep. The gouged sand and pebbles below it fell away, cutting under the dirt held in place by roots and dense clay. I could imagine the hill restored, the soil filled with artifacts and skeletons. I was beguiled by the permanence both burial and terrain pretended. I knew that slow changes were inevitable, but they worked unnoticeably on the land during our lives. Seeing the toppled headstones, the emptied graves, and the avulsion of the hill in our time proved to me that there was no safekeeping in soil.

BURIED ARTIFACTS and vanished peoples led me to archaeological digs. The area had been Oneida tribal territory until the 1780s when the State of New York purchased the land from them. Their villages had been near the rivers all through our valley, and the hills around Poolville, Earlville, and Sherburne had all been native settlements at one time or another. In high school, I went with my godfather, Dr. Hosbach, to a place known as the Cameron site. A longhouse had been found and the excavation had been divided into a grid of carefully measured squares. In our roped-off portion of forest floor, we carefully scooped out the earth, cutting the sharp corners perfectly. A screen was set up beside us to sift the soil through holes just large enough to catch beads. Wampum beads were made of shell from channeled whelk found in Long Island Sound and Narragansett Bay. Most had actually been made by European settlers. They had been a unit of trade and were rather common to find. We uncovered the clay layer between two and three feet down and a portion of the central fire pit. The rest of the pit lay in another grid square and had to be left buried. We could tell by where artifacts were found how deep the dirt had been at the time of the settlement, and surprisingly little topsoil had formed since the area was occupied. I sifted the soil carefully over the galvanized mesh, examining every pebble. Below the sieve tray rose a pile of filtered earth that looked like ground coffee. For the full day spent in dirt, our plot yielded only two wampum beads and a broken arrow point, but I couldn't complain. I had dug down far enough to sit on the undisturbed ground beside the ash of a family fire for the first time since the house had been filled with stories and the smell of smoke.

Underneath the topsoil was clay. It was light-colored, and we could see where posts had been. Wood rotted away aboveground, but below the surface it was transformed into black clay. We dug out the post molds, all that remained of the wall poles, marking their size and location on the archaeological map of the site. When all the plots had been excavated and the posts recorded, the shape and construction of the longhouse would emerge. I looked at the grid, the vanished house continuing into other blocks of soil. I began to realize that the ground must have been filled with bones and artifacts everywhere. We walked slowly back to the truck with our spades, empty-handed and searching the ground as if we had dropped something. Unmarked burials lay throughout the forest, extending under the cleared fields, being plowed up or excavated. Our fascination with hunting the dead inclined us to scrutinize the turned earth while hoping that our own bodies would never be found scattered this way.

WE PATROLLED UP THE STEEP HILLS in single file and spread out, our empty rifles at the ready. It was 1994, and another war with North Korea seemed imminent. We had arrived from Okinawa, Japan, for joint exercises with South Korean Marines inland of P'ohang. It had just rained and the trees and earth were dark, the air damp. The crests of the sharp, rocky hills were aswarm in high fog, the recent rain rising as steam from the warm ground or the rain clouds themselves descended, still heavy with water. I was unsure of which part of the cycle I was witnessing, only that the hills took on the invisible possibilities of mountains, the peaks of which could be miles up. We stalked into the mist, losing sight of the small valley below. My map showed the contour lines shrinking in warped ovals, and I estimated us to be only a few hundred meters from the top of the hill we were moving on. We ascended into the cloud to the sound of boots stepping, each one of us almost alone on the packed dirt path up, straps on backpacks creaking as if we were suspended from parachutes instead of weighed down by them. The swirling vapor left us floating. I could smell the rain, the rock sweating. Tiny beads of water formed on the frayed threads of my uniform as I walked. The moisture was visible moving as soft specks in the pulsing air like schools of fish in a shoal. I had been at higher altitudes, but never so far into the atmosphere, never so able to touch it as it worked. The Asian oak trees swayed, filtering the wind that pushed over the hill, and made the sound of distant coastal waves. We were near the top, the air cool on my face and moving fast, and I stopped to get a physical head count down the column. The terrain had opened up into a clearing with short grass and three mounds the shape of the hill upon which they had been piled.

I had heard the Korean soldiers warn us that we might discover some burial mounds up in the hills. They were not noted on maps, few of them known to anyone at all, placed without permission on the slopes over hundreds of years. They were rural grave sites, and the path that we had chosen must have been for family funeral processions ending at this spot. At the base of each grave sat a single stone, unmarked. They looked ancient, although they could have been a year old. We had been told that the dead were buried sitting up, and that we should never stand on the graves, as they were weak in the center where the head was near the surface. I could see that one of the mounds had a depression in the top where the heap must have collapsed. I looked into it expecting to see the dome of an exposed skull. There was just clay loam and fine shards of stone. I imagined men and women seated inside the mounds, held up by settled soil, their clothing almost empty and pressed to bones all coming apart underground. Their families had mourned them in the space where I stood. They had covered them with soil here.

I formed the platoon into a defensive perimeter in the wood line around the clearing, and we ate in silence, sitting together on the hill in the clouds beside the dead, sitting in their earth. A Korean woman later told me that a grave with a sunken center meant that the deceased had stood up and left. I didn't ask about the bones.

It began to drizzle, and reports of an incoming storm canceled training. We withdrew down a streambed as heavy rain began to fall. When we had hiked up from the valley days earlier, the streambed had been dry, scaled with dusty plates of smooth stone that looked as if they were composed of gray chalk. They scraped against one another, sounding frail and ceramic as we stepped on them. But the water hardened them, glazing their surfaces, transforming them into dark leaden tiles washed clean. They became slick. We moved to the banks, preferring the mud for footing. We could hear the rain smack into everything now, the branches of trees whipping from their trunks and shaking their leaves. All at once it stopped, the sun instantly warm on our wet uniforms. In the center of the valley, we could see trucks coming for us in a slow line down the road.

We loaded into the cargo beds, our packs crowding us, rifles all held straight up, everyone facing one another toward the center, our backs to the outside. I heard ringing and turned to see a funeral procession on the shoulder of the road, a man with a bell in front and several men carrying shovels in back. Held up on long handles was a box covered with flowers. It was like a wooden crate and inside it, legs crossed, sat the dead, passing us toward the hills we had surrendered to the storm. It was still sunny as they crossed the bridge over the stream. They thinned into a line on a path as we began to drive away. The manic clouds cloaked the hills again, and the sky went gray. The rain fell in sheets. The stream was beginning to flow with runoff, brown water pulling topsoil from the high ground. It was proof of the diminution of the topography and its burials. The valley filling and emptying.

I kept watching the procession, as if they would stop, turn back because of the weather, the heavy rain driving them home to sit in shelter until the winds died down. But they didn't. I watched until they disappeared into the clouds and, far away, we turned into another valley.

A YEAR LATER, when I was on military leave, my wife and I drove into the Shenandoah Valley of Virginia to go underground. A cavern had been discovered on August 13, 1878, by locals digging for the source of cool air in a sinkhole near the town of Luray. It had since been a tourist attraction. We had never been in a large cave, and so we got in line with people who collected postcards of places like this. They carried disposable cameras and stood in front

of things to have their pictures taken. When there were enough
people waiting, a guide led us down steps into the underworld
and spoke of the consistent 54 degree F. temperature. I knew that
somewhere beneath the rock chamber was the magma and heat of
the earth's molten interior. Outside, it was 90 degrees and humid,
the sunlight quietly burning the surface of the hill. This space in
between was always 54 degrees. I did not understand why.

Inside, the guide stopped and we looked at the places where he
pointed. It had the look of both a natural phenomenon and a built
environment. Columns, floors, walls, and a roof enclosed a coral
world of reduction and deposit. The space had been hollowed by
the gathering of acidic waters in the limestone mass and then the
slow drainage of the dark lakes deeper into the world. They had
given most formations names such as Castles on the Rhine, Em-
press Column, Giant's Hall, and Skeleton's Gorge. I wished that I
could be alone in the space with my wife, or without anyone. It
just felt like an odd room robbed of its mysteries, another looted
tomb. I wanted to see it as the first men did, with nothing but a
rope into a hole, the caverns of darkness expanding, unknown,
beyond the frail light of their candles.

I was sorry to discover that the experience was so banal. The
cavern floor was smoothed with a dull glaze of calcite. It seemed
to have been worn by hands and feet, though much of it was out
of reach of the shuffling lines of visitors. There was only one discovery that truly intrigued me. A skeleton had been found in the
cavern. It was incomplete, and it was a girl.

The skeletal fragments lay in a small pile, mineralized, fossilized, and in disorder. A piece of cranium lay beside a piece of pelvis, the growth plates in the hip showing her to be in her teens, and the calcification covering the bones estimating her to have fallen into the cavern more than seven hundred years ago. Anthropologists at the Smithsonian, now the custodians of the bones, guess that she had been buried on the surface and that the ground beneath her grave had emptied into a cavity at some point, eventually taking much of her remains to the cavern floor. It is their explanation for the missing bones and their disarray. There is no evidence of predators or scavengers in the history of the cave. No suggestion of murder or mishap. Just some pieces of one girl. But there are also no published thoughts that she had willed herself down, that she had imagined the cavern and tried to enter it, alone, through a vent of cool air, finally arriving inside in pieces. No one thinks that she ended there on purpose, to die in lightless solitude under dripping water, safe from wind and men, her body slowly accepted as part of the washed underworld.

BY 1997, I HAD TRANSITIONED from active duty into the Selected Marine Corps Reserve, and we trained for wars we no longer expected to happen. On sleepless weekends with my LAR unit, I would alternate between precision gunnery ranges and Virginia forests. On a patrol, I came upon a cellar. Miles of reconnaissance through overgrown thickets revealed the foundations in what had once been settled lands on the Quantico Marine Corps Base. Southern farmers had cleared the area of trees and plowed the hard clay soil, depleting their families as they toiled, burying them in holes and covering them up. Most traces of prior occupation had been bulldozed, and forest had largely reconsumed the fields. It was spring when I found the two homesteads. I saw daffodils deep in the forest and headed for them. They were an early breed, small and subdued, but they betrayed settlement, yards, and home. Someone had planted them and doomed them to a perennial life, immortal in the place that had been surrendered by the short lives of people. They continued to multiply and bloom for over a hundred years, expanding into misshapen patches. The grasses had not yet reemerged in the early spring, and the daffodil leaves spread out as a dark glossy green mat on the forest floor, alone in the cold, and blooming sparsely. The bulbs underground remained in the dark, dividing until they crowded themselves with offspring and ceased flowering.

There behind the daffodils lay the cellar of a house. The rocks were slipping inward, and the basement was little more than a dip in the earth, water gathered in the center, bricks collapsed at one end where there had been a chimney. I began to walk in expanding rings around the ruin, hoping to find an ash dump, an old bottle, or the location of the barn. What I found was a line of erect stones. They stood at the head of depressions that looked the same as the cellar. Graves of a family too poor to buy cut stones and carved epitaphs—but their daffodils were still blooming.

My mother had planted daffodils around our houses in Poolyille and Sherburne. I planted more there, and then in the yards of places my wife and I lived in Maryland and Michigan.

They always remind me of her. The daffodils still came up where she had put them in the ground with her hands. They would come up for hundreds of years. They were safe beneath the surface. No one would know who had planted them, but seeing them blooming under the trees, people would know that someone had lived there. If they look in the spring, they will find the depressions left where our houses had been.

IT WAS APRIL 2003 and we were in the desert waiting to invade Iraq. The Marines played baseball with a sock wrapped tightly in gray duct tape. My father would have been pleased to see another use for it. The field was a parking lot made with pebble fill brought in to minimize the dust on trafficked routes in the area. Bursts of powder came up from boots as Marines ran on it. I went to the earth berm that was pushed up around the camp by bulldozers. It stood about twelve feet high and had crumbled to a sharp peak at the top. It wrapped around the tents like an abrupt rectangular ridge of psychological safety. We couldn't see the outside from the inside, and that gave us some comfort, but it was just a pile of sand. There was nothing on the outside but desert, a great uninhabited emptiness that we had come to fight over. The plastic bags, MRE wrappers, and empty water bottles from waves of transient units rested against the base of the berm, brought and held there by odd winds from the east. I walked over a space disturbed by a thousand boots, but there was no trace of anyone having ever been there at all. The dust and sand moved relentlessly across the desert like a film of rough liquid being dragged by invisible rakes. Pointless and purposeful. I knew, as the desert knew, that my conquest of footprints would be erased as soon as the wind returned. A desert, like an ocean, cannot be owned.

I found a piece of clay pottery, left exposed in the sand, and picked it up. Evidence. It was probably more than one thousand years old, rough, gritty red clay from a riverbank somewhere else, moved against the plan of the river, wind, or desert to a place where it could be identified as an object out of place, human. I thought, as I sat on an abandoned sandbag bunker in the berm, that it was all for nothing, this life. All of this dust hurrying to be earth again.

I was listening to dust. We were waiting to invade a land composed of it. The static coming over the radios sometimes sounded like the wind blowing through large trees, but in my comm helmet there were no natural lulls, no pauses that winds give themselves under the churning of clouds in the fall. The static was caused, in part, by dust particles in the connectors. The dust was, in its own way, communicating.

Kuwait was sand and the fine swirling fragments of what had once been sand. The moving rock was in a continuous reduction. It was making itself smaller and smaller by wind-driven collision with other rock at rest. The friction of the detritus was on a scale too negligible to seem important to us. These impacts went without our notice, though we could hear the sound of detrition all around. The actual sand behaved like material of comprehensible substance, stopping at obstacles and easily filtered by cloth, but the elemental sand behaved like the air, moving with the same amount of access to space. It was invasive and small gaps in our tent allowed billows of powdered sand to blow in. As it met the calm interior air, it lost its way and settled onto and into everything. We could see it pour in through the places where the bright light found holes. It felt better to go outside, where the fine dust was not visible. We could still taste it on our lips, but the lack of visual pronunciation made it seem possible to escape in the open desert. At night, with the flashlights off, it was more disturbing as it seeped into our lungs, invisible. It caught under our eyelids and seemed to solidify in the moisture deep in our nostrils. We wrapped our heads in our T-shirts to sleep, and it felt like drowning in dry space. Our gear spread around us, we looked like mummies left in odd positions in an unfinished tomb. Every surface became abrasive with this dust that had once been stone on the other side of Arabia. Some of it had been bone.

A week later we were sent through Iraq to the Iranian border. The hardened dirt flats were covered with sheep droppings. They littered the desert plain in swaths, scattered for miles, random as pebbles strewn from the sky. They seemed as perdurable as rock, imaginably lasting for centuries, rolling imperceptibly as winds moved dust, gathering in clusters and spreading apart again. Women swept them into piles with palm fronds and carried them back to their clay ovens as fuel for cooking bread. They burned like dry oil, as if fossilized just short of coal. What remained curious was that there were no plants in this in-between territory. No grass or water for miles near the befouled paths of flocks. We would sometimes come upon a shepherd walking beside his bobbing carpet of sheep. They moved as if connected by short strings, ungraceful but responding like a scarf to wind when he tapped his stick. They seemed incapable of disappointment, their toil distraction enough. After they crossed a road it was speckled as if each sheep had been shitting continuously at the sight of a clean space. It was magical. The small spheres churned and spun inside these animals were left spilled like a universe on the pavement after the flock passed into the hills. The pellets were still dark and almost glossy with moisture, as if, finding no grass, the sheep, their heads low, had been sifting the desert surface and compressing the dust into tiny balls of mud. The droppings cast oval shadows on the dry road as the sun came up. It was the cleanest filth I had ever seen, and it was only scarce near the villages, where it had other uses.

I could see the town ahead. On my map of Iraq it was called Jassan, and locals confirmed that to be its name. The erosion of mud construction at the site over hundreds of years had raised the ground level so much that the town now sat on a hill composed entirely of the remains of towns before it. The settlement was sculpted from the surrounding dirt, and the land and town were a matched dry orange-tan. The human impression felt temporary despite a long history of occupation. The village could easily dissolve back into the desert, the mound slowly flattening back into the expanse of nothing kept level by the wind. It changed as we got closer.

It was like a head buried above the eyes in the dirt plain, its skull cut open to reveal inside a brain built with mud bricks. Curving passageways wound through the settlement as if they had been carved into the soil by water. All of its intended straight lines had been weathered dull and constructed without noticeable measurement. The town was almost a natural formation.

The doorways were indented into the walls in regular intervals. The doors themselves were not decorated and showed no individual marks other than the composition of found materials they were made from. Wood from crates of tomatoes, cooking-oil cans beaten flat, and sheet metal from old refrigerators. There was no way to tell what lay inside. The town looked like an anthill, and I could imagine that behind the doors in the alleys people were burrowing deep into the underground, building crypts in the cool earth. But I was told that there were no basements in the town. No sunken spaces hidden from the desert. Nothing but surface and what stood above it.

On the south side of town was an oasis that nourished a dusty flourish of palm dates and was the reason for such long settlement. Little rain fell, but the desert sun was unable to dry it out. The rusted hulk of a tank stood its ground nearby, the earth around it dark with oils it had bled and the orange stain of iron, a nameless memorial to the war with Iran. There were trenches and minefields to the east along the border and ammunition bunkers surrounding a garrison to the west. The oasis sat between them, unaware of the scarred earth around it, oblivious to the burned tank on its poisoned piece of dirt, its rust inching toward the palms. The water rose in the spring, unaffected by wars, or dust, or thirst. It was an exposed aquifer, forced up by invisible pressures and subterranean rock formations, arriving at the surface as a perpetual pool inexplicable to generations of people wandering the desert, amazed to see a hole in the dirt reflecting the sky. All this water moving under us.

The bunkers west of Jassan had been cleared days earlier by Marines. My unit staged in between them and I was uncomfortable being so close without inspecting them myself. Most were filled with ammunition spilling from boxes, but no one could tell me what was or wasn't inside the one nearest my vehicle. It had been entirely ignored after the security sweep, and the battalion headquarters had already moved into the abandoned Iraqi base. The vanished army had been here until, suddenly, they weren't. Their footprints were still visible in the dried spring mud.

A hideous dog briefly guarded the entrance as I approached. It was one of many that crept warily around the compound living on garbage. I was glad when it retreated sideways along the open ground instead of falling back into the concrete den. At the doorway, I pulled my pistol and held it at my side with no justification to do so other than that I was at war, it was an enemy bunker, and I expected more unpleasant dogs inside.

The stairway down was coated with recent dust, but inside, the bunker felt ancient. It was like entering an empty tomb, looted of its valuables but still built to house the dead. I descended the steps into the dim gray, and the walls of the passageway were covered with Arabic. Men leaving evidence that they had gone below. The graffiti thinned with the light as I went down. Underground, there were chambers filled with air that didn't seem to circulate and floors covered with a filth of dust and fragments of paper. I couldn't read any of the handwritten notes. The air was cool but smelled of breath, almost damp, and mingled with old sewage that had lost the potency of its offense. In the center of the bunker, built hastily with concrete blocks, stood an uneven wall, a final defense inside the underground. It was curious. Men had been afraid in this space. Enough to build a wall they would never make a stand behind. I remembered seeing pictures of a wall of rough stone found piled between temples in an Aztec ruin. It could only be imagined as a last resort, a final barricade, against some imminent threat. No bones were discovered on either side of it, and no evidence of occupation was found after its construction. The stones divided ghosts from their memories. I peered around the wall with great anticipation. There was no one there. Just newspapers and ammunition. Cigarette wrappers. Old maps.

It was like a cellar without a house above it, gray as late dusk inside and never able to be brighter than that. I was not sure, as I wandered its rooms, if I was alone. I kept expecting to find a man, the last man, in a corner, armed. If he was the one who had stayed . . . would he defend the cave? I was the intruder. I headed back up the steps into the bleached light, the dry heat, and the endless open sky.

The border was a mere twenty miles east of Jassan, exactly where it had been before the Iran-Iraq war, only not exactly. Neither country accepted the location of the boundary, and so it was considered a disputed border . . . and we were to patrol it, our conflict disregarding their dispute. We were to somehow make clear the separation between states that had been unclear to each

side for twenty years. We were to do this as agents speaking for
Iraqi leadership that we had exiled while not speaking to Iranians
at all. We were advised that the United States had no diplomatic
relations with Iran and that we were restricted from conversation
with them, while at the same time we were assigned 150 miles of
their border. The road had old land mines along much of it. Years
of wind had exposed many of them, but we were wary of what
we could not see.

The war with Iran had produced miles of trenches and fortifi-
cations. They had been abandoned for two decades when we came
upon them and they were little more than crumbling mounds of
earth. Command centers and bunker compounds had been built
with burlap and woven plastic sandbags filled with dirt. The dirt
had probably come from the trenches dug nearby. Time and pressure had pressed the soils in the bags into solid blocks that held
their form even after abrasive winds had worn away the cloth from
the exposed outer edges. They stood as compressed dirt walls, and
facing the earthen hills of Iran a mile or two away, they seemed
like minor reflections of the natural terrain.

I found a thin steel helmet with a bullet hole in it and fragments of artillery shells exposed by the wind, but there was no
further evidence of war beyond the dirt molded stiff in sandbags
and ditches slowly filling with dust. It had been a war fought in
dirt and, for Iraq, in the open. A war of artillery, and of holes in
the ground engraving the surface with trenches and, somewhere
else, with graves. Men trying to dig places to hide, trying to move
into the ground, to get underground, hoping to be safely buried

before they were killed. Hiding in the earth was of some comfort while they waited to be laid beneath it. I walked through the battlefield as if I were a tourist. I looked at Iran in the near distance. It had battled Iraq with artillery shells that we had sent them in support of the shah, and Iraq had fired back with shells that we had later given in support of Saddam. We were now hunting that same man, Rumsfeld's old ally, who was, at that moment, hiding in a hole in the dirt, writing orders to his lieutenants requiring their resistance to terrorists we blamed him for befriending. He was hiding in a hole in the yard of a house that had no cellar.

I walked back to my vehicle, making no imprints in the hardened dirt. The traces of war were being absorbed. The dead had already forgotten being killed, and the survivors were slowly forgetting the dead. We would leave without leaving anything. It wouldn't be long before the trenches filled in and the bunkers wore down. There were sheep droppings all over the battlefield. Flocks had passed over this land like soldiers, before the wars and ever after. I had driven past thousands of sheep, walked through them near villages and in the empty borderlands. I found traces of sheep everywhere—in woolen rugs, meat, dung, and cloven tracks—but I didn't see a single sheep bone until the ruins of Babylon.

THE MOUNDS OF DIRT around the exposed remains of Babylon were composed of blown dust trapped in layers by pieces of pottery. There were pits dug into the undulations here and there, made either by archaeologists doing test digs or by thieves burrowing into the fragments hoping to find something whole. In either case, the wounds cut into the ground were fascinating. One day I walked across the pocked field and found my way into one of the holes. It was twelve feet deep and showed no signs of having reached the floor of the ancient capitol. The years had built up without noticeable delineation, all the clay shards and bone packed in the dirt appearing as one layer, one moment that lasted for a thousand years. I wondered if these mounds were simply everything that had been discarded by archaeologists excavating the Ishtar Gate and the walled interior of the citadel, French, Germans, and British fingering through shovelfuls of leavings and hauling all the common matter out to this field and dumping it all over again. All these shattered pots and bones of butchered animals, too ordinary to recompose, left in disorder, everything discarded. It seemed unlikely as, walking on them, the mounds formed geometric shapes. They were rounded squares, dipped in their centers, as if the thick layer of dirt had been draped over the walls of empty rooms. In one of the pits, I could see the bricks of a wall, cuneiform marked on them, and asphalt mortar still holding them in place. It was difficult to imagine the people pouring their trash into the empty sections of city for centuries after its decline, eventually filling buildings and covering their walls with the waste of later occupation. I found no skulls underground in the silt of the city, just jawbones and teeth of vanished flocks consumed.

How was it possible that such immense places could be lost enough to require rediscovery? When Rome was finally unearthed beginning in 1803, many of its stone streets were under sixty feet of debris. How was it that no one noticed the dirt deepening, covering everything? Pompeii was entombed in a pyroclastic surge in AD 79 and lost until 1594 when a man found it digging an underground water channel. Sands massed over the tombs of Egyptian pharaohs, no one left to worry about their afterlives, everyone buried slowly after them, the Acropolis left barren on its rock, the jungles grown over the temples of Machu Picchu, and Ta Prohm, Angkor, no one staying to guard the gates or leave fruit at the statues. All the gods and men worshipped, armies raised and bled away taking empires and losing them, tombs filled with stolen treasures and looted, the seats of civilizations built and surrendered, all of us defending our homes and leaving them behind to be destroyed. The earth boiling up, dunes deepening, and water rising over our eternities.

I stood in the pit looking at its walls. In some ways, it seemed appropriate that Iraq was now left with fragments that could not be reassembled, teeth and jaws, its histories broken down to unfamiliar objects symbolic of consumption instead of memory. You invade so many places in your life, you are a constant intruder, and you keep all of the places you enter, and you let them all go.

DURING MY SECOND TOUR I found myself on the other side of Iraq. It was not Iran that worried us there but Syria. In Ramadi, the water table was just below the surface of the city. All the buildings sat on concrete slabs, but no one had a well. The water came from the only building with a basement.

The water-purification plant on the shore of the Euphrates was built around a concrete pit filled with pumps pulling river water in and pressing it out into the tangle of pipes that trickled into homes. When I arrived the morning after a firefight, the plant was damaged and abandoned. A cloud of chlorine gas had passed over a section of the city from the punctured tanks outside, and bullets had hit the water main inside. The city was getting thirsty and repairs had to be swift. I walked inside to find blood and water.

A group of Syrian jihadists had assaulted the North Bridge vehicle checkpoint guarded by Marines and Iraqi Army soldiers. It was well planned but based on information about our security that was one day older than they needed. The attack began when men dressed in black threw grenades into the back windows of a building we were using to check city visitors in. The grenades were deflected by mesh, just installed the day before, and they fell back on the assailants. The explosions initiated the coordinated attack by the rest of the Syrians as they shot one Iraqi soldier dead and put a bullet into a Marine lieutenant's helmet, stunning him for a moment before he led a counterattack, driving them back into the water plant. Marine reinforcements quickly cornered them as they attempted to retreat to their van. In the parking lot, a teenage boy reclined against the van door, dressed in black and strapped with bandoleers of ammunition beside his machine gun. Around him spread a pool of his blood. There were problems back at the water facility.

One of the attackers died in the cellar, shot through the heart behind throbbing pumps, and another had fled, mortally wounded, out the back door. He was bleeding fast enough down his left leg to make a perfect imprint of his naked foot, in blood, with every step. I followed the trail as it went from concrete to dirt and across a large puddle where his footprints pushed deep into the mud. They were, for a few steps, clean again. The blood reemerged on the far edge of the water and then stopped in an oval stain where he had died.

Nearby, Marines from Weapons Company, First Battalion, Fifth Marines, found a girl covered with damp blankets during a search. She had second- and third-degree burns over 40 percent of her body and had been lying there on the concrete floor for twenty-five days. Her mother had been cleaning her, but the girl was not healing and infection would likely kill her. They said she had set her dress on fire while lighting incense. She was three years old and doomed.

The streets and homes of Ramadi produced scars. They were the permanent scratches of living in a hard place. Children started in with injuries early, and there was usually evidence of their pain etched somewhere on their skin. What could not be seen was still there. As the little girl was being wrapped in gauze by our corpsmen, I stepped out of the room. Tied to a mirror above an outdoor sink nearby was a plastic daffodil. It bloomed forever without ever touching the ground, and it was colored blue, unlike any daffodil that exists on earth. I thought of my mother. In the hallway lay a goat on a leash, and in the courtyard of the girl's house sat her older sister, chained to the wall, laughing with estranged madness. She scraped at the dirt with her hands and stared at the sky. The family had not mentioned her while we were working on their young daughter, and I had the sense that they would not know how to mention what I saw. I stood by a grapevine in silence as the sister shrieked and spoke to no one. She looked at nothing in particular, and she seemed not to notice me standing before her in her roofless cell. I stayed at a distance that I judged to be farther than the length of her chain and then went back inside to the crying of the little girl, and the worry and hopefulness of the family as they watched. That was easier for me.

On my next visit, I asked the father about his other daughter. My interpreter explained that he claimed she had gone crazy from the sound of bombs and had to be tied up because she would wander off. There had been a mental health clinic in the city, but it was abandoned, and I wondered how much wandering off that had caused. I researched options for her care, but Iraq was deranged and not yet prepared for the insane. The family kept her, fed her, and cleaned her as she laughed at our world. I turned my back and focused on the injuries that could be repaired. She seemed self-existent, but I wondered if her laughing was a crying or if it was a blissful detachment that protected her from the rest of us, kept her safe in her wild despair aboveground. She scratched at the hardened dirt, hoping, maybe, the earth would open beneath her enough to let her into a quiet cavern.

In Iraq, dirt was the environment. The soil was capable of rising above ground-level, billowing into atmospheric clouds, moving, the landscape shedding its skin. In June, when my mother was watching seedlings emerge from moist earth, I wrote home about the desertic soil:

> It is now hot enough to sweat spinal fluid. Truly miserable and not yet even July. Dust storms have poured out of the dry spaces to the west. The air turns opaque with an orange tan of migrating particles. They move with the freedom of the air that moves them and cannot be kept out of anything. Eyes, nose, weapons. Dust seems to seek the places that it becomes most noticeable. When the wind finally thins, the entire city is left covered with a fragile layer of fine powder. The resident dust beneath is revealed to be a different, older hue of dirt by the first footsteps of the next day. More gray than colored, as if it has aged by settling. Our trudging begins the blending of sediments. Of dunes and riverbeds. Of bones and buildings. Mountains and of what lies beneath. There is something to be said about being dust. It is where we're all heading.

Northern Africa had the highest fecal content blowing in its winds, Kuwait had grit, Los Angeles had petroleum soot, central New York had my dander, and Iraq would have death in its dust. The Pentagon was still denying Gulf War syndrome as veterans hollowed out and died from it in VA hospitals. T. S. Eliot wrote, "I will show you fear in a handful of dust." There was something else in the air with all of that dust and ash.

→ ←

I HAVE SEEN an aftermath photograph of the D-Day invasion at Omaha Beach, bodies of soldiers half-buried in the sand. I have seen men digging trenches and graves, and I keep forgetting how much dirt is composed of the dead and how much the living are subsumed by soil. Adam was made of clay. In the tomb of the first Qin emperor are ten thousand terra-cotta soldiers buried in the edge of the Gobi Desert, the only survivors, and somewhere in the dunes of Arabia are the lost armies of empires that emptied their citadels to vanish into the sand. The human record is filled with soldiers filing into the unknown, so few returning, and no one ever able to convince them not to go. I know something about how it ends, and the soil underground smells like the last place we go. I have already dug my own grave, stood inside it, and looked back out.

CHAPTER 5

BONE

IN POOLVILLE, THERE WERE ALWAYS BONES SCATTERED on the railroad. I would sometimes walk down the tracks with my mother looking for wild trilliums. A friend had told her that some were there. State prisoners had come through and cut the trees along the river as part of some environmental restoration program, and the trillium bed was now exposed to direct sun. They are a delicate shade plant, and the sunlight would kill them if the vigorous new brush didn't choke them out first. They could be rescued and transplanted. This was a mission my mother could not resist. The river ran like a loose wire along the taut straight lines of raised track. The railroad had been built on a high bank of crushed pumice that was interrupted only by steel bridges at the places where the river crossed the line. The trains were still running then, and the rails were worn to a bright shine on the top. I would pick up an occasional loose spike and take it home. We had sung "John Henry" in school, and I had rooted for him against the machine. The song ended with: "And he died with a hammer in his hand." I wanted to go out that way.

We were half a mile from the intersection of Willey Road and the tracks, and we came to a dead deer draped across a rail. It had just been killed, and I could not look away. I had never seen a deer that close or a dead creature of that size. Its immense dark eyes were open and had just begun to gray, its blood red on the black gravel. Over the following years I would study the spot as the deer was absorbed into the porous volcanic rock piled beneath it. The skeleton first surrounded itself with a mat of tan hair, which spread and grew thinner. Then the bones fell apart, bleached, and began to fragment. Within a few years it was difficult to find any evidence of the deer on the spot where it had died. Just a handful of small whitened pieces of bone in the gravel.

That day my mother pulled me along and we stopped at the bolt-pimpled bridge that crossed the river. The concrete supports on either side of the trestle directed the water neatly through the gap, and the effect was of a tight belt on a large dress. The current flowed faster through the pinch and dug the riverbed deeper to handle the canalized volume of moving water. The secrets in the middle of the river were vulnerable to my observation through the spaces between the wooden railroad ties of the bridge, and I searched for fish. I could see the silver flashes of suckers tearing at the algae on rocks and the long shadows of northern pike laying nearly motionless beside waterlogged branches, their pectoral fins working hard to keep them still. The inelegant carp lolling in the sun-warmed mud holes always drew my attention by their size, though I despised them. They were bottom-feeders and ate trout eggs. I considered them the ruin of the river and tried to hunt them to destruction. I often forgot that the river was much larger than my part of it and that the carp would fill the niche that I emptied from the hundreds of miles of water above and below the town. Fish could swim and were not bound to anything other than the water itself. For all of my travels, I was bound to how far I could walk between breakfast and dinner. I would catch or spear the carp and leave them on the shore, with too much air, to die in the sun.

In the field behind our house, I would look for arrowheads. It was called surface surveying. Many Native American artifacts had been found by an archaeologist in the field back near the river, but I never found anything. No bones. In high school American history, there was a chapter in our book that spoke of the confusion of armies meeting along a road during the Civil War. There were no fields to pour into, and so there was no proper battlefield. There were just trees and dense underbrush and 170,000 troops running through it shooting blind. The battle became known as The Wilderness, and the dead were scattered throughout a vast forest and left where they lay as Lee retreated to regroup near Spotsylvania and Grant pursued him after three days of disorganized fighting. The book showed a picture of a farmer with bones piled on the edge of his field taken after the war, and the chapter mentioned, plainly, that the dead were still plowed up each year, their bones forever unnamed.

IN HIGH SCHOOL FOOTBALL, we were sent onto the field and told to be brave. We knew that winning was better than losing. We thought of our physical selves in a singular sense, not composed of parts. The bones, veins, and muscles were joined beneath our skin, the complication of our anatomy invisible. I remember nothing of the mumps, chicken pox, or rheumatic fever except lost school days in bed and ginger ale. Ailments just seemed forgettable.

Coach Virgil had eaten a worm during practice, and we guessed at the significance of the act—something primal and daring. "Good protein," he said. The next day would be our homecoming game in Sherburne, and we needed inspiration. Worm eating would do. For seniors like me, it would be our last homecoming and the beginning of our leaving home. We would be watched. There was the possibility of as much brief glory as could be achieved at the age of eighteen. Self-preservation of any kind was ruled a tendency toward cowardice.

The armor had drawn me to the sport. The helmet and shoulder pads that shielded me in the combat of adolescence. The pads on arms and thighs. The colors of my tribe and my number, which made me unique in their mass. There was a safety in the layers of pads and plastic plates, and they separated me from the belief in injury. As I put them on for the game, I grew more powerful, my strength swelling to the size that I became with my uniform on. It was a war cave, the locker room, the smell of decaying sweat left in unwashed clothing, the sound of cleats clicking on the painted concrete floor, and the scrape of shoulder pads glancing off of lockers, the boys made less graceful by their unusual insulated size and their voices changed to that of young men rehearsing for violence. It filled me and I was ready for the clash of lines. The air in the locker room was dense, and as we pressed out the small door, our blood was rich with something like growing up.

The field was lit by lights on tall poles, surrounded by darkness, and it seemed, always, to be a surreal place. Our cleats tapped like claws on the sidewalk, and then we turned off into the grass, trudging silently down from the school on an unlit length of hill. The helmets in front of me caught the light of the field ahead, and there was a robotic creak and slap of shoulder pads as we moved together out of step. In the dark, it felt like there could have been thousands of us. It felt like we were equally indomitable and doomed. Spartans toward the Gates of Fire. There was, on those nights, as much romance as war was ever painted to have for young men. You could not have convinced us that we were going to play a game. You could have impelled us to rush to our deaths.

The field was strange with light falling from all directions, the blades of grass oddly lit from all sides, dew sweating through the turf. We formed our line for the opening kickoff, and it felt like we waited for a long time in the tension of our first action. We began our slow advance behind the motion of the kicker and then broke into a mad run behind the ball as it rose away like a slow bullet. We collided with the other team as we ran, following the ball with our eyes and forgetting to avoid the obstacles in between. Forgetting that we were terrestrial. The receiver was in my zone, and I headed for him as he began to make choices. He picked a course toward me and I reached out for him, both of us almost stopping for a moment. The pressure of my lunge was all on my planted leg, and my knee was struck from the side by a teammate who had lowered his head and hurled all of his force in the direction of his last glance. I heard the muted sounds of ropes breaking as if below the earth. My leg seemed to unravel around the bones, and I fell, the opponent carrying the ball past me. There were no pads on the side of my knee. No armor. I heard a whistle and struggled to stand, straightened myself, and limped to the sideline. Two others would go in as the defensive ends, and I would try to work out the sprain and switch in later. I was full of the rush of fighting and could not believe that any damage had been done. I paced the sideline slowly, trying to will strength back into my knee. It seemed unable to support me. I could not run or pivot. No one noticed me as I hobbled behind the sideline, and I cannot remember if I noticed what was happening on the field. I didn't tell anyone I was wounded. We were losing.

I remember, as the team ran into the locker room at halftime, that I staggered, alone, and came in late, and was noticed because I was late.

Whatever benefits usually awarded by adrenaline or focus

were now gone. The team returned to the field and I behind them, a friend bracing me. The pain had come fast and the swelling was increasing. I swung my leg without really stepping with it. Something was very wrong. My constant motion had initially kept the blood from gathering in the injury, but there was no stopping it now. I had to sit down on the bench. The EMT in the resident game ambulance lifted my leg and, despite the forward bend below the knee, said that it was a serious sprain, gave me Motrin, and left me. I sat trying to work the blood out of the swelling and continued to disbelieve my injury. As it worsened, I watched for its improvement. The leg would not bend on its own.

Two teammates supported my arms and helped me back to the locker room at the end of the game. I had been silent for the entirety of the contest after the first play. The ambulance was gone and an assistant coach finally realized that I was crippled. He knelt in front of me and lifted my calf. My foot came up and my leg extended beyond straight. The pain shot up my back. He looked frightened, which was of little comfort. He called my parents and they came to pick me up and take me to the hospital.

I lay for the next day on my bed with my leg raised and immobile because the surgery could not be performed immediately. The surgeon, Dr. Ivan Gowan, was the sports-injury specialist for the nearby university, and he was my best hope. The prognosis was dark. I would walk with a limp. There would be no more contact sports. My interior and exterior cruciate ligaments had been ripped apart and a tendon torn from the bone. The perfection of my youth had definitively ended. My leg could be repaired but not restored. My incredible vulnerability had finally been exposed to me. It would take a year to recover.

The hospital was being renovated, and the room that I had been wheeled from was not the one that I returned to. I awoke slowly from the density of anesthetics and painkillers to see colorful cartoon children painted on the walls and a mobile with animals hanging over me. It was a room in pediatrics that was a temporary fill for the wreckage rolled out of the surgical ward, and I thought, in my bleary squinting, that I had died. My leg was mummified in a heavy pressure wrap and elevated. There was a tube draining blood from the knee. It began to hurt. I was trapped on my back in bed for a month of staring at a room that smelled like crayons, rubber, and alcohol. My father told me, at the time, that I was being unpleasant.

When the swelling ebbed, they removed the wrapping and I finally saw my leg, shaved and orange with bruises, stitches in two lines along either side of my right knee, stains of sterilizing liquids. I had no power over its movement, and I regarded the limb as if it were not mine. I had not been able to move it in weeks, and now, unbound, it seemed unwilling to move at all. Doctors smiled as if it looked excellent, wrapped it again and encased it in a fiberglass cast, from my hip to my ankle, bent slightly at the knee. I was released from the hospital to lie in a room of my choosing somewhere else. I lay at home and stared blankly at study books for the SAT. It seemed that years passed and that I was aging rapidly as I lay waiting to be well. It was almost impossible to shower, and I felt my skin developing a paste born of inactivity and decay. I thinned and weakened, my vitality draining into the bed, and I began to believe that my life was drawing to a close over a football injury. I was told that I could return to school on crutches.

I had survived childhood without ever hurting my knees. I had scraped them and banged them, but bruises and Band-Aids were not injuries. They were small side effects of play. Now I knew something about my composition. I hobbled down the halls swinging the sticks as everyone walked by. There was no parade for the fallen player returning to his school. No note of the sacrifice at all. I was just back as if I had not been gone, and noticeable only because I was damaged now. No one cared if I had been brave.

When the hip-to-ankle cast was finally cut off my leg, there was little more than bone remaining under the skin. The muscle had atrophied from long dormancy, and it was the first time that I had concentrated on commanding a limb to move with no result. It lay on the bed dead to me, looking as if it had been transplanted onto me from a corpse. I was truly shocked by my inability to will movement from my own leg. I was an invalid. I hobbled into physical therapy to begin my recuperation, angry at my disability and harried by a new vanity. I was intent on erasing the damage. I made myself believe that the prognosis was incorrect, that the expectations were based on less ambitious patients, and that full recovery merely required ignorance of pain and more will. I punished myself for being weak, for falling inglorious on the field, and within six months I was running again.

→ ←

WHEN I FIRST ARRIVED at the trailer I lived in after college, a goat had greeted me. It was chained to a steel ground spike and was moved around the property to keep hard-to-mow corners from being overgrown. A goat will eat anything. A goat will not complain. It had incredibly intelligent eyes, large and dark with horizontal sliver pupils, and it would look into yours as if wanting to discuss philosophy. I would toss it apples from the tree. This small act animated the goat with what I could only see as joy, and if he saw me working in the yard, he would stand stretched to the limit of his chain and call out to me. No one there knew that I was quite fond of the goat. One afternoon in fall, a local friend, John Murray, came to the trailer.

"Put on some pants. We need to bury that goat," he said as if the chore were my fault. I had spent a long day digging a new garden bed in shale soil for a painter. I had just washed off, and I was reluctant to dig another hole. I didn't know the goat had died while I was out.

The owners had called John while I was working, and the two of us were to take the goat to one of the empty stone wells in the pasture, throw it in, and cover it with a pile of hay from the stables. We did this with some difficulty. It was a large animal and heavy with muscle and bone. We lifted it by its legs, struggled it awkwardly onto the bed of a pickup, and drove it down to the edge of the pasture by the river. As we pulled the goat from the truck by its legs, its horns caught in the gap between the truck bed and the tailgate. John kicked it free, and I couldn't manage the sudden weight of the carcass. The goat fell with a thud and lay swollen and rigid, as if it were solidifying, filling with sand. We looked at it, then grabbed its hooves and dragged it to the hole. I noticed that there were already layers of hay deep in the pit. John said that the animals on the farm all ended up in here. There were already many sheep packed in wet hay following the rotting roots of the missing trees down into the earth, the rock rings now serving as open graves. It felt like a sacrificial act, dropping an animal into a hole built with stone. It also felt as vulgar as anything I had ever done.

Someday this site would be excavated and archaeologists would be at a loss to explain what we had done. It was dusk and natural sounds became noticeable as people went indoors. The river flushed past us filled with the fine bones of fish and rolling pebbles. We stood at the rim of the stone circle looking down at the goat as it lay contorted in the pit. We covered it with hay, drove back to the house, and I walked up the hill past the leash and the apple trees to the trailer in the dark.

ONSLOW BEACH was the North Carolina shoreline along Camp Lejeune Marine Corps Base, where I trained to be a Marine. At low tide it was covered with bones. In the empty winter months, when I wasn't training on weekends, I would spend solitary hours searching for fossilized shark teeth. The beach was whipped with cold wind, and sand would rise up in it, stinging my face like freezing rain. It was rare to see anyone else there. The teeth were black when wet and gray when dry and they were often as sharp as the day that they had fallen to the seafloor twenty-three million years before. They had absorbed the chemicals of preservation as the pressure of gathering sands formed sedimentary rock, and bone was given the preferences of immortality. The sinking of the earth reversed at some point and began to rise instead, the aggression of waves grinding the sand loose again and returning it to the beach. The ocean had a way of separating things at the shoreline, and the teeth would wash in sorted with objects of similar size at low tide. Bones have a long life in the sea.

In the disintegration of larger things, there were fragments of ribs and other bones that were smooth and looked as if they had been sculpted from graphite. I had no idea what they had come from, but I kept a few as I walked the beach. The ocean had forever been full of predators, and the land was composed of the dead. I had been on both sides of the shore, wading in from one and crawling in from the other. Life began there.

I knew that the world was wearing down, and that what was worn off was piling up. I wanted it to be imbalanced in favor of piles, the cumulative somehow increasing more quickly than the reductive, the earth expanding, our work contributing to a rise in the land. To think this way you can never visit the shores of the sea where the collision of mass is so visible. The solidity of rock can be seen being randomly damaged, the violence of water so continuous, the planet's instability revealed to be obvious, and we are content only because we live lives too short to register the speed of ruin. We tread on the dead, some so long in the earth as to have become stone, but we only think of the few we have buried, the ones we have witnessed being buried. Every time I dig, I expect to find bones, but I know that the rest of us becomes unremarkable, reduced to a fertile dirt, our skulls emptied of all our wonder and our hollowed eyes unable to be amazed by the absolute dark of the underground. Unable to remember or to be afraid.

MY MOTHER DREAMED of whales. Before we went to Maine one year my father wrote, "Judy is whispering something about a very long boat ride, next year, to see whales. I am pretending not to hear her." My wife and I drove to meet my parents on Great Wass Island, where they rented a summer cottage for a few years. We arranged to take a lobster boat out to Machias Seal Island far off the coast. The seas were choppy and I recalled the storm aboard the USS Fort McHenry. I was getting sick as the small boat rode the swells, feeling worse with the knowledge that we were still only on our way out. My father, on the other hand, after making much of his expected misery, became visibly delighted. He stood looking out at the sea like a captain. He had just finished a novel with Melville in it, and oceans had been much on his mind. Moby-Dick had originally been simply titled The Whale, and he had read it many times. He had a metal sign screwed to the door of his workroom that said CALL ME ISHMAEL. The island was ten miles from the nearest shore but more than twenty from the port where we departed. As my mother searched the ocean for whales, my father looked forward as if he were steering a great ship, and I looked back toward land.

We never saw any living whales at sea, but everyone in the town of Jonesport knew about the dead whale on Great Wass Island. It had washed ashore or beached itself in the early 1990s, like the pod of gray stones that were already there, and it began to rot, tides and seagulls picking at it. Each year, people and storms took pieces of it away. Its immense vertebrae sat in yards and flowerbeds throughout the nearby town, and by the time I found it there was just a skull. There was a heavy mass of bone at the base of the head, and its eight-foot nasal bone aimed up into the air. The beach was all cobblestones that ground things between them when the waves came in, and the rest of the great animal had been taken farther inland by people or drawn back into the sea. The last bone was too large to be carried off in either direction, and so it lay on the stones with the driftwood like an anchor dropped from a ship.

Scientists believe that whales went back into the sea from land, losing faith in a world of dust, giving up their legs but keeping the strange stretched bones of hands in their dorsal fins. They still have pelvic remnants, femur and tibia rudiments of hind legs. They are still forced to surface for air. It is their weakness. They sing into the water at the creatures that don't know what it is to drown. In the deep, they speak to land at the bottom of the ocean with the slurred sounds of shores moving apart.

On the other side of the island there were massive outcroppings of granite that declined toward the waves, a solid beach, slick with seaweeds and rough with barnacles. At low tide, their midriff masses were draped with seaweed and they seemed, for hours, to hiss as they dried. When I went down into the pits and cracks where the foundations of the island had split open, I could hear the beds of mussels breathing and crabs laboring over empty shells in deep crevices behind rockweed curtains. As the sea slowly filled the spaces that it had left, the seaweed lifted and began to sway like hair being pulled underwater. The island seemed to sink rather than the ocean to rise. The rough stone was the worn peak of a submerged mountain or part of a great henge pushed inland by storms. Either way, what it had been was destroyed and it was now just an island with edges resisting further consumption by the sea.

Below the rock, I believed, there was just more rock. Above the tidemark the stone slabs lay revealed, scoured by storm waves and saline winds. This was the place between worlds, desolate, contested, and surrendered by both. There were no soils, no seaweeds or grasses. At the base of the rock lay driftwood and sea wrack, empty shells and the debris that did not survive a life in the sea. On top, the outcrop buried itself into the thin earth of the land. The cap of peat was held together by small pines punished for extending their trespass toward the salted waters below, their dried roots exposed, crowning the rock like a thorned warning.

In between the exposed stone were thin crescents of granular sand and smashed shells. My parents would place their chairs on these beaches during low tide and read in the sun. They rubbed their toes in the warm, ground-down bones, shells, and stone at the edge of the ocean and then slept while I picked mussels from the rocks for dinner. They would wake and talk, my mother rubbing my father's bald, sun-reddened head while he said things that made her laugh. Her laughs were shameless and had chickens and shore birds in them. High and fluttering or one of those deep, pure laughs that come from somewhere under the sea. My father would laugh like an owl hooting until he became breathless, his head tilted back, chest shaking, hands on his stomach, mouth open wide. I was too close to the slap of waves and too far from them to hear what they said, but their laughing was large and seemed to reply to the calls of seagulls flying past. The tide would slowly return, taking the rocks back under and driving my parents up onto the porch for drinks. It is an important line, the division of water and land, that which is on the surface and that which is below it.

MY WIFE AND I FLEW to London in 2001 for a New Year's vacation. We went down onto the shore of the Thames River where I was told not to touch the riverbed because its alluvial soils still held the plague. The river had served to clean the city since it was Roman Londinium, and the history of London's occupation lay sordid in the Thames's wet bed. The city, once darkened by soot from the burning of coal, had emptied all of its tarnish, murder, shit, disease, and intrigue into the passing water, and as the river slowed against the incoming sea, much of the debris sank, settled, and remained perpetually drowned at the bottom. The tide was out and the wide channel that cut through the Greenwich Pier section was allowed to drain, exposing the edges of its guts. The shore that always stayed above water was pressed against the stone walls of the city in front of the Old Royal Naval College. This was common ground, and the piles of sand and polished pebbles were picked clean of artifacts. Below the waterline the mud, almost black with the condensed filth of offscourings, was dense with the evidence of man. Scattered in between rocks were pieces of clay-pipe stems, and I went about collecting them in a bag. They began to appear in the 1600s and were popular through the 1800s. A dozen pipes could be bought for a shilling and came packed with tobacco with the expectation that they would be smoked once and then discarded. As I got closer to the water I began to slide on the muck. The river had stopped receding toward its center and had pulled far away from the land of footsteps. It was in those last few feet of retreat that it gave up its dead. I thought, at first, that the strange pattern of bulges under the water was just sunken sticks, but it was the offal of London, now a tight blackened puzzle of bones packed into the clay. Ribs, joints, vertebrae, and the sawed-bone remains discarded by butchers and cooks had been embedded in the riverbed for as far as I could see. I imagined them continuing under the sullen current all the way to the opposite shore and then all the way to the sea.

"COME. WE KNOW where they are under the dirt."

In May of 2003, near the Iranian border in the town of Badrah, Iraq, locals beckoned my Marines and me to follow them to a mass

grave. Men filled Toyota pickup trucks and hurried to an empty, lifeless expanse outside of the small town. They could have exhumed
the grave without us, but there was still an underlying fear of retribution by Ba'athists that seemed to require our presence. It may
have also been a simple desire for others to bear witness to what had
happened to them there. The grave site was surrounded by nothing
more than a low rectangular berm, but it had clearly been forbidden ground during Saddam's rule. It looked just like our base camp
in Kuwait. We stood nearby as Iraqi men dug into the yellow-white
lime powder in search of their relatives. They gathered the bones in
the clothes of the dead and laid them in rows for families to examine. There were no forensic teams or police, just men with shovels
and us. The people in the grave had been executed in 1991 following the revolt against Saddam that the United States had encouraged
during Desert Storm but had then failed to reinforce after our brief
invasion. Following the rapid U.S. withdrawal into Kuwait, Saddam identified and executed everyone associated with the uprising.
They had been buried here without proper Islamic funerary ritual,
but relatives had never dared recover them for reburial. Families
could identify the remains by the clothing still preserved on the
victims. The bodies were collected on squares of thin white cloth,
the corners then tied together to make a sack for them, blessed by
a cleric, and hurried to ancient cemeteries as far as Najaf to be in-
terned. American warplanes would later bomb that cemetery while
fighting Muqtada al-Sadr's al-Mahdi Army, the combatants using the
graves as cover, conflict following these murdered people to their

final resting place. An older man kept pointing at a pile of bones
with a skull wrapped in a blue veil. Men expected men to be killed,
but the execution of women even violated the protocol of tyranny.
"Woman," he kept saying as if trying to convince me that it was
true. I kept nodding my somber agreement. "Woman."

It had taken a Marine working in a Civil Affairs unit a long
time to hire a local Iraqi man to exhume the graves with his back-
hoe. At first he believed that the man was reluctant to cooper-
ate because he was being contracted to work for Americans, the
enemy. Like the bodies in the grave, there would be consequences
if he were later listed as a collaborator, and Saddam had not yet
been found. It was not that. Through a frustrating negotiation we
learned the truth and forgave the man his reluctance. The man was
feeling guilty because, twelve years earlier, he had dug the graves
for the execution. When he arrived at the site, he knew exactly
where to dig. Only bones and cloth had survived, and the skulls
all had blindfolds still tied tightly over the hollow spaces that had
been eyes. Telephone wire bound the arms of the dead just above
the spilling bones of their hands. As the Iraqis lifted the skeletons
up, dust rose out of the holes and I stepped carefully upwind. I
knew what most of that dust was.

A YEAR AND A HALF LATER I stood by the Ramadi dam
on the northeast corner of Camp Hurricane Point sweating in
my heavy uniform and looking down at the fish in the lock. My

team and I were escorting the Iraqi dam workers to assist an assessment of the dam's condition. They called it a barrage. *Barrage* means several things in English. To Marines, *barrage* only means falling mortars or incoming rockets—so we called it a dam. Its operation had largely been abandoned due to violence in the city during our two-year occupation of the area, and we were hoping to restore the flood-regulation infrastructure built in 1955. It still had a functioning fish ladder. The dam had first been damaged by a U.S. airstrike in 1991 and had not yet been completely repaired. What the workers needed to access was causing too many base-security problems, and I began to realize the futility of the effort. More good intentions damned by hostile circumstances. There was a lock in the dam to raise and lower boat traffic, but it had been shut for years and the water within it was a placid mixture of azure blue and jade green as the Euphrates pushed around it, wild with hurling itself through the dam gates, falling twenty feet to continue east through Fallujah and Baghdad. I kept watching the fish in their deep concrete cistern. They hardly moved. Despite the enclosure, the water was translucent for about four feet and the fish were dark, suspended in it at different depths.

The water began in the melting snow of Turkish mountains but on its way south had gathered the sewage of every town including ours, the blue-dyed water being pumped by Iraqi contractors directly from the Porta-Johns into the river just above the dam. Below the dam was the inlet for the Ramadi water-purification plant. Somehow, in this world, these fish lived. If we were not here, someone would be fishing for them. There were old nets and line on the ground beside me. I hadn't been fishing since high school and missed it. The bones of fish lay in a pile, their scales spilled down the slope, dully reflecting the sunlight like weathered sequins.

A boat was nearby, its stern pushed up on the bank and its bow sunk, angled sharply underwater as if preparing to dive, its pilot booth facing down into the river. The boat had once systematically dredged the gathering sediment from the base of the dam, repositing it on shore. The silt drew my attention. It seemed as if it had been sifted, the piles of fine gray filings larger than dust and smaller than sand. It looked like pulverized lead and was so completely dry that I could not imagine it wet, moving in the river. We were using the deposits of sediment as a quarry for fortifying outposts in the city. As I headed back to the headquarters, Marines were stacking sandbags heavy with the bottom of the Euphrates. We were building barricades to protect ourselves from Iraq. Iraqi silt in American bags kept us from one another. It was hot outside, the sun bright. We were living in graves, our bones still slick with blood and held alert by muscle to keep them from their rest. It would not be much for us to lie down and go quiet, the bags emptying mountains over us.

A mile downriver, the bodies of people with names were kept in the new morgue beside the Saddam Hospital (renamed Ramadi Hospital), but those that were brought in from the city were left in a trailer outside. The corpses were laid on the floor of what had been the refrigerated trailer of a meat truck, but the air conditioner no longer worked. I would have to check the morgue each

week and photograph the unclaimed bodies. They were foreign
fighters killed by the United States in gun battles, people killed in
car accidents on the highway nearby, murders, homeless children
caught in crossfires or used to lay bombs, and women who had
died as victims of family shame. Some of the men had been tor-
tured. None of them had any identification. I was looking for Iraqi
contractors and city political leaders who would often go missing
for ransom, rivalry, or terrorism. Rarely would we find anyone
we were actually looking for, but I always found someone who
was missing from somewhere. It was 100 degrees F. or more in
the summer, and I would put on a dust mask, which was useless,
and carefully climb into the boiling trailer on the side of the door
that did not have the liquids of bodies dripping slowly from it. I
squinted as though the smell hurt my eyes. It didn't, but somehow
I felt that I must squint, closing up as much of myself as possible.
I would hold my breath before going in and come back out to
breathe. The bodies would be blackened but not by fire, their teeth
glowing white as the skin had tightened and pulled away from
their mouths. Their eyes lost volume and the lids would sink,
eventually cracking open to reveal that the sockets had emptied.
White molds were spreading over their faces. The corpses would
remain strewn on the floor for thirty days and would then be
taken south of Ramadi and buried en masse, without a marker.

I never touched the dead where they lay, wearing numbers and
waiting to be covered with earth. I was a foreigner sent to witness
the end of these unknown. I could not know if it was important that
we knew who they were after they were dead. In their heads, their

memories were quietly rotting. It is for a brief moment that the living and the dead should share the surface. These dead had stayed too long, abandoned, forgotten, or lost. If I stayed in the trailer, I might see them shed their skin and break into pieces. I could watch dust and earth conclude on the floor and lay there until someone opened the door again. I sometimes imagine, now, that the entire earth, just beneath us, has a layer of bones that we have left. It begins in the Thames River and runs under the ocean, under the fields and forests and deserts. In the blown dust and at the bottom of ponds, the bones are always there. We brought them to the war and left them.

WHEN I RETURNED from my second combat tour in Iraq in 2005, my wife was offered a teaching position in Michigan. I packed my collections and her books, and we moved to an eighty-acre wreckage of farm just north of Reed City. To call it a city is an exaggeration. To its west is the town of Evart, known for a salt mine and a bottled-water plant. There is the Evart Flea Market, closed now, which is a stand of conjoined covered tables heaped with debris and hubcaps hung from trees. Lines of toy trucks rust like hulks in a miniature junkyard, and rain pours onto the piles of magazines and books in a back corner. On dry days, the shaded space smells of wet pulp and a permanent damp. In the orbit between towns is the flotsam of declining farms. Trailers near the road with children's toys spilling from porches and hoards of dismembered machinery in their yards.

But Reed City was thriving once. Its farms had been profitable, and small machine shops, oil production, and logging kept paychecks coming in. A railroad ran through from Fort Wayne, Indiana, to the Straits of Mackinac, and in Reed City it crossed the line that ran from Saginaw to Ludington. Twelve passenger trains had stopped here every day. There had been an opera house, a theater, and numerous mercantile stores. But they were all gone now. A chemical spill on an oil field north of the town poisoned the groundwater in a plume for miles, and a tanker on the railroad spilled its entire payload of coal tar creosote, black with toxins, onto a baseball field when a valve cracked off in winter. The streams had been famous for trout fishing, but now, if you can find a living fish in the Hersey River running through Reed City, the EPA has banned eating any for decades. The county has one of the highest rates of rare cancers in the country. The town has been quiet about stories like these. "Cost of business," an old man said to me as he recounted the damage. "Everyone was working when the rails were hot." Train service stopped completely in 1984, and the rails were torn up and taken away.

On the site of the old theater where locals used to take their dates to the balcony for kisses, there sits a Yoplait yogurt plant. The completion of Highway 131 a mile to the east, bypassing the town, sealed its fate and drew regional business to the Walmart and Lowe's twenty minutes south. An unsentimental culture has emerged here, given to scavenging and buying plastic home decor at the Dollar General. At a corner store you can still find such oddities as Crackling Jumping Monkey Fireworks, a bag of army men, scrapbook stickers, bandages, and plastic aquarium plants. Across the street a family has a small T-shirt shop where you can have names ironed on. In the window is an orange shirt with the words I HUNT THEREFORE I AM printed on the back. Down the block the men at D&E can repair a 1960 electric pump in a matter of minutes with parts no one can find at Lowe's, Home Depot, or Menards. They are some of the last of a pack of original repairmen who can eye a solution for obscure country calamities with a sense of responsibility toward local economic hardship. They price things on a scale based on how you walk into their store. They keep everyone in water as a public service if need be. There are no young men working in the store, no understudies. Just a space lined with neat bins of metal pipe fittings. It will close one day.

People die with their stories every day, taking them and leaving a history of gathered objects. Tombs full of offerings priced again and open to the public for redistribution. Farms are stripped down, tools first, traveling into the basements and garages of the survivors, gathering again, metal hoarded like money. Some of those things are valued only for their melted weight now. On the other edge of town is a welding supply store, its cluttered windows dimly lit all night, and across the road is the scrap-metal recycling yard. Sorted long sections of steel pipe and truck axles lay spilled out beside refrigerators, car doors, lawn mowers, and washing machines in the sheet-metal pile. The short steel is most interesting, consisting of cast-iron and foundry-steel machine parts not to exceed two feet in length. Rims for wheels, gears, pieces of farm equipment, bent tools, and blades in a mass so complex it looks as if a colossal clock has been gutted and ground up. Who knows how many things this metal has already been, how many times it has been melted down? The scrap is all aftermath, and the metal from our farm came here, too.

The old farmer who had lived in our house before us had been a collector. Our farm was a surface graveyard of metal debris. There were two large oil tanks left from the days when a well had been here, and there was another tank that had been cut up and dumped in a heap, its bolts still running in straight lines down the sheets of steel beside the jagged edges left by the torch. It had the appearance of a ship that had been flattened in a field. I had the standing tanks cut apart with torches, and as their bases were severed, they slumped over, looking like amber sections of a whale that had been beached a thousand miles from the sea. The raw crude that still coated the interior with tar reluctantly caught fire, and the segments smoked. Before the tanks were scrapped, I had shoveled the sludge gathered in them into buckets to discard in October on hazardous-materials collection day. It was viscous and rank, filled with bird and rodent bones, the field mice curled and the sparrows glued down with their blackened wings spread out. It was, in fact, the same black remains of ancient life that had drowned animals in the La Brea Tar Pits, the dead sinking, their bones rubbing together in the pitch.

The tractor shed beside the barn collapsed, and I dismantled it. In the oil-darkened dirt of the floor, I found bolts, screws, and plow blades. I dug up the soil and sifted out the metal. Old valves, latches, hinges, and a mass of padlocks all frozen together in rust came up, and there were bullets from various rifles, lengths of chain, and nails. I took them all to the scrap yard in crumpled metal pails I'd found stacked in a corner. They had once been used to collect the sap from sugar maples. Behind the old hay barn along a crescent of trees tracing a deep streambed lay all the derelict farm equipment—a baling machine from 1910, a corn harvester from the 1970s, a tiller from the 1940s. Thrown down the slope into the stream was all the trash discarded since the 1960s, including more than three hundred white five-gallon buckets that had brought excess whey from the yogurt plant to the pigs. The slope was sharp with metal and glass, spongy with years of fallen leaves, and littered with bone. I called scrapers to come cut up and haul the unrestorable equipment and had Dumpsters delivered to get rid of the dump. I saw one coin as I began to rake the garbage and paused, tapped the dirt, and uncovered two more. The locals were all convinced that the farmer, like all the old families, had buried his fortune. I thought that I had finally found it and dropped to my knees to dig with my fingers. I found a rotted sock full of pennies and nickels as I dug into the heap. One dollar and twenty-seven cents is all there was to the fortune I found.

In the first spring that we lived there, I discovered that the sill and floor joists had rotted under the house and the cellar walls were failing. The pressure of years of swelling Michigan clay had cracked the weak sand mortar, and it fell away from the foundation as the glacial fieldstones shifted within the walls. I had already put in a new basement floor, but that would not solve this. The entire house would have to be jacked up by hand, the sills replaced, the joists sistered to new ones, and concrete walls poured.

I cleared all of the volunteer growth around the house and pulled away the broken concrete blocks that had held up an old front porch. The house had the usual offerings in its drip line—shards of glass from broken windows, pieces of bottles, flakes of white paint, granular bits of asphalt shingles from its roof, rusted nails from its siding, and a marble. Recent leavings included a pink plastic fly swatter, a small crushed reindeer decoration, and a plaster statue of the Virgin Mary that had lost most of her paint, leaving one eye to watch me and the other blank. In a patch of tiger lilies sat a large solid block of concrete. It looked to have been a step onto the missing porch, but it lay at an odd angle. I rolled it over to break it into pieces with a sledgehammer but froze, hammer in my hand. The block fell toward me, crushing the lily leaves, revealing, under the clinging dirt and earthworms, an epitaph: JOHN KURTZ 1862–1944.

It was the man who had built our house, a Civil War baby who had died during World War II. I was about to excavate the foundation, and a burial was not what I needed to find. I assumed that it had been a temporary marker brought home after a proper gravestone had been made, but I had no one to ask. I moved it to the front lawn and set it so that it could be read again. His grandson, John Peter Kurtz, had left the house to his widow, and we had bought it from her. There were bones all over the eighty-acre plot from one hundred and fifty years of farming and eleven thousand years of life after the melting of the glaciers.

There were stories for some of the bones. In a small swamp, I found the skulls and piled ribs of a herd of cows that Kurtz had lost to a lightning strike. Along the banks of a ravine lay the remains of the cattle and pigs that he had butchered in his barn. Locals showed me the beam on which he had hung them to drain their blood into buckets, the threads of ropes still dangling from it. But there was one story that was repeated most. Kurtz had owned two Persian horses. They were the pride of his farm, and in the winter of one year they disappeared. Kurtz organized a massive search. He circled the county in an airplane looking for them. They were lost without a trace in the falling snow of Michigan. Years later there was a severe drought that parched crops and dried up swamps. The small pond behind Kurtz's house evaporated, its deep mud hardening and splitting open. In the center of the pond lay his two horses, drowned when they had fallen through the ice in the winter. It is said that he walked out to the carcasses, took off their bridles, and walked back to his barn.

In the attic, I found the skeletons of bats, in the walls those of mice, in the chicken coop, the spine and ribs of a deer killed in the road during the winter and left by a neighbor for the barn cats to eat . . . and the skeletons of cats. I never found the remains of John Kurtz, but I was told that the ashes of his grandson had been spread in the front yard under a bush, unburied. I found the cracked leather bridles hanging on a nail in the barn, and some-where in our pond lie the bones of his horses.

CHAPTER 6

WOOD

TREES SEEM TO BE RANDOM, THEIR ARRIVAL IN FIELDS
and the top of hills unexplainable, their growth mysterious. It is
hard to imagine the wood of trees while they stand, but inside
there is something magical happening. The growth of trees is not
repetitive but additive, each year recorded in their flesh. Cut wood
can be burnished like clay, polished to show its grain like stone,
and on the shore, bleached driftwood looks like worn bone. Wood
is known for how it burns more than for how it grows, but it is
trees that most clearly mark time. The destruction of a tree by ax,
rot, or fire is an assurance that memory is not intended to survive.
Trees grow with us.

ONE DAY, while we lived in Poolville, my family went for a
drive. There was no particular reason for it other than that my

parents wanted to see the countryside in winter. My brother and I sat in the back of the station wagon as we drove out into the great white cold of central New York. It was before Christmas because there were boxes of books in the back of the car that my father had not yet donated to the library for the tax year. The car whistled as we went and always felt frigid in the back, the large empty bay incapable of holding any heat. The roads farthest from the village were plowed last, and my parents chose to drive onto one that had not yet been cleared, identifiable only by recent truck tracks and a row of skeletal maples lining its shoulder. We moved on the confidence my father had in the new snow tires he had bought. He relied on local wisdom for all mechanical matters and would quote mechanics as if they were philosophers. He had grown up in Brooklyn and somehow maintained an urban perspective on the natural world despite his long tenure in rural territory.

It had been little more than momentum that had kept us from being trapped by the deepening snow. The tracks we had been following turned off, my father hesitated, and the car slowed to a stop. They decided that they had seen enough, and my father tried to turn around. The wheels spun and revealed the smooth ice below the snow. My mother offered advice, which was to gun the engine and rock in their seat. My father got out and looked at the road as if something was wrong with it. I got out, too, and we stood examining the polished ice and tire treads packed smooth with snow. They talked strategy. I suggested that we use fallen branches from the maples as traction and went to gather some, but when I returned with an armful of sticks, my father had already taken action. He had arranged his old books, open, packed in front of each tire. I was shocked. I thought that my mother, a librarian, would never allow it, but she sat in the front, far from town, resigned to accept forfeiture.

I stood outside, still holding the sticks, as my father got in, started the engine, and hit the gas. The wheels stripped pages and threw them in a plume behind the car. A few were mangled, but many simply tore free and were thrown like large sheets of confetti. The paper did not look like snow and was noticeable on the road. One of the books was by Dickens, a duplicate he had found in a box of books bought for a few dollars at an auction. My father got out and we looked at the pages blown over the snow. He could tell that I was horrified, but he smiled and said, "Dickens would be proud to know that his book had been sacrificed to save little boys." We had watched *A Christmas Carol* that year, and I had seen *Oliver!* in London. I guessed that he was right.

We were eventually rescued by a plow and went home to soup and less confidence in snow tires. A farmer walking along his field in spring would find, spread along his fence, pages of Dickens caught in the barbs with the dry leaves of fall.

I SET OUT TO CHART the land around our new house as soon as we moved to the wilds beyond Sherburne. It was summer. I disliked the blinking open country in the bright sun. The grass hardened and went pale, the ground prickling with the needle stumps of broken stems left dry from years before. I could hear them give as I walked on them, like the splintering of delicate fish and rodent bones. In the cleared land, everything was exposed. In the meadow, spiked masses of mint, frail clumps of forget-me-nots, and marsh marigolds huddled along the trickle of water, painting a dark trace of green through the grasses. The stream was a depression in the land but not a division of it. It was different in the woods.

I followed the streambed from the meadow into the woodland, and the light changed. Inside, the hemlocks and maples stood tall and old. The land sank toward the vein of water and seemed to have emptied into the streambed and washed away. That is, of course, what had happened. Water took everything away over time, then brought it all back. There was little underbrush, and the stream had cut a trench into the shale. It was filled with stone, and the water was transparent in the shade. Nothing grew in the water or along its banks except rashes of moss. Roots roped up the slopes like cords of muscle toward the trees on either side and were hard to walk on. I had to decide whether to step on the flat rocks in the stream or follow on the banks above where the ground leveled as forest floor. I chose the stream.

The forest spread undisturbed and beyond measure, and I felt like I had found a place before maps. I drew my own map of the forest, without a compass, and gave names to the terrain. It was a kind of storytelling. I had done the same thing when I walked the Sanger-field River. The river cut through the hills, pastures, and towns, and I named its bends and pools. For me, the river was an island. It could not be claimed by anyone and defined itself through the land of people, unoccupied, holding them at bay with its long shores, a thin ribbon of ocean. The forest, with a stream running through it, was not a river. But I made the forest into an island, too, and explored its edges as a shore where it met the fences and fields of the enemy.

The forest sank down a hill as if it would eventually end in a great pit, and I followed it down. The canopy thickened with the large limbs of older trees, and I came to a point where a branch of stream fed into the one I was walking in. The shale was exposed now, ripped open and showing the sedimentary layers that had grown it, growth rings that began in the rot at the core of the earth, thin lines that split apart to prove that they were insular events though pressed together like memory, and I, seeing this rent open, the chronology of the rock below the forest betrayed, felt deep inside of the world. I could no longer reach the roots that gripped the top of the shale cliff and had to backtrack to gain the high ground between the two branches of stream. On top, the ground was spongy with fallen needles that were slow to decay, the color and feel of damp peat moss. It was like the bow of a soft ship and had on it two great hemlocks. I sat on the tip looking down the stream as it continued into the deep and wondered if anyone had ever seen what I saw or if they had ever known that it was important. On my map, I decided that this was the center of the forest and named the spot. Reading *Robinson Crusoe* here would be different from reading it in a room.

I would need bridges to join the land on either side of the fork in the stream below, and I studied the two trees that stood there. The point faced east, and if I could cut one tree to fall to the north and one to the south, I would have perfect bridges over the ravines. I had my elegant Plumb hatchet with me, given to me by

the poet Paul Nelson, and I began to chip the trunk of the hemlock
on the north side. The tree was almost three feet thick, and my
ambition had made no reasonable consideration of the entirety of
the effort to fell it with a small hatchet. I labored for three to four
hours, swinging the blade into the base of the tree. I had carved
a brutal gouge into the living wood, and the ground around the
tree was covered with an explosion of bright shards of fresh meat.
They were the brightest objects in the forest and proved that man
had come. I had come into the forest and done this. In the very
place I had sought for its absence of me, I had made myself apparent. The chips had showered over the bank and littered the stream
on one side, the flakes of hemlock and shale lying together in
natural ruin, pages torn from different books. I had small crumbs
of wood in my hair. My chopping had slowed and become unpro-
ductive, most strikes glancing off of the sap-slick bite that was not
even half of the way through the tree. Hacking is not like sawing.
The wound is made large, and it feels like an act of killing.

The trees darkened with the end of the day. I was only a mile
from home, but it was a hard mile and I was tired. The water that
crept through the rocks in the quarry pile became the slow stream
moving below me. I walked back out of the forest on the high
bank and then followed a trail that I had cut through the brush,
staining my fingers eating blackberries that grew along the edge.
The juice was like ink on my skin and wouldn't wash off for days.
I didn't mind the meadows now that the sun was low in the west.
The grasses were lit with yellow light and looked lithe. A softness
had returned to the ground.

Back home, I went out to the barn and sharpened my hatchet, adding a small square nail to the top of the wood handle to tighten the head, and went into the house with the last light.

I left early the next day and walked quickly. My arms were still heavy from the efforts of the day before. Back in the shade of trees, I heard the drumming of a woodpecker. The tree stood as I had left it, a great yellow notch on the side facing the stream, and a mat of chipped wood around it. I had accounted for the denser growth over the open space made by the stream below to help pull the tree over the ravine, but that was all of the accounting that I had done. I finished chopping into the hemlock when I judged the gouge to be halfway through the trunk. Nothing in the stiff movement of the spire gave any indication that the hemlock had acknowledged my labors to sever it from the earth. The remaining fibers held the timber firm and straight. I looked up at it. Staring up at trees in a forest is like staring into a hole. All of the lines decrease toward a center that does not exist. It is an anomaly in the rules of perspective. If the trees were to continue into space, they would never touch. But seen looking up, they formed a cone, and I felt like falling, detached from the ground.

I chose a spot about eighteen inches above the cut on the opposite side and began to smack the hatchet into the bark. I stayed on the side of the tree that was away from the point of land in case I had to dive out of the way when the tree leapt from its stump. I didn't want to fall into the chasm of eroding shale. There was no wind, and the forest carried the drumming echo of the hewing. The sound of each strike glanced off the other trees as if I was cutting into all of them. Deeper in the forest came the sound of a woodpecker boring into a tree, and a mile away my father was typing in his workroom. I heard a snap inside of the hemlock and backed away. Then nothing. I looked up but could not tell, in the sparkling manipulation of light through boughs of needles, if the tree was swaying. I may have been swaying instead.

I went back to it as if approaching a wounded animal that might still stagger up and turn on me. I swung back into the wet wood until I heard the tree begin to bend at the notches, tearing itself with its own weight and losing the muscle and arteries holding it alive to its roots. It fell as a slow explosion with a high-pitched creak that sounded like the strings of instruments being dragged across one another by heavy anchors dropping into the ocean, moving slowly at first and then gaining speed. The timber twisted in the air as its boughs pressed into those of the trees on the other side of the rift, but the weight increased as it fell horizontally and it smashed down. Its severed base lurched free from its stump and drove into the dirt beside it. It was still held up by a wilderness of branches on the other side, but they broke, almost all at once, and the log settled as if it had released its last breath. I emerged and stood on the bridge. It had fallen very well, and I walked out onto it with my hatchet to trim off the limbs on its topside. I was twenty feet above the streambed, and I had to watch my balance as I swung at the branches. I looked back from the other side once I had cleared the path across. Sun now burned a large spot on the point. I had let it in when I took the tree, and it seemed to heat the forest floor. I had cut a hole into the center of the woodland and ruined the balance of its prose. I had revealed myself to be the enemy.

I abandoned the notion of cutting down the second tree, and I didn't count the growth rings on the first. You can't watch a tree grow by staring at it, but you can remember when it was a smaller tree. The story of a tree is time.

On my way back into the meadow, I found a straight young hemlock and cut a wide circle around it with my hatchet. I dug with my hands, feeling the roots and rocking the sapling loose from the forest floor. The earth was made of fallen pine needles, and the roots reached into them to pull life from the history of trees. I took it back and planted it on the point beside the stump of the tree that lay across the stream. I looked down. The water was quietly cutting through the bedrock and slowly separating the continents. The sun was reflecting off of the water now, because of the hole in the shade that I had made, and I could no longer see through it to the bottom.

BY THE CORNER of our land in Sherburne was a stand of quaking aspen. Locals called them poplar, but when the wind blew, their leaves shook all together and made a rushing sound like waves withdrawing from a pebble beach. They actually quaked. The aspen grew quickly, straight, and the grove expanded from the roots of large central trees that had volunteered at the edge of old fields. The wood was soft, and the trunks felt like tubes of wet pulp when I chopped into them with my hatchet. As the aspen grew tall, their lower limbs withered, drained of their sap, and fell off at the slightest touch. I had finished the tower on a stone fort nearby and the height had given me a taste for getting aboveground. There was no particular purpose in doing so, but I looked up at the close columns of straight trees and thought that I could build a platform tied between them.

Up the hill was a crowding of maple saplings that had been fighting one another for light and rain in the shade of their parents. There were a few hundred and I had already thinned out the crooked trees to encourage the success of straight ones. The remaining saplings were still serried, but I had relied on natural selection to solve that. I went into them, brushing through their precinct of gray poles. I needed a matched pair about twenty feet high that I could use as the legs of a ladder. The trees that were tall enough were closest to the old trees by the roadside, the heirs apparent, and I had already thinned most of them so that the best would have more space. I couldn't bring myself to cut any. They were the bones of a proto forest I had been crafting for four years, and they were spaced perfectly. I crossed the road and climbed into the density of saplings farther up.

I had cleared some of the trees in this stand as well, dragging out saplings to build bean trellises for my mother's garden, and the trees I had left had thickened. The sharp stumps from my harvest had not yet rotted, their gray spikes marking the small clearings made when they were cut, the forest floor opening a little there, but the spaces above closed with new growth. I found two trees that were the right height, near other trees that would be able to fill their absence. I chopped them down, trimmed off the branches, and dragged them down the hill.

Back at the aspen stand, I lashed steps to the saplings with baling twine and raised the ladder to a thick branch high above, pressing the sharpened points of the legs into the soil. I climbed carefully, feeling the ladder shift and sway, and lashed the top to the branch. On the way back down, I smashed off all the other branches so that the trunk of the tree stood clean, and the ladder, standing beside it, was the only way up. I began to gather straight saplings from along the field, carrying them up the ladder and laying them into the notches of other nearby trees as if a fan of limbs had grown, a gray cancer radiating from a tumor on the aspen. I tied other maple poles across the main braces, building latticework like a spiderweb.

The platform moved with the trees, the saplings bending like limbs and rubbing against one another, the leaves rushing all around, and the twine straining and relaxing with the swaying trunks. I lay on the raft looking up, dreaming of girls who would never lie next to me there in the wind and leaves. It was a weightlessness, this place in between the daring of limbs and the seriousness of roots.

IN COLLEGE, I WORKED at a lumberyard over the summer. I enjoyed stocking the warehouse but could not stand the sight of badly piled lumber. The contractors rarely cared what they got, or, for that matter, what they were building. They put houses up quickly and ran before the ground settled and walls cracked. The rough farm carpenters took the bent boards to build crooked additions to their drooping barns and sagging houses. They didn't know to notice the difference. But the serious carpenters would sort through the whole pile for the straight boards with the fewest knots. They examined the grain and edge, holding a board up to one eye and peering down its length as if it were a rifle scope. I didn't blame them, as I did the same, but they left their rejects in haphazard piles, and I would restack the lumber meticulously, keeping the worst pieces out. I had come to love the sound of boards slapping into tight stacks. It was like an immense musical instrument as the smack echoed off the corrugated metal roof. In every pile, there would be perfect boards, and I would sometimes save them for myself as I worked. I did not like that the piles were always being disturbed. A well-stacked pile should stay that way, but they were always being shifted, and boards would leave sticking out of the windows of cars and leaning on the tailgates of pickups. When enough had left, I would bring in a new pallet and cut the straps binding the wood tightly together. As soon as the straps were loose, the perfection of the block of lumber ended and its decline began. Rocks separated differently. But wood had been alive, and there was something restless about it. It had bent in the wind once.

I liked that the wood had all grown somewhere. The boards were born as natural verticals and refined by man, trees split and traveled hundreds of miles to be divided further into houses and barns. Often the board on top of the next one had come from the same tree, had been severed from the other by a blade. They

would sometimes be sold together and remain in the same building, maybe nailed to each other for whatever life there was left
for wood that could no longer grow. Others would be sold apart,
as they had been sawed apart, and would travel away in different
directions. I enjoyed matching unique knots and tracing them out
of the lumber as invisible branches that probably still lay in the
path through the forest where the tree had fallen.

WOOD KEPT ITS STORIES, and I was aware of forest when
I stood inside wooden spaces. A military range tower was like
the bridge of a ship at night. The front looked out through Plexi-
glas that had not been cleaned for fifteen years or more. Along a
wooden table there was a PA microphone and a radio or two to
send instructions to the line of shooters below and report fires
and trouble to Range Control miles away. There were no windows other than those facing the range. Men sat here leaning
forward to look at the same ground, moments of scrutiny followed by hours of boredom. The tower had this one purpose. It
was a watchtower, and so we watched. It seemed to be the same
tower wherever we went. The range towers at Quantico, Virginia,
were like those in Okinawa, Japan. The same as those at Fort Knox,
Kentucky; Camp Shelby, Mississippi; and Camp Lejeune, North
Carolina. It was as if the booth had traveled, submerged in the soil,
ascending again at the edge of every range we trained on. No one
ever witnessed these acts of transportation, but the room, elevated
on its welded-steel framework, was there again. We climbed the

stairs and opened the door to find the same smell and the same wood. We felt the same inside. The table that ran the length of the room beneath the windows was the tower's record. The plywood looked glossy, burnished by thousands of forearms rubbing oil and sweat into the pressed wood. Visitors also began to carve into it. Names, units, weapons, and jokes were cut through the first layer of veneer with knives, and they darkened as grime gathered in their depressions. The messages looked like ancient prison graffiti, etchings in smooth stone or the bark of trees. The grain in the wood was traced with pens until it looked like a magnified topographical map. The map of the range looked the same, its liquid lines curving around the hills, tight together where the slopes were steep and far apart where the elevation barely changed. A line for every five or ten meters of height or depth. Laid over the map was clear plastic with the arbitrary range span drawn on it, the right and left lateral limits of gunfire beyond which bullets could travel into other ranges and training areas. Every type of ordnance had its own template. Some munitions exploded and considerations had to be made for shrapnel flying far from the point of impact. Bullets ricocheted. Everything we fired with such precision could go astray. It was all part of the calculus of death, and there it was on the table beside the names, units, and the tracings of wood grain.

Before these lands were purchased for military training grounds, they had been private property. The range at Fort Pickett, Virginia, fired into the space that had been a town. A cemetery was still marked on the map, though we could not see any gravestones from the tower. Most ranges had been farms; generations of people clearing the land had left no markings of toil or crops or cattle. No epitaph but the names carved into the range towers one hundred years later or on graves in places too dangerous to read, surrounded by live fire. No one came to visit these dead, their burials long forgotten by the departure of families unable to return to a place anyone could now call home. The graves were just outside the right lateral limit of our range as we fired 25-millimeter rounds into the mounded dirt of empty bunkers and the tangled steel hulks of old military vehicles. What we were doing was known as precision gunnery, three-round bursts fired at point targets. The bullets searched for the dead in the soil, blowing it into the air in sudden clouds that obscured the point where the metal had entered the ground. The earth around the targets was powdered, leaded, lifeless, and discolored, as if the planet had vented something toxic at these ruptures. Low brush and grass encircling the impact areas had blackened with fires in the dry summers. Plants were growing back into the burned patches but their leaves seemed to hover above the charred surface, not dense enough to reclaim the space. We stared at these mounds from the tower, waiting for them to erupt again, and in the forest grown up at the edge of the range were the gravestones marking where the farmers and townspeople had gone underground, their town submerged, traveling invisible to us who had never seen it, to appear again in someone's dreams of youth.

I HAD LEFT HOME and hurried to wait for the war, training in forests for combat in the desert. My light armored reconnaissance company was having their last two days near family while packing equipment at our reserve center, Camp Upshur, on the Quantico Marine Corps Base. It was March 2003, and there was still frost on the ground in the mornings and the dormant grasses, wild cedars, and thorny vines in the field behind the headquarters building were lambent with frozen moisture when the sun was low. Cedar Run Creek cut a crescent around the camp in the mud beyond the field, but we could not see it past the tree line running along its banks.

Despite the uncertainty of what waited for us across the ocean and north of Kuwait, I was not worried about fighting. My Marines were tight and dangerous. I had a measured confidence in our battle skills, but I was wary of operations in a chemical environment. The media and the military argued over our projected casualty percentages. They debated predictions about the tactics of Saddam Hussein, who they finally agreed was completely unpredictable. They said that we would be gassed. They showed photographs of the bodies of Kurds killed with chemical weapons and left unburied. It was the cheapest way for a third world nation to even its odds against a technologically superior force. There were chemical agents designed to attack skin, nerves, lungs, and blood. Then there were sarin gas, anthrax, and other invisible, odorless, and fatal plagues that kept our focus on breathing as much as fighting. You can't fight the air. Saddam had these weapons, which was why we were attacking him. Marines packed while I watched the motion from the edges and read new reports about the effects of Iraqi chemical agents that were likely to be used against us.

The ring of consultants around Washington were wild with hy-
potheses. Every specialist had a theory that he or she had been cul-
tivating since Iraq had been mentioned in anger. They had written
books. Apparently, the Iraqis would have a difficult time deploying
their weapons accurately against agile units like mine. That seemed
reasonable in part because I wanted it to be true. Winds would
make gas and particle clouds less effective. We were to hope for
winds. Stationary elements with high troop concentrations would
be targeted if the Iraqis knew where we were massing. That was
also sensible and obvious. Analysts espoused common sense as if it
were unique to their own insights, and the only difference between
most theories was the argument over which had the sense more
common among them. All that I could think about was how all of
these scenarios would be applied to our lives. Ranking retirees were
being interviewed in succession, and they spoke of the difficulties
that fighting in chemical conditions presented. None of them had
ever experienced these "conditions," but they could imagine them
for us. They could explain the difficulties in lists, usually in threes.
Those with no experience would say, "Based on my research . . . ,"
and those with no research would claim their military training
as legitimate experience. They weren't talking about foxholes for
this war. No one mentioned the digging of holes for survival. I
was imagining experiencing the conditions without fair use of air.
The awkward rubber boot shells, the activated-charcoal protective
pants and overcoat heavy with sweat, the rubber gloves filling with
moisture, and the hooded mask in 110-degree heat. Trying to save
the Marines who had been exposed as they convulsed and tore

at themselves in the dust. The reluctance of medical evacuation by units not in the contaminated area. The sweat, the goggles on our masks slowly going opaque with condensation from anxious breath, and the knowledge that a command center somewhere was marking our last known grid as a "no-go" zone to be bypassed by other units using upwind routes. Our only hope would be to attack, with our survivors, forward into the clean air of enemy positions. Nothing to worry about there but bullets.

Weapons of mass destruction had been established as the reason for invading Iraq, but there was not much specificity in the language. Casual language, in fact, was the first weapon used. No one had heard of improvised explosive devices (IEDs), and none of the specialists were imagining them for us in interviews yet. No one really knew anything. We said our farewells and boarded buses.

WE ARRIVED AT CAMP LEJEUNE as it took on the depression of an abandoned place. Almost every operational combat unit had been deployed to Afghanistan or Iraq, and only transient units and bitter nondeployable Marines were now residents. Anyone projecting a positive attitude was marked with great suspicion. Empty parking lots. Silent buildings surrounded by the coughing of vents from buried hot-water pipes. White paint curling away from concrete blocks. The businesses outside were hibernating until the troops returned with tax-free pay. If they could survive for seven months, they would thrive. The Marines in the desert were thinking the same thing.

The next morning I sat on empty aluminum bleachers and listened. I was alone there, but Marines waited nearby for training to begin. I could be alone just five feet from someone. It was raining lightly and the bleacher seats were gritty with sand left by a history of reluctant boots. The area was a field classroom without walls built in a forest clearing. Such classrooms appear near helicopter-landing zones, live fire ranges, and wooded training areas throughout the base. The rain running off the metal roof tumbled down a single gutter, emptying into a puddle at the bottom as if by surprise. The hurried water rattled more like a solid falling through a thin metal pipe than a liquid. There was an occasional rise of laughter above the murmur of Marines in groups. It was good to hear them at ease. There had been so much tension in the anticipation of leaving our home lives for this war. The familiarity of Camp Upshur and the comfort of regular life had been entirely too close. Even then we were too close. At a distance, the laughter had a particular unison like the sudden lift of birds startled from the surface of a pond. The sound returned to a murmur before the next joke, the birds fleeing from the pond having nowhere to fly but back onto the pond. I stepped in to explain that the threat of a chemical or biological agent was not as probable as had been threatened. The Iraqis had very limited delivery capability, and we were not a rich target due to our speed and tactical dispersion. My opinion based on my research. Some might have called it a theory. The Marines needed to be concerned but confident and methodical. Anxiety would make them clumsy and vulnerable. They were also not as worried about bullets or dying a Spartan "beautiful death" in combat as they were of suffering a poisoned breath. We formed a line and entered the gas chamber with our masks on.

The tear gas (CS) was heated until it filled the room with a fog of particles. It burned on contact with moisture. My seal was good. I would not die . . . if I could get the mask on in time. We were instructed to remove our masks and perform the procedure of masking in a poisoned environment. It was Sunday and people were attending church services at 0800 while I stood in a small room with fifteen Marines. My eyes were closed. I was holding my breath. A young lance corporal had not even taken off his mask yet, and we were waiting for him so that we could don and clear our masks and breathe again. My mask was in my hands near my waist. An instructor was yelling through his mask at the lance corporal. He sounded like he was underwater. I held my breath. I could feel the burn of the CS powder as it found the slight ring of sweat around my face where the rubber edge of my mask had just been. I sensed the strange absence of my second face, which left an uncomfortable impression along the line where it was tightened. People were in church a mile away and I was holding my breath. Ten seconds more. Someone took a small breath, coughing. My eyes were closed and I couldn't tell who was suffering. The lance corporal got his mask off, and we could all put our masks back on. My eyes were still closed, and I used my strained breath to blow the CS out of the mask as I brought it to my face again, moving quickly to tighten the straps behind my head. The lance corporal was fine. Now he knew. He wouldn't die either if he could get his mask on in time. We all stood in a line and walked outside to

unmask. I felt the cool, damp air on my face. My hands burned in
the moisture, but I had to smile. I was not coughing and I could
almost see because the procedure works. If I could get my mask
on in time, I could die a proper death from the lead in the air and
not the air itself.

North Carolina is essentially a beach that continues for fifty
miles inland. I had forgotten how much of Camp Lejeune was sand.
It got into everything. My floor slowly grew a thin coat of it. I could
feel it on my feet when I walked around my room in the dark. I
disliked the feeling. Sand is an irritating symbol of desolation. The
day continued to darken as a sign that time was passing. There were
few other signs. Rain came with a strange violence, and lightning
set glow to the sky, reflected by the even pools of water surrounding the barracks. Marines were running in the half-lit moments of
night, and there was a slow motion to it. I stood by my open door
watching for a while. Every room felt damp. We were waiting and
losing hope of action, surrounded by sand and far from the desert.
We had to go. Anywhere but where we were.

Out in town, we bought better holsters than the ones we were
issued, extra ammunition pouches, and other items we would not
be given by the military. A veteran wearing a POW/MIA hat was in
the store watching us pick out gear.

"Sandbox, huh?" he said.

"Any day now," I replied.

"I'll take the goddamned jungle over that," he said.

"Were you in 'Nam?" I asked.

"I was all the fuckin' way in 'Nam. Wasn't any further into

'Nam to get than where I was. But you couldn't even draft my ass to go to a desert."

He wore an old woodland camouflage jacket. He looked at me as if he were squinting into the sun. I wanted to know how being sent into the tropics to fight regiments of disciplined troops in mud, heat, and insects could be better.

"Not a fan of sand?" I asked.

"I like the beach, but I don't want to fuckin' fight on one. Hidin' in water is called drownin' where I come from. Jungle was bad, but we could hide as well as them in those trees. You get out in that desert . . ."

"Well, they won't be able to hide from us either."

"Man lives long enough in sand, he's gonna know how to look like it. Good luck, Marine."

As he left, I noticed that he limped.

The next day came and I waited in the parking lot by the Second Marine Expeditionary Force headquarters. It is pressed directly against the edge of a river. Water from the ocean pushes its fingers into Camp Lejeune from the east and backs up the flow of rivers from the west. I could hear artillery in the distance as water sloshed against rocks implanted along the shore to keep the sand from returning to the sea. The rocks were composed of shells densely compacted during some ancient gathering of ocean sediment. The water, the rock, and the sand all products of the sea at one time. Me too, I suppose. The artillery thudded again. I could hear both the TV broadcasting the beginning of the war live inside the HQ building and the noise of practice in the near distance blending in my head. The dull echo of impacts continued to thump through the fog on the water surface. It seemed to be both close and far, a reflection of the war for us then. The sun came out late, and the sky had a lingering gray stain of torn rain clouds. The moisture would not depart. It clung to metal and skin and got too personal. When I came in from a run, I couldn't stop sweating. Moisture wants to gather into drops. Wants to run back into the sea. Lejeune is always unnecessarily humid. It is a relentless, unforgiving environment. We called it "the hate factory." It was the perfect hell in which to forge a being that just doesn't give a fuck. A Lejeune Marine.

Smoke from a huge range fire several miles away arrived, adding a density to the air. It was thinned by wind and distance and moved diluted and invisible in the breeze. It reminded me of my parents' woodstove and there was something comforting about the trace of home. Smoke and fire. The strange pleasure in proximity to destruction that draws us to war must also have ties to this smell. Wild animals flee the scent of smoke in the woods. Marines rush into the woods to find the source of the fire but not to put it out. A fascination with damage. Smoke would be constant in Iraq, its varied odors inescapable.

THE LAND BETWEEN KUT and Jassan was a barren expanse of powder. We had been training in the brush and forests of North Carolina for this treeless landscape known as Hawr Ash Shuwayjah. It was said to hold the downpours that fell on it in the spring, and it also caught the flood of rainwater that drained off the dirt hills of Iran to the east. The ground was chalky silt and seemed hostile to permeation. It was too level to allow the gathered waters to run off, and so for days they covered miles of desert in every direction, slowly evaporating and, maybe, sinking into the soil.

It was the dry season in 2003 when we got there, and the empty plain lay as a lake of dust covered by a fragile crust of dried mud. On our maps the area was labeled as a marsh. The road from Kut to the Iranian border cut through the dead floodplain in a straight line. It had a culvert every few miles to allow imaginary torrents to pass under it, and the hardened silt was gouged out on either side of the pipe as if by rushing water. During the four months that we patrolled the route, puddles of red-orange water sat in the depressions left at the ends of the pipes. The liquid was like the drainage from a bruise. It did not seem to evaporate and led me to think that the entire plain had red water just beneath its blistered husk. In other places, Iraqis scraped salt from the top of dry desert pools. It was slightly yellow, and I could see it in low piles in the middle of dirt circles. No one scraped any of the salt here as it formed around the stagnant reservoir of blood, and nothing grew.

These dry flats were dangerous. The crust was sometimes like a sheet of ice and would crack, pulling trucks into deep, wet mire just below the surface. They were called *sobkas* and were formed when the brief lake that lay on the dust sank into it and was sealed over by the chapped skin of mud left by the hot winds. Sometimes it was tar. The last exposed water evaporated into nearly invisible clouds to be carried over the hills. It would rain onto Iran or fall as snow in the mountains of Afghanistan, moving always east with the winds or south with the rivers. It was to cross the world forever, rising and falling. Some of it had fallen on New York, and on Michigan, taken in by trees, and it would eventually fall there again.

There were towns beside oasis pools where palm trees grew. They were thick and tall, primeval-looking and dull with dust. Clusters of orange-yellow dates dangled under their umbrella of ancient fronds. At the edge of one oasis lay the trunk of a fallen palm. It had been cut down with an ax with what looked to have been a great effort. Someone had tried to burn it, with almost no effect other than blackening a small spot. I looked to see how old it was, but there were no growth rings. Palms do not grow that way. The only tree I could find in the desert could not be burned, and its years could not be counted. A palm tree is like a desert.

AFTER MY SECOND TOUR, I returned to Sherburne to see my parents. My mother had kept the gardens well, and the interior of the house appeared unchanged. The rest of the land was being transformed though, and I had been away from my trails for a long time. Beavers had come and dammed the stream, raising the water in the swamp. It had grown huge, with the look of a lake that someone had poisoned and filled with nails, the gray shards of trees stabbing through the surface. In death, the trees had lost the elegance of trees. They were no longer beautiful. They were just dead matter, skeletal. They were down to their trunks, broken, cracked open and peeling, bark slipping off in sheets or in small pieces.

I could not tell how deep the water was, only that it was three or four feet deeper than it had been before the dams. Trees that drowned had become brittle, and they dropped in a way that was different from trees that fell in forests. These trees hit the ground and broke into sections, suddenly fragile despite their veins and fibers, as if they had been cast in plaster or fossilized while still standing. They looked like portions of petrified forest. Around the bottoms of trees that had not even fallen there was the work of beavers, bark all torn away and dents gnawed into them. All the nocturnal labor to build the dams was revealed to have been left incomplete, but not without lasting effect.

An immense ancient tree stood gnarled, the long growth of its roots smothered by the water they had reached for. It was the only sculpture left, the other straight trees decapitated at various heights and fallen into the flood or onto shore. Most trees seemed to fall away from the water, by design of the beaver, landing on ground where they could be stripped. It was as if something had exploded in the center of the pond, the concussion of which had knocked over everything along its edge. There were submerged stumps where trees had been sawed down, years ago, cut into sections and left abandoned. The swamp's expansion had covered the old shores. The last owners had auctioned off their property, taken their profit, and moved to a city, their rural efforts here left unfinished. Their timber still lay under the trees dropped by beavers, as if there had been a mutual agreement to lay everything to waste. As if somehow the owners and the beavers had colluded to deforest the land.

The water was thick with leaves and branches, the detritus of a living world dumped into it, and instead of floating, it sunk. Nothing floated now but the geese chanting their awkward lyric. Moss, spongy with cold rain, crept from stumps, and fungus petals flowered from the pulp. Along one side, poured down from the road, lay a spray of fresh wood chips, mechanically cut. I walked up and found that road crews had trimmed trees and ground them down, blowing the pieces into the damaged forest. The new chips covered the flakes of wood shaved away by beavers and hammered by woodpeckers.

I crossed the dam, looking into the dark water. The bed of the swamp was littered with pieces of branch, stripped of their bark, sunken bones of the trees that had shaded the swamp when I was a teenager. In the corner, I could see the square outline of a stone outpost I had built. It looked ancient, the rocks all soft with algae and a pall of rotten leaves. I remembered building it to look out over the swamp beneath the shadows of some young maples. The trees were all gone. I passed through the old tree line along the field that had once produced the bulk of the profits of the farm. In the late eighties, a man had cut the field for a few years, making round bales, a new technique at the time. He had left a number of them along the edge of the field when he had failed to pay for the hay. They remained and were slow to rot, still visible in two lines as they were consumed by the field quietly reclaiming its own, pushing roots into its dead, grass growing on the mounds of wrapped grass. Exactly thirty of them, little more than humps, looking like burial mounds.

The field itself was beginning to lose its purity. Volunteer growth was pushing in from its borders, and evergreens had appeared magically in its middle, almost equally spaced, unopposed. The hay was in decline as perennial plants took root along with berries and shrubs. I found a bright white ribbon tangled in the grass and tied to the base of what remained of a red balloon. Fragments of crimson rubber lay around it from when it had burst on the sharp stalks blowing the words HAPPY BIRTHDAY apart.

It had been years since I crossed behind the dome of the field out of view of the house. I could only see a thin sliver of the hill across the road. The slope had been a bare pasture down the center opposite the house, but it had almost completely filled in with brush and saplings, gray with empty branches now instead of tan with grass. It looked like a scar on the hill the shape of a square. It would eventually be impossible to tell that the slope had ever been cleared. In the tree line beside me, an ash had pushed up a large slab of shale. The rock leaned against it, almost vertical like a gravestone, cutting into the trunk at one spot, the bark growing around the intersection like lips. The stone was the first sign of the boundary wall. Here, on the far northern corner of the old field, the fieldstones emerged. Around the rest of the border the wall had mostly been consumed by growth, but here it lay exposed, shards of rock, some rounded, picked from the rows after plowing and laid at the edge of the property. It was no longer possible to know if they had ever been stacked carefully. They were made remarkable only by the lines of trees that had grown beside them, safe from the plow. The broken stones were spreading from the pile, slipping back under the earth like flounder. The rocks, trees, and I are what remains, all of us representing our part of the boundaries.

At my stone fort, the land seemed far more open than it had when I first pulled the fieldstones from their silent pile, laboring to change their placement one last time. I had cut an opening into the overgrown pasture, planted maple saplings and a few hemlock in the marshy ground, the view beyond the stream remaining obscured by dense brush and hawthorn trees. I stood there now. Forest had grown over the clearing, the underbrush killed off by the shade. It had been a space secluded by low growth, but now I could see through the empty underneath of forest, all the way up the ridge to where the road curved around the shale. The stand of aspens, high upon which I had tied together the platform of sapling spears, was dying off. Maples were pushing through and choking them out, the aspen falling and their shallow roots peeling up from the ground to stand vertical like peacock gravestones.

The maple that defined the corner of the land was still there, a steel pipe marking the spot in its roots where nothing changed. It was showing its fatigue, pieces of it breaking off and littering the ground around its base. It was not dead, just older, its center hollowing and the rings of its youth rotting as the rings of its late age continued to form, keeping count. One more year. The great tree

was being replaced by its offspring, young straight maples growing with no memories of the old forest here, or the loggers, or the
pasture that followed, or the farmers, all leaving the one tree to
mark the property line. The one tree that brought the forest back.
These things happen. I was understanding. It was giving the sun to
its young, as parents do, declining itself into shade.

The topography of the land was revealed, but I had to keep moving to maintain a sense of it. The trees screened the view and kept
changing what I could see as I walked, as if I were looking through
blinds with thinly spaced slats. The straight saplings I had left standing on the hill were trees now. They kept the light high above, and
I was sorry to find the wild apple trees dead in their shade. They
lay in piles of dark twisted fragments. They looked damp, almost
charred, bark fallen off, small. With the pieces remaining I could
not reassemble the trees to be as large as I remembered them.

I circled back to the swamp.

There was a message in the change that had occurred since
I had left home after high school. Having been so long absent, I
could see the evolution of wilderness. The trees had risen or fallen,
sixteen new rings sealed in the thickening trunks of the standing
wood. I had a point of reference. I had seen trees when they were
young. The land was not ageless. I went back inside the house for
dinner. It was comforting to see home preserved, constant, and
safe from the evidence of nature's wild.

CHAPTER 7

STONE

THERE IS A PHOTOGRAPH OF ME IN AN ALBUM THAT my mother compiled, in which I am wearing bright red rubber boots, Wellingtons, and pounding on a rock with a stick in each hand. I can't guess where I got the small branches, as there are no trees in the picture. The land is dark with dense grass and looks wet. Behind me stand the sarsen stones of Stonehenge in the south of England. I am beating on the edge of the sacrificial rock, and smiling.

A FEW YEARS LATER, we returned to England. In the Lake District, far from London, we stayed in a cottage rented from the Cookseys. They kept horses in their walled farm pastures, but sheep were raised all around them, and there had been plenty of them on the grounds over the years. The buildings stood clustered along the edge of flat meadows that spread out from the base of a slope plush with trees. I was six. One day my parents hiked up the hill through the forest behind the barn, carrying my brother, and I went ahead of them as a scout. We followed an old wagon trail that had not yet filled again with saplings and came to a clearing on top of the low ridge. A stone wall separated the small passage from an emptiness of pasture that fell down the other side of the saddle. It felt like we were much higher than we were. We sat down to rest, and I placed my hand on something smooth under the folded layers of wintered grass. Parting the thatch, I found a sheep's skull. It was discolored by years of rain, the hollowed eye sockets stained the bister of dirt. As I felt through the grass on my other side, I found another. I had sat down directly in between them. The skulls still had their blunt horns and rows of loose teeth, darkened by the shaded earth, but I could not find the lower jaws for either. There were no other bones at all. It was as if they had been left as no more than symbols of death, skulls placed on the ground in the corners of Renaissance paintings, the empty housing of the mind enough to represent the loss of body, of impending mortality. I carried them both down the hill to our cottage.

We stayed in an addition to the main house, and it was made of stone. My father would write during the day, I built stone forts in the pasture walls, and my mother took up crochet while she watched my brother. She had large skeins of local wool yarn in a basket, and she sat on a couch with her back to the sun looping the yarn with hooked needles, entranced by the repetitive movement of her fingers, somehow counting the knots. It was like a trick I could not understand, something requiring a gift I didn't have. She chose undyed off-white wool, which had the natural color of sheep in the fields around us. She would joke that she was crocheting a sheep back together. As she crocheted the strands into patterns it was like she was making large snowflakes in summer. At the end of the day I would lay out the separate squares in a grid to show the progress she had made on the afghan. I remember her being very proud of it. My father, who could not much comprehend the manual making of tangible things, was dumbfounded. Although their fingers were both laboring over white rectangles, eyes focused on the progression, laying compositions out, pieces of a whole, they could not see the parallel. I didn't see it either at the time. She stitched it all together near the end of our stay and told me that it had in it the wool from four entire sheep. Maybe more. She mailed the afghan home to Poolville wrapped around the two sheep skulls I had found on the hill.

One of the skulls still sits on a bookshelf in Sherburne, and one has come with me to Michigan. I am not sure why my parents mailed them home and kept them. We brought very little back with us from England. My mother carried in her luggage two stones she picked from a stream. My father carried books. I have long thought them to have been merely decorative curiosities, but the discovery of these two skulls must have meant something else to our history. They have become familiar in our home. I have held them like Hamlet, and though I never knew these animals while they lived, they have earned a place in our memorial, moving always with us, as present as our own skulls. These sheep, never considering perpetuity, remain in my life and will, one day, pass to my daughters, who will not remember them being found under dead grass on an English hill but will, instead, place their discovery on a bookshelf in the house they grew up in. It is, in this way, as if these beings had lived and died here as one of us.

AT HOME IN POOLVILLE, the sun came out after a heavy storm and dampened the snow. I went outside to build with it, taking a shovel and a plastic form for making bricks. I tamped down a spot with my boots and drew a circle in the level snow with two nails connected by a piece of my mother's yarn, one nail stuck in the center of the plot and the other cutting the trace, the stretched yarn keeping the radius equal. It was a bright purple yarn that my mother didn't much like, and I was allowed to use it when my efforts required string. I packed snow into the red plastic form to make tight blocks and laid them in place along the line of the circle. I offset the second row, centering the blocks over the ends of the ones below, and continued up until the wall was as tall as my head. I had left a doorway at the bottom and capped it with a piece of board to support the wall above, just high enough to slide under. I packed the moist snow into the wall like mortar, adding an inch around the exterior and smoothing it so that the whole shape looked like a cylinder formed as one shape and not composed of many pieces. A widening circle of absent snow grew around the site as I quarried it for the fort, and I spent more and more time carrying new snow from the field beside our yard. Inside the turret I was pressing handfuls of snow into an arch above my head to build a roof. It was like working with clay, sculpting, and I carefully patted it into place and then smoothed it. It became thinner as it extended toward the center, and as the hole in the middle closed I struggled to pack the snow without breaking the delicate bond of hundreds of handfuls.

I leaned a rough ladder to the top on the outside and slowly added snow until it was two feet thick on the roof. I tested it, standing on it but not jumping. I began, again, to lay blocks until the walls were up to my shoulders, and then I smoothed the battlement from above to match the part below. I built a small barricade in a ring about four feet from the base but tired of carrying the snow from so far away and began, instead, to pound tight balls in my mittens and stack them inside. It was getting dark, and I had spent the entire day working on the castle. I was allowed out that night, before bed, to wet the outside walls with cold water from a bucket. I took one last look from the kitchen at the great white shape lit by the yellow light of the back porch. I was proud of it but went to bed thinking of ways to make it bigger. It needed to be like the stone castles I had seen, as hard as stone. Ice was the only rock I could make.

The cold returned with the night, and the snow crusted on the surface and powdered beneath it in the field. The fort was solid ice and impenetrable, but the snow would no longer support further construction. It fell apart in my hands as I tried to pack it into the mold. Snowballs would deteriorate in flight and come apart like comets trailing their cold dust through space. Conditions were perfect to be besieged, and so I invited attack from the older boys in the village. I called out to the younger tier of soldiers, and they came from the two directions that the town offered by way of its main street. We ranged from six to ten years old, and the "big kids" were in their teens and bored enough on a snow day to accept the sport of beating on us.

They threw chunks of crusted snow and boulders of frozen slush tossed from the road by plows. We exhausted my supply of snowballs and fell to the torture of being overrun. A large boy, cheek reddened by a well-aimed impact, went to work on razing my fort. I could only watch as he threw himself against it. The incomplete barricade had already been laid to ruin during the fight, and when the second story finally broke apart he kicked it down in pieces. Everyone watched. My humiliated army disbanded and retreated to their homes to shed jackets and warm hands; the older boys headed away in a group. But the one boy stayed raging at my monument. The walls and roof would not crack, and he was hurting himself as he tried to force its destruction. His fury was from something else, though I was too young to understand it. He tired and left without a word. My parents had watched the battle and watched still as I surveyed the damage. The base had sustained almost no injury, and its smooth ice walls had the burnished glint of dull beach glass. The top lay around it in fragments, and there was an expanse of footprints encircling the site. The sparse red trail of a bloody nose headed away toward the street. I went in for dinner.

It remained cold for a week, and school kept me from the important labors of empire. A warm front came through, and the sleet that fell changed into rain. The roads turned gray with wet filth, and portions of the yard showed the brown ground again. I had removed most of the snow around my fort in building it, and the fragile layer that remained disappeared quickly, leaving the white mound solitary. I could monitor the decline each night as the yellow light from the porch reflected on the ruin in its field of darkness. It thinned and weakened as the rain continued, and the roof fell in. As spring came, I watched out of the kitchen window as the last white ring of wall sank into the cold grass of the yard. In the morning, after another night of rain, it was gone.

AT THE OTHER END of town from the tunnel and dam, near the railroad crossing and the junkyard, the water seeped under the Willey Road bridge toward the Poolville Rural Cemetery, where it was rejected by a stone wall built to keep the river from the dead. When I was eleven there had been a drought for months in New York, and our river was low and showing its bones. The rocks that once caused bumps and swirls on the surface now cut the water like dull plows gouging furrows into the slow flow. Crossing the bridge, I entered the solemn path that traced the rectangle of grass and graves. The lawn was brown and crippled by the heat; yet the coughing of a lawn mower resounded from the far corner of the plot. An older boy pushed the mower down the rows, exciting dust into clouds. It was usually cut by my fifth-grade teacher, Mr. Gunther, but on this day it was a boy I did not know. An old woman bent toward a stone tablet clenching a handful of black-eyed Susans and Queen Anne's lace. They were both flowers impervious to drought. The stone seemed to lean slightly toward her as well, the two close to touching. She was almost always there when I cut through the cemetery to go fishing, but at different headstones. It might be that I hadn't noticed her to be different women. I was told not to stare.

The earliest gravestones were by the road. Most of them had crumbled and been carted away, leaving nothing to mark the graves but slight depressions in the ground. MARY SKINNER, 20 MAY 1801, 19 YRS OLD was the oldest one that I could read. Many tombstones had been reduced to Neolithic markers, acid rains and winters feeding on the inscriptions cut into them, taking names away from the record. They had been made of limestone, which was easily cut and carved but also withered with erosion. "Weathered off," people would say. The slate stones had all cleaved long ago as water found its way into their pressed silt layers and then froze, shattering them. The thin sheets of stone had come apart like pages of a book all washed clean of words. Several had been swallowed by the earth and had sunk so deep that only their curved crests marked their places, their epitaphs preserved underground with the remains that they were to note. Children were buried under stones with seated lambs carved on them.

All of the old graves had small dips left where the earth had settled after the pine boxes buckled, the space inside of them filling with dirt. The boy pushed the mower over them, rising and sinking and rising again as if he captained a small boat on the low river beside the cemetery. He passed me closely this time, as he cut the edge of the rectangle, and the dust blew onto my wet boots, quickly forming a darkened film of soil. I didn't know anyone buried here.

I turned from the path and went down a breach in the wall, beside the maintenance shed where the old barrier had washed out, and stepped into the water. The river hastened past, stripping the damp dust from my boots to mingle with the mud that I stirred from the riverbed. It was pulled away downstream in the current, alive again. I began to follow it toward the pools behind the cemetery where the river cut through the Tackleberrys' pasture. I thought that the trout might gather in the deeper water basins and wait for the rains to return. The water was too thinly spread over the rocks above and below the basins for fish now.

There were no trees or shade in the pasture, and I had to be careful to keep my shadow from crossing the water. Trout would scare if a shadow passed over them and would not bite. I lay behind the tall grass on the bank above the pool watching my bait writhe and sink in the water. I had carried the worm from the compost pile behind our garden, and the worm was made, partly, of leaves from our yard. Some of the dust that I had brought from the cemetery would settle on the mud bank. The pools were always lined with gathered soil, and who knew how far it had come and how much of it belonged to the dead. I hadn't thought of it until then. The sun behind me made my head sweat into my hair. The grass was long on the steep drop down to the river, but on top where I lay it was gnawed short and even by cattle. Around me flat piles of cow manure were baked dry. The world smelled of earth, and at the edge of the field was the pile of gravel, ribs visible emerging through it, where a cow had been buried by the farmers. Even the animals were placed under stone.

MOST OF THE STONES that I remember were cornerstones, because finding them was such a great pleasure. I could hold any rock, turn it in my hands, and know where it was needed in a wall. But a cornerstone had a certain destiny. Discovering a cornerstone was like finding the right word for the hole in a poem.

Near our house in the shadow of a hill in Sherburne was a pit scaled with fieldstones picked long ago from the old hayfield beyond. It was close enough to supply the rock I needed for building a wall beside our driveway. The slabs on the top were gray and bleached, dry lichen clinging to them in oval patches; nothing grew through the spaces between the stones. I began to peel the clean rock from the pile and search through the damp pieces below for anything with a straight side. The fragments of bedrock that had risen through the dirt in the field were mostly oyster-edged shale broken from subterranean masses. Fractured along the flat layers of silt sediments, it surfaced as crude plates. Crooked edges could only be buried inside of a wall as fill for stones that had at least one flat face. The stones were packed in dirt, and as I dug into the base of the pile, I had to pull them from the earth a second time. A hundred years of water draining through the heap had carried soil into the pockets between the slabs, filling them in. I felt along the rocks for their edges and lifted them up by one side as if opening a tomb, finding underneath another stone packed in dirt. The farther down I went, the more moisture clung to the stone. A small spring drained somewhere below. I could hear it moving, muffled by depth, making the sound of water spilling into small bottles.

I hauled a number of good stones out of the hole, slipping on the pile of discards as I did. I had been careless in tossing the bad rock aside and had difficulty finding a stable path to carry out my quarry. Near the bottom of the pit I found a promising cornerstone, and I was eager to free it from the vein of rocks that it was caught in. The stone was thick, and I had no way of knowing how far into the bank it went without digging it out. I pulled away the chips of shale and dirt above it and threw myself into loosening it. It was pinched in the hillside, and I could only force it back and forth a few inches with all my strength. I was fourteen years old and the rock itself weighed only a little less than I did. I removed more plates of shale. The pile of stones above would eventually collapse, and I was trying my luck digging below them. After half an hour, I had burrowed a small cave and I could see the rock that held the cornerstone in place. If I moved it, the slope would give and the stone and I would be buried together. I went to the barn to get a chain.

I found an old rusted length of dog leash and returned to the mine. I looped the metal links around the stone twice, then walked out of the hole to a poplar that stood at the edge of the spill. I took the slack out of the chain and lashed it to the trunk. I figured that I could use the stone as its own leverage against the weight of the rock clamping it into the hillside and that if I could lift the cornerstone instead of pulling at it, I could upset the balance of things and slide it out ahead of the collapse of shale shingles held above it. The taut chain would swing the stone and keep it from slipping further down the slope with the tumbling disorder of dirt and detritus. I stood between the tree and the stone and heaved on the chain. Shale slid out from under my feet, and I seemed, as I stayed in the same spot, to be losing ground as I pulled, everything but me wanting to move down and be covered up. The hole, by its declination, had created a center of gravity, and I felt caught in it. As I struggled to ascend the incline, I kept descending.

Finally, the cornerstone came loose, the chain swung with it, and I stumbled into the hole as the hill emptied to fill it. It all happened quickly and my shoes bulged with dirt. I staggered up to see the stone hanging from the chain like a tooth resting on the slope. It was dark against the surface stones and had the smell of the underground, a faint moist smell of things that had rotted too long to stink. The stone was large and weighed about ninety pounds. I began to roll it out of the spill, lifting it on an edge and dropping it forward. It struck the stone slope with a hollow boom each time it fell, and there was the sound of an adjustment in the connections of the stones below, as if they were rapidly changing temperature. Each clap of the rock's impact brought the smell of gunpowder from the dry stones. I strained and fought the stone out of the pit to the tree, unwrapped the chain, panting, my arms covered with dirt and scrapes. The cornerstone lay there, in the open, the corner of nothing. I had ruined the ceremony of its sleep, and out in the light it seemed more damaged. But its corner edges were perfect, and it was flat on top and bottom—as if it had been cut to be a gravestone and left unfinished. I pushed it to the house in a wheelbarrow.

I had prepared the base for the wall, spreading gravel to allow rain to drain. Water kept in a wall would destroy it, creeping into the balance of fragments and then freezing in the winter, the ice expanding, carefully pushing the stacks apart until they were a mound spreading back into the ground. I placed the cornerstone first, then laid the wall. It was a very satisfying kind of attention that I paid to building it. I stacked it all by eye, and the rocks made a sound like shards of thick pottery being piled. The sound of building was like the sound of ruin. It is quite a thing to build a wall, a futile declaration that man might permanently imprint the earth.

I turned to building a castle—far from the house. I walked a quarter mile down the stream from the place where I had removed the cornerstone and found a level site under a massive basswood tree. There was another spill of fieldstones there that had been dumped by farmers after plowing and I began sorting it into face stones and fill. I built a small, round turret first, just large enough for me to sit inside. It lacked ambition so I dismantled it, re-sorted the stones, and built a much larger structure. Although it was dry laid, stacked without the use of mortar, I shimmed it carefully and there was no movement in the stones once they had been placed. The walls rose up five feet and I leveled them on top to fit a roof. The first roof was built with aspen logs—soft, wet wood but straight and easy to cut. I got a summer job at a lumberyard and tore the log roof off in favor of one made with rough-sawed hemlock boards that I could buy with an employee discount. I was also exposed to other materials that expanded what was possible and I bought four sixteen-foot 4×4s and built a twenty-five-foot turret in the corner of the fort with a sharp peaked roof on top. I planted trees and dammed the stream in front to have a small moat, and then built a bridge. I worked on the grounds around it for several summers, adding a Quikrete floor capped with smooth stones and a door with an antique metal floor-grate as an armored portal.

I couldn't work on the fort during the winters—the snow blew too deep in the depression made by the stream—but I would sometimes forge my way down there, clear the snow from the doorway, and sit inside listening to winter. It was satisfying to see the straight walls, the stone so tightly stacked. On the outside, the walls widened toward the base and I had placed them like shingles to run the water off. Without the turret, the fort would just look like a mound of stone, a cairn. I wanted to live in it, the cool rock surrounding me, but I could also imagine being buried in it. It was my work, this crypt built of stone, intended for perpetuity like any grave. All anyone would need to do would be to lay me inside and fill it in.

WE TRAINED FOR DESERT OPERATIONS in a spread of volcanic wastelands of eastern California where there were no trees. The rock formations were blackened by their birth as lava, and reminded me that the earth's crust floated over a stewing red boil of iron and stone. How far down? It was the iron core that kept us all from falling off of the world. Molten mountains churned like hot paste beneath the cooled surface, clotting over fissures in the land that slowly drifted on it. I could see it here, where the underground had come to the surface.

The Marine base at Twentynine Palms was an immense landscape of shattered rock, and there was a salt flat made famous by the filming of car ads near its edge. It was not far from the meteor crater where Charles Manson had conducted his demonic ceremonies. The salt pan was white, and it reflected the sun with enough metallic brightness to lift above the ground and ripple. One day I stood and watched as a storm swept toward me over the burnt rock. The thunder had the sound of the shift and fall of great shapes, a crumbling echo of larger places. There was a warm weight on the breeze that was pushed ahead of the rain, and it smelled of damp and ancient dust. The gray line of water advanced across the plain, and I could hear it come like the spread of waves on a beach, the drops striking everything at once. I was inside the darkness of rain for only a few minutes, and then it was gone. It had moved past like an abstraction, without lingering, and leaving no marks. The heated rocks quickly shed their coat of moisture, and the water-darkened sand began to lighten again. Except for the thickening of the air and the smell of wet gunpowder, there was no way to know that rain had just fallen.

In Twentynine Palms Marine Corps Base, there was a combined arms range where we conducted company-size assaults into a rock valley supported by battalion heavy-weapons assets. It was unforgiving ground, dangerous, and as close as we could get to combat without having an adversary shooting back. Marines had been killed training there. A crescent of tall rock outcroppings contained the valley in a jagged bowl, and its floor was veined with sandy wadis, channels cut by centuries of water draining from rainstorms in spring and left dry for the rest of the year. The rock that lay strewn throughout the area was sharp and it looked to have been cracked and split by explosions rather than by natural decline and erosion.

"Second Platoon, you are the focus of main effort and will spearhead the attack on the final objective."

I was the Second Platoon commander and I could not have been more pleased to be given that assignment. It was an honor to be the main effort, although that would often ensure that we would take the highest casualties in combat. I gave my platoon the order and we took up a position at the mouth of the valley. Behind us we heard the plunk of mortars fired out of their tubes and we waited as they arced through the air, almost slow enough to see. When the rounds reached the peak in their trajectory, the call, "Splash," came over the radio and we could time the fall of the mortars exactly from there.

Far in the back of the valley, puffs of gray smoke appeared and we advanced before the sounds of the impacts reached us. Machine guns opened up from the top of a hill above us and we ran underneath their fire as mortars continued to fall ahead of us. The terrain was difficult to navigate and I hurried back and forth between my three squads to keep them in line with one another. Marines kept getting separated in the wadis and coordination became difficult with our supporting elements as we pushed deeper into the broken ground. We would appear rushing over a ridge only to disappear into a dry streambed. There was only one radio in the platoon and I adjusted supporting fires with it while controlling thirty-five Marines by voice and hand and arm signals. It was my first true experience with chaos. Two Dragon missiles fired across my front as I pressed my forward squad on, and .50-caliber rounds raked the ground just ahead of us, sparking on stones, shifting on my signals. At the rear of the range, 60- and 81-millimeter mortars struck the objective with a smack and thump.

The air was sliced with bullets and we all hurried forward with a slight crouch as if there were a ceiling of lead inches above our heads. I ran, pulling my radioman by the cord attached to my handset mic and he stumbled after me, the weight of his pack making the going harder for him than for me. The objective was close now, on a mound above me capped with the thump of mortars. I called for a cease-fire and broke into a dead run up the slope of the objective, the curled radio cord stretched straight to my radioman and my platoon spread out behind me, bounding over spills of rock and the expended rifle shells from a thousand final assaults on this last hill. I was out of breath, my mouth dry with running and yelling, standing victorious on a small plateau of gravel dimpled by impacts and littered with aluminum mortar fins. It was an exhilarating victory against nothing. The shattered rock, a notional foe, beaten. One of my squad leaders, Corporal

John Trotta, arrived at the base of the mound and looked up at me. He was my most skilled Marine and had consistently proven his prowess in training exercises. He looked serious, brows creased with examination.

"Everyone all right?" I asked, suddenly concerned by his apparent lack of rapture.

"Sir . . . all due respect, but, in the future, I would feel better if you wouldn't assault the objective alone with your radioman."

"So you didn't find that inspiring?" I replied.

"Oh, it was inspiring, sir, and you would have been the shit in the Civil War, but times have changed. The officers go behind the troops now."

"I defer to your wisdom as always, Corporal Trotta."

We had discussed my enthusiasm before and it had become the subject of considerable banter between us. Trotta was convinced that I was doomed to some inappropriate and unnecessary heroism, and took it upon himself to protect me from it. He watched as I picked up a red stone and slid it into my pocket. He was accustomed to me doing that but he never asked why I kept rocks from the places we went. Nearby were petroglyphs left by the first humans to migrate south after crossing the Asian ice bridge thousands of years ago. People passing here had been drawn to mark the volcanic outcroppings with stone tools, the dry desert preserving the etchings as if they had just been made. My platoon sergeant brought up the last Marines and we checked scrapes and bruises. The valley would be attacked again, Marines rushing across it, tripping on the sharp stones as bullets sprayed overhead. The rocks would remain, except for the one I took.

WHEN MY UNIT ARRIVED in Babylon as the quick reaction force (QRF) for the First Marine Division, we set up near the helicopter landing-pad beside a shallow concrete-lined pond. It looked poisoned despite the sparse presence of lethargic gray fish. The area had been a visitors' center for people touring the ruins before the invasion, and it would be again when we withdrew. My first sergeant organized our headquarters in an abandoned café and I put my tent on the dirt beside it. Shards of Nebuchad-nezzar's bricks lay all around us. The soil and fragments were what remained of one of the most storied cities in history. Now it was the seat of the First Marine Division as it retrograded, and the Polish division which was to take command of all coalition forces as we withdrew. The military situation was comical. To our south, Nicaraguan and El Salvadoran troops in Karbala refused to take orders from the Spanish military nearby in Najaf due to old colonial resentments. The Spanish refused to take orders from the Polish, demanding that if Spanish troops were to be employed under coalition command that all orders would have to come to them by way of their ambassador, meaning that the Poles, sta-tioned in Babylon, would have to contact their own ambassador in Poland, who would then have to contact the Spanish ambassador in Spain, who would then have to contact the Spanish military in

Najaf and order them to respond to a tactical situation. The Poles, on their first mission outside of Poland, were the third largest international force in Iraq after the United States and Britain, and they were key to allowing a U.S. force reduction, but they came with political difficulties of their own. We were told that if the Polish force took a single casualty, they would likely be pulled out of Iraq. So for several months my unit patrolled outside of their perimeter to protect them from possible exposure to insurgents in order for the myth of a "coalition of the willing" to survive.

The region around Babylon did not feel dangerous yet, and we were able to relax for the first time in six months. My Marines and I walked through the ruins with an official Iraqi tour guide. The museum there had been looted but the actual structures had been left untouched. Saddam had been rebuilding the city with his own bricks, but his reconstructions looked sterile and cheap beside the original foundations. I stood in the space they called the throne room, and they said that it was here that Alexander the Great had died of malaria. Nebuchadnezzar and Alexander were in this dust. I kneeled down and took a handful of it in my hands. It was like the earth along the Iranian border, the bank of the Tigris in Nasiriyah, the entire fertile crescent gone dry. But Alexander had died here and so had the hanging gardens. I wanted to find something that I could be sure the two kings had touched. I asked the guide and she said, "the Lion of Babylon." I was taken aback by the name. I hadn't heard it since it was used to swear my as-sassination in Jassan. I followed her to an open area and there on a pedestal sat a large basalt sculpture of a lion wearing a saddle and crouching over a man. It was unclear if the man was being mauled, but his situation didn't look favorable. The guide said that the sculpture was meant to have an elaborate saddle, on which the goddess Ishtar was to ride. It was guessed to be Assyrian and brought to Babylon as a gift or taken as a trophy. The basalt could not have come from anywhere nearby and it weighed so much that even the British quit their attempt to carry it off a century earlier. I found it interesting that Ishtar was the goddess of love as well as war. The guide moved on with a group, but I stayed with the lion for a moment. The statue had been damaged during World War I when soldiers fired a cannon at its face on the rumor that it was filled with gold. There was nothing inside but basalt. It was the largest single piece of stone I had seen in Iraq. I looked at it and touched the mouth on the side that had not been smashed.

"At last we meet," I said. "I got your fucking note."

WHEN IT RAINED at our house in Michigan, the basement flooded. You couldn't tell looking down the stairway because of the old clothes and firewood covering the floor, but everything darkened. The sodden odor of rot thickened in the water-swollen space below, and the thin passageway down to the cellar became the mouth of a cave lit by a single bulb.

I had already beaten the cast-iron stove into pieces with a sledge and taken the two chimneys down, brick by brick, from the roof three stories to the cellar. Years of ash and flaked creosote spilled out as the hollow brick pillars came apart, and I carried it all up to a Dumpster in buckets. It took me a few days, working with a local boy, to haul out all of the firewood that had been left in the damp cellar for fifty years. The bottom of the pile had turned into black pulp and the cut logs lost their form as we picked them up. The rotten wood smelled wrong, like an early stage of oil.

The thin layer of concrete, discovered beneath the wood, newspapers, garbage, and clothing, came up easily with a pickax. At some point it had been spread over the clay as a floor. Then the work began. I stamped the shovel down into the moist clay to cut it into loaves. The clay would hold together in clumps, and I would struggle them from their grip on the shovel into five-gallon buckets, then carry them up out of the cellar. I needed to put in a new concrete floor, and that would require going down thirteen inches below the base of the walls. The foundation consisted of boulders dragged from the fields by teams of horses in 1880 and laid in place with pulleys from above. They were so large that I did not worry about them collapsing in as I dug away the clay beside them and then down a full foot beneath where they rested. It felt like I was digging a square grave for the house above me. I was in the tomb as I dug it, becoming part of it as the clay covered my gloves and boots.

On a shelf stood a collection of sealed mason jars containing beets, corn, pickles, and chicken legs, canned in the 1950s. They were now the only relics that remained in the cellar from the centennial family farm, and I was glad the space was finally clean down to dirt alone. It was a pure cavern again, elemental, the raw wood floor above, the gray stone walls, the orange clay, and the ash-colored circles on the floor where the chimneys had been. I was digging further down into the unknown than the original builders had. The storms came again before I had the new concrete floor poured, and the cracked walls ran wet with rainwater, silently filling the indentation I had dug. The floodwater was deeper than my boots, and I had to wait as it slowly drained deeper into the earth. Peering into the basement, I could imagine the black water having incredible depth.

The stones in the cellar walls had been collected from the fields and saved for the foundation. The rounded rocks had been gathered until fall, then covered with brush, fallen branches, and discarded lumber. After the snows came, the pile was ringed with buckets of water and the wood was set on fire. When the stones were hot, the farmers would throw ice water and shovel snow onto the pile and the stones would all crack, the rapid cooling splitting them open, their curves cleaved. In the spring, the rock pile was quarried for cornerstones with two flat edges and other rock that had been fractured into useful shapes. There was very little decent mortar mix here and an abundance of sand. A country sand mortar became popular at the time, as it was cheap and basements were intended only as places for cool winter storage of food, firewood, and a way to keep the house aboveground.

A square had been dug by hand in 1885, and teams of horses had dragged the largest stones from the fields. Some of them weighed almost half a ton, and they were dropped into place with winches to serve as foundation stones. In a small fallen barn, I found the skid sleigh that had probably been used to tow in the

rock. All the evidence of effort was still present, the people vanished, the cellar walls breaking apart and releasing their stones. I
ran steel beams under the house and jacked it three feet above the
foundation on nine stacks of rough-cut blocks of maple, oak, and
cherry. I chipped away the powdering sand mortar and began to
carry the stones back out of the cellar, piling them beside the field
they had once been pulled from. I would replace the walls with
poured concrete, but as I carried each rock out, I thought of how it
had been carried in. I tunneled under the floating house until the
hole was picked clean of stone, the clay walls pitted with shovel
marks.

I had to leave my house balanced in the air to go back to Sherburne. Passing into the mountain through Tuscarora Tunnel on
Pennsylvania's Route 76, I headed east. The passage is long and
square, not round like an organic hole produced by the burrowing
of creatures. The accuracy is that of an urban structure, the applied
science of imposition, mechanically cut and sheathed in the familiarity of concrete, formulaic rock of our own making. The tunnel
did not communicate with the stone it had been ripped through.
It was a preconceived thing, unnatural in the geologic evolution
of the mountain.

The lines of light running along the corners of ceiling still left
the gray road dim, as if the glow couldn't fall quite that far, the
rock beyond the tiles somehow absorbing the tubed discard of
photons. White tiles on the walls had popped off in patches, always patches. You never seem to see the first one drop or a group
of them just letting go, their gridded scar dark on the bright wall

as if there were a hole formed into the mountain. Did they break off together? Maybe they do. There is, in this interior, the feeling that the moment we pass through a tunnel is the moment of its entire history. A tunnel is a place hidden from time, compressed, weighed down by the rock above. We should be able to see the tiles all fall at once, the rock caving into the space, and onto us, in this moment. But nothing ever happens. We drive noticing the flicker of several lights about to burn out, a short section of tunnel dimming, the mountain trying to darken its center again. The missing tiles are the only evidence in the tunnel of the mountain surrounding it, the pressure from above. We hollowed through it as if the rest of the mass wouldn't notice what was gone, wouldn't note the space inside with no mass in it. It is the opposite of when we drive over mountains, our ears popping to compensate for the lack of pressure at higher altitudes, our heads trying to re-create the pressure below before our ascent, then giving it up again as bubbles when we descend.

Strange, all these absences, all this pressure, everything being judged by mass, weight, and distance from the center of the earth. Rock is so fragile, laid cool over the melted world. We revel at the solidity of stone as it falls away around us in pieces. That we can hold a fragment of rock, turn a pebble in our palm, sift sand through our fingers, shows its constitution. A mountain is a pile of sand, wearing down, flattening out, becoming particles and amassing again, not really stronger than anything, the weakness of its bonds no more lasting than the memories of insects.

→ ←

BACK IN MICHIGAN, I continued to clean up the farm. I emptied the old tractor shed filled with what the old man had left,
still leaking. The dead farmer had tried to pour it all on the land,
but not all at once. Two hundred seventy-three cans, buckets,
and bottles. I had to count. There is only one day every year to
turn them in at a county collection. I took loads of contaminated
gasoline and diesel sloshing and hissing in the truck. I felt like
a suicide bomber as I drove them into the facility. I took more
loads, the rusted cans of paint knocking against buckets of oil,
transmission and hydraulic fluid, blood stopper and dehorning
paste, antifreeze and motor lubricants, tar, primer, sealant, concentrated pesticides, toxins, and granulated herbicides. There
were white and yellow sludge-filled buckets, rank with the rotted flesh smell of raw oil and nameless poisons, their labels lost
to the damp years and mold. Hazardous materials. He couldn't
take them with him, couldn't throw them away in his day. "You
never know what you're going to need," I can hear him think.
"It's already paid for." He had known what was in those tanks
and cracked bottles, wasn't worried about them as he died of
cancer. Nature needs governing. Weeds, flies, worms, disease.
All the cures he brought here, from factories, to work the land,
I had to remove with gloves. They spread his ashes here on the
farm, somewhere. But I was erasing him as I worked.

I took down the shed and hauled it to the back field, where I
was building a bonfire pile with all the unpainted wood. I stood
the boards and posts on end, restoring them to their original positions as pieces of old trees cleared from this very field and cut

into the skin of barns. I dug up the soil where it was dark with oil and put it in buckets for disposal, old manure iridescent with petroleum, then picked up all the metal parts, bolts, tools, and nails and drove them to the scrap yard. Finally a bulldozer came and I had the area leveled, the top few feet of earth moved to a side yard and built into a berm to serve as a windbreak. While the bulldozer stripped the soil from the low mound, another gravestone emerged.

This one was more disturbing than the headstone of John Kurtz I had found by the front porch. It looked like a concrete lawn ornament, a seated lamb weathered featureless on a block. For a moment I thought of the plaster Mary that had lost its paint by the house. Then I remembered the lambs from the graves of children in Poolville. I rubbed the dirt on the base looking for a name or a date and found both. BARBARA SULLIVAN, 1931–1932. I felt safe guessing that the toppled headstone of Kurtz had been a temporary marker brought home, but this one left me wondering. It could have been a backyard burial. A baby girl one year old. An old farmer who had been born in our house remembered her name. He had been three years old when she died, and the story was told over and over in his youth. He confirmed the memorial to be temporary, that Barbara Sullivan was in a cemetery a few miles away. She was at peace beneath a stone.

ROCKS WITH VEINS sometimes look like wood grain. On a cobblestone beach you can find some gray stones with white rings through them. They are the lifelines of nonorganic matter still marked by evidence of growth. My mother had picked some from beaches in Maine, stones that looked like gray eggs, and had kept them in a basket. I had brought them from beaches and rivers in the places where I traveled and kept them in a basket in my home, an imitation of hers. Sedimentary rock had growth lines. There was one such rock used as a paperweight on my father's desk. It looked to be one from Maine, a white line circling it. It appeared not as a layer that continued through the rock but as a ring existing only on the surface, an orbit incorporated onto the planet, its movement halted by my father, who placed it, still, on his desk.

CHAPTER 8

BLOOD

I WAS ALWAYS TOLD TO STAY AWAY FROM BEES. THE
fact that they could hurt me only made them worthy of closer
examination. Once as a boy, I found a bumblebee living in a hole
beside a barn and I watched it come and go. I decided that it was
a creature that I could capture, something I could outwit without injury despite its dangers. I was told to stay away from bees,
wasps, and fire, but I believed that they all required secret scrutiny
of the most cautious kind. The almost solitary habit of the bumblebee removed me from the true fear of a swarm, and I waited
nearby with a minnow net for it to return. It was flying back and
forth to a cluster of wild phlox, its legs thickened by the pollen,
and it moved like a slow bullet toward me, its wings invisible with
effort. I swung the net and knocked it down. It fell onto the driveway, heavy enough to make a sound and an impression in the dust.

It was stunned, but I thought it was dead. I did not know that a bee could be stunned. I had a jar cleaned of its strawberry preserves, the tin lid still fragrant with fruit, and I carefully reached for a wing of the downed insect. I picked it up, examining it before placing it in my jar, and it awoke, curled, stung my finger, and escaped as I retreated to the house. My hands were small then, and my finger quickly reddened with swelling. I had to admit that it hurt, that I was possibly at fault, and that I required aid. My mother made a salve of baking soda and a wet towel, and I was told to hold it on my hand and rest. It took some time to feel better. Worse were the words she left me with as I was humbled with surprise, injury, and discovery:

"Now, what did we tell you about staying away from bees."

AFTER MY FOOTBALL INJURY, I carried heavy things. I reconstructed the myth of invulnerability with stoicism. At Vassar there were no physical challenges to overcome. I needed to seek the greatest possibility of my destruction in part to prove my invincibility. A friend gave me a pamphlet, and I sought out the Marine Corps.

My parents came to visit me at school near the end of my junior year and took me out to lunch. My father asked me questions about classes, and my mother asked about my plans. She always carried a calendar and obsessed over exactly what was happening, and when. I said, rather casually, that I would be spending the summer at Officer Candidates' School. My mother asked if it was some kind of corporate training program, and I replied that it did have Corps in it. I told them about signing up to be evaluated by the Marines, and there followed the longest silence in parenthood. My father had stopped chewing, eyebrows raised almost over his forehead, and stared at me as if I had spoken well of Hitler. My mother took a deep breath, her hands clamped to the edge of the table as if she were watching an accident happen in the street. Her father had been a Marine, had gone to war and almost not come back. I said that it was no big deal. If I graduated from the program, I was not committed to joining the Marines. I was further interrogated about the contract, and then they left for what must have been a terrible drive back to Sherburne.

I arrived in Quantico, Virginia, in June to the undisguised delight of my recruiter, who had become a minor celebrity for signing the first Vassar student in history. No one thought that I would show up. He greeted me with the last smile I would get, and I went inside to yelling and a shot of every inoculation known to medicine. From that moment on, every question was delivered to me in anger, and every response I gave was wrong. This was to continue for ten weeks. We referred to ourselves in the third person and became merely "the candidate," our names lost to us, and unlike enlisted boot camp, where the Corps hoped to break everyone down and then build them all up, retaining as many as possible, OCS was designed to burn us out, hoping to emotionally and physically wear us down and make us quit. This was 1989 and the Marines didn't need any more men for wars. I had found the right place.

One day they showed us slides of lieutenants killed in Vietnam. They were taken by coroners for records of some kind, and the images were macabre. Just dead men laid on a white cloth somewhere. The pictures were flashed as a slide show given near the week when candidates were allowed to quit. The images were meant to scare us, and they should have. An instructor paced as the dead appeared on the screen behind him.

"This is the consequence of your job," he began. "These Marine lieutenants were all leading their platoons, and this was their reward. You should expect no better. There's a bullet waiting for every one of you . . . and it's up to the one shooting it to miss, because you can't dodge it when it comes. You'll be in front. First to go and last to know."

An image came up of a man who had been hit in the face with an RPG, a softball-sized hole clean through the middle of his inflated head, his cartoon features ballooned to each side of it.

"His last words were, 'Follow me,' and those will be yours, candidates."

The mangled bodies continued to appear, one with a young peaceful face that showed no trauma. He looked to be asleep and unharmed. Below his shoulders, there was no body.

We ate without speaking, carried telephone poles on long runs through the woods, waded up to our necks in miasmic mud, climbed ropes, polished brass, cleaned rifles, marched. We could not eat enough to keep up with the exertion, five minutes per meal, and we began to consume ourselves. We lost weight, and our limbs got slim and hard. I didn't shit for twenty-two days. Candidates were injured, went down as heat casualties, quit. Anyone who went to the infirmary was not likely to return, and the next day his bunk would be empty, the candidate gone without ceremony. We were told that pain was weakness leaving the body. I had twisted my ankle in the fourth week and was worried that my injury would be discovered. We were running five to seven miles a day. There was a roll of duct tape in the cleaning-supply closet, and I made a brace every night after lights out. I remembered my father's lesson: Anything could be repaired with duct tape.

On our last forced march through the Virginia forest, it was in the high nineties and saturated with humidity. My ankle hurt but the boot kept it supported. I was severely dehydrated, heatstroke rising in me as we got to the end and caught sight of the parade deck, the last place I had to stand. Several candidates had already fallen. My heart was racing with blood that must have been thick as oil. I got dizzy, and everything was too bright. I thought of the lights as I went into surgery for my knee in high school, the dead lieutenants, how I was about to fall, and how I couldn't.

We assembled on the paved lot in ranks, exhausted, exultant, above ourselves. One of our instructors walked the lines. I kept my knees slightly bent as I had been told, to avoid toppling. I closed my eyes for a moment and opened them to find him staring into my face.

"You can sleep when you're dead, Women's College," he said, and stepped away.

I forgot to pass out. He was uncharacteristically pleasant. It was his last wasted day of yelling at us. We were not being trained, we were merely being thinned out. The instructors probably had a feeling of diminished returns on their time. But they played their role, and we never knew how much of it was an act. He stood and did an impersonation of the instructor in *Full Metal Jacket*.

"What makes the grass green?!"

At the top of our lungs, and with true elation we screamed, "Blood, blood, blood!"

IN MY LEAKING TRAILER after college, I cleaned the estate grounds in exchange for rent. I removed stacks of warped lumber, cracked plastic planting containers, parts of lawn mowers, and mossy cinder blocks. I stacked the piles of firewood into tight cords and planted a garden. The overgrown yard by the barn was raked and mowed. The last monumental piece of debris was a derelict Ford Bronco, baby blue, that the father had insisted on saving despite its worsening condition. It had been parked at the top of the hill beside the barn for years, with a blue tarp draped over part of it, and it was full of wasps that had converted the seats into hives. There was no money to tow it away, so I asked another tenant on the property if he could pull it to the top of the path down to the meadow with his pickup. We could then pull his pickup around behind the wreck, chain the rear of the Bronco to his truck, and ease it down the road out of sight by the gate at the bottom. It could still be towed away someday if the owners ever cared to do so. Everyone agreed to the plan, but someone would have to steer the Bronco. The steering fluid had drained out and the column was rusty, so small adjustments would take great effort. That was not the problem. The problem was the wasps.

The colony of yellow jackets that had settled in the Bronco was considerable. A crack in the loose driver's side door produced a steady flow of wasps, hundreds, and the truck could not even be approached on that side. When we pulled the tarp off, the entire truck vibrated with the hum of insects inside, and we had to back away quickly as they orbited the hood in search of the disturbance. I agreed to steer the truck.

I went into my trailer and put on three layers of sweatshirts, jeans, two layers of sweatpants, two pairs of socks, boots, a scarf, an extreme sports bike helmet that I had found in a Salvation Army store, ski goggles, and winter gloves. It was July and I boiled in the density of inappropriate clothing. It was difficult to bend my arms and legs. There were no brakes anyway, and I figured there to be an unlikely requirement for dramatic steering, so my immobility was of little concern. We looped the chain to the front, and I opened the door to an explosion of wasps.

I sat on the seat and I could feel the hive crush and stir through my clothes. The wasps hovered and dove at me, and the compartment filled with them. It was like seeing molecules of gas heated. I almost felt that I had changed scale, become smaller, the wasps larger at this distance than they should be. I recall nothing of the short trip to the top of the hill except that I went there with every wasp on earth.

The pickup pulled me slowly forward and then stopped. I had to assume we were at the top because I could barely see through the wasps on my goggles. I wiped them off with my glove. A log was wedged against the front tire and the chain removed. The pickup then took its new position behind me. One man fastened the chain to the back and gave the thumbs up, and another kicked away the log keeping the Bronco from rolling. Then they pushed. The Bronco crept forward, reaching the limit of the chain, which promptly lost its hook, slipped off the pickup, and began to rush, gaining speed as I fought the steering wheel to stay on the path. The latch on the driver's side door was broken, and as the Bronco bounced on the ruts, the door swung open and the seat springs compressed and expanded like a billows, blowing out more wasps. The hive swarmed like static around my face. At the far edge of the pasture was a small cliff, and it was approaching fast, the truck speeding as the limp door smashed into the lower gate to the meadow and slammed back into the cloud of wasps, throwing glass over me. I was in the meadow now, pulling with all my might on the steering wheel to turn away from the cliff that dropped into the river. The door hung at an angle from a hinge and I tumbled from the seat covered by wasps as the truck hit a tree. I began to run, somehow sensing that my clothing was getting thinner as they stung into it and that they would find a spot I had missed, something coming loose around my helmet and wasps pouring through a hole near my neck. I ran to the sound of three men laughing so hard they were bent over and holding their knees.

→ ←

AFTER A THREE-YEAR TOUR at Camp Lejeune in the infantry, my wife and I moved into a little house in College Park, Maryland, our first home together. I had wanted to audition for *Homicide: Life on the Street* because it was a good television show and it was filmed in Baltimore, only thirty minutes from our house. It was, in fact, the only local show at the time, and it was probably the only chance I had at a significant role. I had given my head shots to the casting agent months before, and I was called in to play an extra. They said nothing more than that I would need to wear shorts and bring slippers and a bathrobe.

I arrived on set excited to be in the middle of the production, and a production assistant boarded me onto a van to go to the hair and makeup trailer. I was informed that I was to play a corpse, which was disappointing. I sat shirtless as my death was applied to me. I was covered with a pale paste where they thought I would be seen in the partially unzipped body bag, and a large hatchet wound was sculpted onto my forehead with wax and opaque shades of blood paints. It was an impressive wound. I dressed in my bathrobe and slippers, got into another van, which might have been the same van, and was driven a block to the set.

In a small warehouse, separated from the Baltimore harbor by a dock where the water rides stopped, was a morgue. It had been built for the show, which often brought its detectives there to examine the fictitious dead. There were extras milling around in lab coats and film crew setting up the room for the shoot. I was directed to a stainless steel table, and I carefully slid into the body bag. Even though the room was heated, the table was still cold.

Another extra sat beside me with a pad as if taking notes on what could only be the most obvious cause of death in history. As I lay there, I did not participate in the bored banter of the other insignificant players and corpses. I wanted to be noted as professional and focused. I heard the actors speak their lines for camera tests while I kept my eyes closed, then stand-ins stepped in as lighting was adjusted and the actors rested or continued rehearsing elsewhere. I remained on the table. I did not speak. I waited as the actors were brought back and filming began. I held my breath and controlled my instinct to shiver until they called "Cut." If anyone had seen me, they would believe that I was not alive.

They began to shuttle people away for lunch, which was set up somewhere down the street, and the actors disappeared along with the crew. I lay on the table. I had no intention of moving until directed to do so. The set lights clicked off and the warehouse grew quiet. I could hear footsteps in the back and things being moved, but the set was abandoned. I sat up in the body bag. I was alone. I had not followed the herd out of the building to wait for rides and had been left behind. It occurred to me that no one was going to direct me anywhere. I slipped out of the bag and off the table, walked backstage, found my bathrobe and slippers, and walked outside. It was December in Baltimore, bitter cold, and I didn't know the area very well. A member of the crew was walking back with a plate, and I asked if there was a shuttle coming back. He seemed surprised to see me and gave directions to the church where the catering was laid out. I would have to walk.

I began to head up the street in my bathrobe and slippers, my bare legs feeling strange as the cold wind struck them. I felt re-markably exposed. I walked across Thames Street where people were Christmas shopping and felt myself being noticed. I smiled at couples as they stared, unsure of what they thought they were witnessing. I had forgotten how my head must have looked. There were many homeless people stumbling around Baltimore, mad with drugs or savage with long disregard. I could have been one of them, insane with imaginary heat in the chill of winter. I arrived at the church where the vans were parked and went in the front entrance. As I stepped through the large wooden doors, I looked directly into a classroom of black children, who promptly went silent. It took me a moment to see that the lunch was downstairs in the church basement. I stood, blanched, a gaping wound on my forehead, in a bathrobe. The children stared as the dead white man descended the stairs and joined the rest of the damned beneath the church.

After we ate, the shuttle returned us to the set, where I lay back on the table and they finished the scene. Afterward, hair and makeup was busy so they just gave me some wipes designed for removing makeup and I dressed in my regular clothes. I drove home with the makeup on. I stopped in a 7-Eleven near our house and bought a soda. The Pakistani clerk gave me my change and pretended not to notice that I had been killed. He was very polite.

At home I looked at myself in the mirror. It was good work, the split skin on my forehead, the drained color of my face. I began to wash it off at the sink, my skin red with rubbing, and the wax wound shaved off with a butter knife. I was alive again.

Later, I watched the episode, eager to see my performance as a dead man. I appeared briefly in the background, out of focus, un-recognizable, my wound unnoticeable, and all the attention paid to details surrounding me were impossible to see. I was as the dead are, blurred, transformed, faded.

A year later I was called in to audition for a serial killer, and re-turned to the set in Baltimore. In the series finale, in winter again, I was killed, the last homicide on the show, and I lay for hours in a pool of red syrup, my hair actually frozen to the sidewalk. I lay there in between takes as the crew piled blankets on me. I wanted to be a professional. I didn't complain and I didn't move. I held my breath while they rolled film. When the episode aired, my parents said that they couldn't watch.

BY THE END OF MAY 2003, we had been told that the war had transitioned into security and stabilization operations. This was a post-hostilities phase and we were to focus on hearts-and-minds projects. General Mattis had ordered our focus to be on school rehabilitation and that required me to go to the city of Kut, capital of the Wasit Province, for which my unit had become largely responsible. It was the only place that I could purchase electrical wire, paint, concrete, pipe, and plaster.

In a back street, my patrol came across the Kut war cemetery. It had been found covered in several feet of garbage by Marines in Task Force Tarawa during the invasion, and they had cleaned and rededicated it to the British. Turkish and German troops had laid siege to Kut Al Amara, now simply known as Kut, from December 7,

1915, to April 29, 1916, and the British casualties were astounding. Over 22,000 soldiers had been killed or wounded; 13,000 captured; and here in this small plot submerged from the street by four feet lay the remains of 450 of them. I stepped down into the graveyard and was surprised to see the intricate carving on the headstones. The dead here had not been killed during the siege but rather two years later, when the British and their Arab allies had retaken Kut. I was pleased to see the equitable burial of supporting troops from the British Empire lost in her efforts. Beside infantry and artillery soldiers lay a man with the title, "FOLLOWER." F. X. D'SOUZA, INDIAN LABOUR CORPS, 21ST AUGUST 1918. His name appeared below an image of a rifle crossing a shovel, bound with a wreath beneath the crown of England and a banner with the Latin motto LABOR OMNIA VINCIT (hard work conquers all). Service was what had brought him from India to Kut, following troops with the toil of carrying ammunition and supplies. I had to wonder where the men lost in the seige had been buried. We had not heard of any other cemeteries and had to guess that they had gone into mass graves somewhere nearby, somewhere just beneath us. This place, full of people tossing trash onto the graves, had been the site of a desperate battle, this soil soaked with blood, this ground heavy with lead. The blood and bullets were still here, and so were the dead.

I had been wearing my flak jacket all day in the Kut market, and hours of negotiating for electrical supplies had left me exhausted. The last purchase I had to make was paint and I was directed to a disgusting street in the meat market, thirty feet from the war cemetery. I brought two locals to negotiate for supplies and they had a long list of paints and plaster needed to restore several children's schools around Jassan. The store was a catacomb of rooms stacked with cans and bags of paint. It was a dark place, brick exposed up to the waist as if worn away by years of flowing water and yellow dirt-rubbed plaster above. On the surviving plaster, finger swipes of paint samples covered the walls at shoulder level like frescos in a cave. Blood-red, grass-green, and sky-blue smudges. The floor was uneven with compacted clumps of dirt, caked paint powder, and clots of oil colors. I politely declined the metal chair offered as the men began to count cans and argue prices. They bent over a calculator converting square meters of paint to dinars and then dinars to dollars. I told them I would come back.

Away from the chalky cavern filled with powdered pigments, the air was difficult to breathe. There was a crooked gutter cut down the center of the meat market that oozed a puss of waste from slaughter, and the street was a blood-darkened orange that looked permanently wet. Wheeled carts of filthy chickens lined the passage and the shit-coated pens showed the success of recent sales with small pools of bright blood around them. Skinned goats hung from doorways. It was hot and I was boiling in my flak. My boots were filling with sweat that had run down my legs. Flies hurried by, wild with the vast supply of death, and their buzzing had a loud electrical sound. I had to repress the involuntary urge to cough and I tried to hold my breath as much as possible. The street opened into a large souk and two flats of fly-coated carp marked the end of the meat market. They drained into a bucket and a man would occasionally pour the water, orange with blood, back over the fish as if to keep them fresh.

Wooden carts of carefully piled fruits and vegetables huddled together under draped cloth canopies, the colors luminous and beautiful. Seeing them reminded me of my mother's garden with its yellow squash, tomatoes, red onions, and zucchini. Along a covered alleyway were bowls of ground spices, red and rust-colored chilies, and mustard-yellow curry powders. There were knives and lines of prayer beads on blankets. Sandals were strung like fruit on lines, cloth was wrapped in piles, and black burkas hung in rows. There was order in the marketplace, a ritualized presentation of everything, a daily museum of transient objects that were endlessly replenished. It is AD 500 and an old man sells cucumbers grown on the banks of the Tigris and brought to market on a donkey. It is AD 2003 and he is still here, like the old man selling seashells and coins in Morocco. I was out of place, like the British war dead left here to be covered with garbage. I turned and walked back up the street of blood through the flies.

BY JULY 2003, the insurgency had begun in Iraq, and we were sent to protect supply lines being attacked near Yusifiah, a small city just south of Baghdad. It was not far from the Euphrates and felt humid. The nights were warm, and in the morning a mix of smoke and moisture hung over the town. The sun rose and immediately illuminated everything standing aboveground. Women were already cutting grasses, and men were preparing shops near the road. Vendors covered ice blocks with cloth, the melting water evaporating through the fibers keeping it cool during the day. They had little to sell: small cages with sickly white chickens, some vegetables, stacks of canned soda, and packs of cigarettes. Two sheep lay dead on a slab of concrete in front of the butcher's hut. Their blood was thinned with water and swept off into the dust, like so much blood for so long here, and the meat hung, skinned and headless, for view. Another sheep stood tied to a stake nearby, but it appeared unaware of the process involving the killing of sheep in the hut beside it. That was a useful thing about sheep—they just didn't seem to notice death.

The region was farmland, fed by a grid of uncrossable irrigation ditches, and tall grasses grew close to the road. We arrived from the apocalyptic Iranian border and were not used to seeing vegetation. The walls of marsh reeds turned some road sections into claustrophobic passages, and we felt vulnerable, even more so than when we had been in the open, because the enemy could easily remain hidden right beside our routes. A few miles to the south was an immense Iraqi ammunition-storage base that was being looted for explosives to use against us. It was too large to defend, and we could only hope to capture vehicles hauling away artillery rounds called in by aircraft doing reconnaissance missions. We patrolled from an abandoned refrigeration facility that had kept bananas, potatoes, and other imported crops chilled for distribution. The space inside was filled with oversized bays, and Marines looked miniaturized on their rows of cots. It was dark and still somehow cool inside, despite its dereliction. We received mortar fire on our first day there as a welcome, and the nearby town, Mulla Fayed, was a planned community built for retired officers of the Republican Guard. We were in a snake pit.

IEDs began to appear as terrorists taught insurgents new methods of attack against our supply routes, and we could only respond with increased presence patrols. Nights were surreal, Iraqi men gathered in courtyards discussing crops and us, few lights on, the grass black as we drove past it. We moved using night-vision monocles, 7-Bravos, our vehicles blacked out to disguise our convoy and make it harder for insurgents to time the detonation of roadside bombs. As cars appeared, we turned on our headlights to avoid collisions, then went dark again. One evening a car hurried to pass another in the opposite lane and smashed into the front of one of our LAVs running blacked out. The car was wrecked but there was only some paint chipped on our side.

The sun had been down for a while, and the moon had not yet risen. I hadn't slept in almost three days and was glazing over standing up, sweating into my flak vest. Cars passed slowly, their headlights catching the shattered glass spilled on the pavement. They looked like crystals spread out on a black cloth, a reflection of the moonless sky and its accident of stars. Locals gathered around the damage. If they felt they could get money by complaining, they were certain to arrive at our gate in the morning. More cars crept past, wondering if they would be stopped, wondering, also, if we knew what they had done. Everyone there knew something about the insurgency. I had enough and signaled to press on back to our forward operating base. As soon as I put my comm hel-

met on and started to move, one of my patrols reported contact. I
halted the convoy and the night went to shit.

The voice came in shrill. I got their grid and turned around.
One man down, helo medevac requested. The bird would take too
long to get to them. I ordered a react force to be sent to their position from our base, another to be sent along a parallel route I
hoped would cut off the enemy's escape. Marines on sleep rotation
went to full alert on base. I tried to get to the ambush site but we
sped past the small road they were on, and I asked if the casualty
was stable enough for ground evacuation. They reported that he
was and I told them to take him themselves at best speed while I
screened ahead along their medevac route. The attack could have
been coordinated with another ambush or IEDs set on the only
bridge that crossed the river to the nearest base with a medical aid
station. That area had been hit before.

I arrived at the aid station moments after the medevac did. The
unflinching corpsman, Doc Negron, was covered with blood and
looked drained as if it had been his own. The others were wide-
eyed, exhausted, and silent with shock. They were huddled in a
group staring at the entrance to the trauma tent, a large inflated
portable triage facility. I could hear screaming and ran inside. My
Marine had been sitting on the edge of his vehicle hatch when it
was struck by an RPG and he was hit in the hip by the blast, a vi-
cious injury that had blown him open and bled him out. He was
a tough kid but small, wiry, and fine-boned. His wounds made
him appear even smaller, younger than he was. I hurried to his
stretcher as medics tried to stabilize him and prepare him for ur-

gent surgery. Negron had saved his life, patching and wrapping him with gauze and tape, enough to get him this far. I stood at his side and he reached for my hand, which I took. He was shaking and breathing strangely, his screaming paused, and he looked at me with complete bewilderment and asked, "What is happening to me?" It was a detached voice, childlike, and I pretended I wasn't worried. I told him that he was hit, but that he was going to be fine. I was sent away by the medical staff, and I backed my way out, watching him as he was carried into surgery.

It was dark outside when I walked out to the crew. They were waiting for me to tell them how it was going to end. I didn't know. They recounted what they knew, which was little, due to the nature of being surprised by an ambush. They had turned a corner near a field, heard the swoosh of the incoming rocket, and then an explosion on the left side of the vehicle, the gunner thrown off, and nothing to shoot back at. The insurgents had fired and immediately run away, using an irrigation ditch as a convenient trench. They were below ground-level and impossible to see. The Marines fired in the suspected direction of attack but with no result. At the time, I could only think of thanking them for their swift response and the rescue of their casualty. I could not think of what else to say to them, though I should have. Storytelling was what they needed most. I went back to my assembly area, sat in a red cloth camping chair, and, believing that my wounded Marine would die, began to compose a letter to his wife. I realized, in the glow of my flashlight, that my hand was dark red with his blood. It was the hand that he had held, and I stared at it. It was drying and cracking at the creases in my palm. I was not able to write anything and went outside into the desert to will his survival. I had the thought that if I wrote the letter, it would pronounce his death. I washed off his blood with a bottle of water in the dark. I thought of Negron covered with it.

We went for over a week waiting for word of his arrival in Germany. When combat casualties were medevaced from their units, they were essentially severed from them. I was not his next of kin, and, even as his commanding officer, I had almost no access to his medical status as he was moved between field trauma stations in Iraq and surgical wards in Germany and America. Over two weeks later, I finally received confirmation that he had survived.

I HAD TO STAND on the seat in the commander's hatch for much of seven months. The light armored reconnaissance vehicles we patrolled in had a chair designed for gunnery inside, but it could not be raised high enough for me to sit and see out. I needed to see the outside. We had invaded Iraq and I had stood for the drive from Kuwait to Nasiryah, Kut, the Iranian border, Yusifiyah, Baghdad, Babylon, and back. All the heat and all the standing, legs strained with balancing the body as the vehicle moved, the blood going down and staying while my heart tried to push it back up. The valves in my veins began to fail and produce varicosity. My legs hurt, my knees especially, bending on patches of lost cartilage and scar tissue. I became very slow to rise after squatting. By then I had been in the infantry and LAR for twelve years. When

I returned from the invasion of Iraq, I needed something done.

"The procedure is quite simple but will take quite some time and will be fairly painful," announced the doctor with a German name and disposition. He had no foreign accent, being that he was not foreign, but I imagined one for him. A very clean man with a slight smile set in place. He would be efficient, had probably been efficient as a child. "Fairly painful." Most pain is unfair, I thought, but apparently mine would be well deserved.

"Will I grow new veins to compensate?" I asked, expecting good news.

"No, but don't worry. There's a good deal of redundancy in the system."

"Redundancy in the system?"

"Yes. The blood will find new ways to get out of the leg through existing veins."

"But there have to be consequences for removing something that cannot be renewed. The other veins will have to be more burdened."

"Yes, but there was always redundancy in the system. The deep system will not be affected. Only the superficial system."

"The deep system," I said, wondering what I might have already done to the deep system. I thought about disregard, and ailments, and consequences for a lifetime of overexertion, and how, now, it would kill me from within. I began to imagine a fatal itch somewhere inside of my leg. Probably the deep system beginning to buckle, I thought. How long did I have before it collapsed all of the way to my heart?

"You'll have to wear pressure stockings in order to reduce the possibility of recurrence."

"Recurrence? Won't they be fixed? Isn't this surgery the solution?" I asked while I imagined wearing a stocking designed to maintain circulation in the elderly. Would I soon join the slow drone walk in assisted-living colonies and hospital wards?

"It may be, but you have a predisposition for incompetent valves, and without serious continuous efforts to prevent further failures, they will allow overpressure, and that will lead to dilation of the veins, and the chain of varicosity will recur."

"Can they be removed?"

"To a certain extent, but eventually you will run out of connections to the deep system, and the superficial blood system will not be able to drain. We are going to suture the valve connecting the greater saphenous vein to the femoral vein. It is called ligation. The greater saphenous must be sealed in order to remove the veins that have already been compromised when we do the microphlebectomy. The section of vein that they use for heart bypass surgery is located in the greater saphenous vein."

"So what if I require that operation someday?"

"Well, you won't have the vein segment required to do it."

I will be fucked.

"There will be problems," he added, as if to clarify.

There was a pause and we waited for each other. Finally he asked, "Do you have any other questions?" I was too distracted by my incompetent valves to come up with much.

"Will I be able to run and carry rocks?"

"Yes. I wouldn't do marathons, but this will not stop you from doing anything regular."

Regular was an unspecific word for activities that I should be able to surmise from its use. Most people sat in offices. I was a Marine. The world of healing was different from the world of wounding and each had a different frame of reference for regularity.

I went in for the operation and watched the lights on the ceiling of the hallway as I was wheeled to the operating room. It is an odd trip because of the static nature of beds in our lives. To lie down and move without dreaming is disturbing. As I was transferred onto the cold stainless steel table in the chilled room full of lights, equipment, and people, I began to make jokes. I had been a corpse on a table before. They were to know that I was unafraid. That I invited this cutting into me that they were waiting to perform. Knives through old scars on one leg to dismantle more of what had survived.

"Remember . . . not the face," was the last thing that I could remember saying through some kind of inappropriate mirth. The anesthesiologist laughed. The gas was working, and I woke up several hours later, surrounded by curtains. I recall the unnecessary blinking, and the slowness of waking while no longer asleep. I was sick with the residue of drugs that had lost their potency, and my head was heavy. My friend Richard Allnutt was there to drive me to his parents' house to recuperate. It was an "outpatient" procedure, but I was left with two bound legs that were, essentially, to be immobilized for days. As I lay there, I mourned the absent body, and the invisible confusion of blood negotiating new terms of passage back to the heart. The pain throbbing attentively at the sites of invasion, the orange-blue darkness of wounds, the steri-strips and white tape across gauze signifying damage, the constricting tightness on the legs from the rubber fibers hidden in the beige of Ace bandages, and the endless indefinites of doctors' explanations along with their professional absence of promises, the solutions recommended, and their bleak relationships to other difficulties. All of this because I had fallen to an old man's disease at the age of thirty-five. I have always healed well, I told myself. I will not be crippled. I was expected to be crippled already, and I was not.

There are small lines on my leg now. They are not noticeable scars, but I feel the hardened parts of skin when I scratch. The long scars from football are clear along both sides of my right knee, but the little scars do not announce the missing veins beneath them. You shouldn't worry about superficial things except that they are the things you can see, and, sometimes, speak to something that you can't. There is a deep system they relate to.

LESS THAN A YEAR LATER I returned to Iraq with fewer veins. Patrols took me through the dirt of Ramadi, and my knees carried whatever I did. Mostly on foot this time, and weighed down with ceramic plate armor and extra ammunition.

A mobile platoon from Alpha Company, First Battalion, Fifth Marines, arrived as our escort for a survey and census mission in central Ramadi. We rolled out from Hurricane Point and the platoon cordoned the south and west as we worked the street, going to each home and inquiring what the residents were thinking and who the residents were. The area was mostly poor judging from the appearance of the clothing, and only a few homes displayed proof of recent wealth in their construction. Children followed us as a swarm to have their pictures taken. The surveys were done more quickly here than in most areas, and I tried to understand why. Then a single shot. We heard shots to the west and the children scattered, some crying, already knowing what was happening more than we did, mothers pulling them into their enclosed yards and shutting their metal gates in a near unison of slams. Within moments the children and Marines in the street had emptied into the yards, the families retreating further into their homes, and our rifles, like the antennas of insects, searched the sky from behind the safety of walls. Armored Humvees raced into the neighborhood from staging areas and jerked to a stop to fill with troops and move again. They brought a thickness of dust that seemed to add more haste to the hurry of our armed response to . . . something. Someone had been hit, we could hear on the radios. "Sniper from the northeast. One Marine down." I was crouching on a pile of discarded rubble, my knee slammed into the shards of brick and concrete. I hadn't worn my knee pads.

Vehicles began to separate, some for pursuit, some for medevac. My vehicle was a late add and did not intuitively belong with either group. The section in pursuit had been tight for months, and although I wanted to go with them, they were not used to us and we might complicate their coordination. I opted to retrograde with the medevac to simplify the situation, but as my Humvee pushed into the penned herd of cars trapped in the street along the route, we discovered ourselves to be late to join either and both were gone. The medevac was moving fast, already out of sight, heading west. The pursuit had already vanished into the streets to the north. We were alone in the center of Ramadi.

The retrograde route was simple enough and went through territory where we had cast a large shadow. But when the city got violent, we didn't own any real estate outside of our forward operating bases. I pulled my gunner, a young corporal from Baltimore, down out of the turret and told the driver to make best speed. The driver was a very young, very blond lance corporal from California who could not have looked more out of place in Iraq. Along with my Iraqi interpreter and black gunnery sergeant, we looked like the crew of *Star Trek*. The main street was scarred by the explosion of bombs left along it for us during the two-year occupation, and traffic crept close to the curb when there was trouble. Suicide bombers also drove their cars with a slow erratic discomfort, so as we rushed past each car along the route, my body tightened involuntarily, expecting them to detonate. None of them did.

We announced our arrival to the gate of Camp Ramadi and hurried to Charlie Med, where all casualties were taken. Marines were gathered in silence near the emergency room, and I went inside pretending authority and not knowing what I would find. I wanted to make sure that the Marine in charge of the medevac knew that we had arrived and that we were accounted for. It was the same field hospital I had been treated in a few months before. There was a cluster of army medical personnel encircling the ser-

geant who was writhing on a metal table. They seemed to be feeding on him. I stood away from them until a nurse placed me by
his head so that he would see someone familiar while the medics
did their work. He barely knew me but I was not unknown. He
looked up and said, "I'm sorry, sir. I didn't want to let you down."
I tried to assure him that my disappointment was an impossible
thing, but I can't remember what I said in the presence of his inconceivable apology.

The round had been fired as a single shot from a sniper as the
sergeant was running across the street. The bullet had entered his
hand and left through his forearm, leaving a discolored mass of
muscle and the sinews of other necessary parts hanging from the
exit wound. There were bone fragments inside that would have
to be dealt with later. Blood dripped from the table onto the floor
as they flushed the exposed interior of his arm. The medics threw
some kind of sand down to keep from slipping on the slick pool
of blood and alcohol.

He asked to see a photo of his family and told me that there
was one in his wallet. We found it sorting through his cut-up uniform, and I held a photograph of his baby daughter and another
of his family together over his face. He was afraid that he would
lose his arm, but I joked that I was afraid he would have to keep
it. I tried to help him pretend his injury was minor. The more he
worried, the more blood he would lose.

I went outside as the helicopter was being called in, and the
platoon had condensed into a silent pack nearby. They seemed
full of something unsettled and beyond words. I knew the feel-

ing. They were, again, incapable of exacting revenge, unsure if they should blame the mission, the leadership, or the city. For the sniper, the little bullet had been very particular. He had made a choice. For the Marines it was entirely random. I went over to talk to them, but they were sullen with fury and fatigue. I was brief. All that I knew was all that they knew. We would have to go back out tomorrow. The sniper had not been found and would probably be waiting for us.

The platoon went in to see their Marine in twos before he was flown away for surgery at another base. He was carried out to an ambulance for movement to the landing zone, and we all watched him go. He had been brave, but all anyone at home would know was that he had been hurt.

Back at the patrol base I lay down on a crooked cot. I left my pistol on my leg and did not sleep. My knees were hurting, but they had not been struck by bullets. I thought then that the history of pain in my legs was of little consequence. I kept seeing the Marines putting wet bulletproof pads into the back of their Humvee. They had been washing them to get the blood out at the medical aid station with a hose after the sergeant's medevac helicopter had lifted off. It was a silent ceremony that I watched from the door of the emergency room. It seemed to happen quietly despite the vehicles rolling past, the shuffle of feet on the gravel road, and the medical staff talking nearby. None of the Marines had said a word.

➤ ⬅

IN THE BEGINNING of our third year in Michigan, the war three years behind me, I was in the back field of our farm. I saw the Canada geese with their fuzzy rows of goslings following them like pussy willows on a branch, and a pair of ducks raised their heads from the grasses around the pond when I mowed the trail. My wife had flown to Russia to do research for a few weeks, and I resolved to catch a duckling for our daughter. We could raise it for a few months and then release it in the fall to join the migration south. Summer had just settled in as I walked out to our swamp. I spied a duck in the field near the pond and moved quickly to separate her from retreat to the safety of the open water. Her ducklings would not yet be able to fly or outrun me. The mother tried to draw me away by feigning injury and thrashing her way farther into the grass of the field as if she had broken a wing. I turned instead toward her point of origin to seek her young as prize. There was, in the weeds, a solitary duckling running away from the sounds of me. I picked it up and held it in a careful cage of fingers as it struggled. It made small sounds, distress codes sent into the wild for rescue.

I washed out an old aquarium and filled it with lush grass from the edge of the pond, bought duckling feed from the farm store, and cut a plastic water bowl down to size with a knife. I placed the duckling inside. My daughter came home from preschool, and we examined the beautiful creature together, stroking it lightly and telling it that it was safe with language that must have sounded, instead, like the purring of a cat. It was covered in brown hair and had an elegant dark brown bill. A mallard. It was a perfect thing. It kept making the small sounds. It did not have enough experi-

ence for bravery. We went to bed, and it just made the sounds of
needing and not having. At some point in the night, the sounds
stopped. The duckling had finally fallen asleep.

I woke early the next day and the house was still quiet. I had
been wrong in thinking the silence was peaceful. The duckling
had been confused by the glass walls of the aquarium and become
entangled in the severed wilderness of grass that I had carefully
piled for its comfort. It had spilled the bowl of water and soaked its
down flat to its body. Once wet, it got cold. It had been calling out
in desperation when I had only heard loneliness. I had not held it
under my arm so that the infant would stay warm, hear my heart,
and close its eyes. It was an immensity of silence, the destruction
of the little thing that I had taken from the wild without meaning
any harm.

I took the duckling outside wrapped in the cool grass that had
chilled it. I gave it an unceremonious burial so that I could hurry
back inside. I did not want to leave my sleeping daughter alone in
the house, even if I was nearby. In the morning, she asked where
her duckling had gone. I told her that the mother duck had found
her baby and that they had gone back to the swamp together. I said
that it was safe.

LIMPING AROUND OUR FARM in Michigan, my knees hurt
all the time. I ignored it as much as possible, still somehow expecting their deterioration to reverse. I relented to have doctors
perform arthroscopy to examine the cartilage and bone inside the

knee, and they confirmed what I knew. The knee was a mess, cartilage gone, bones arthritic and forming calcified spurs, repair simply impossible. The knee could not be healed. They echoed the diagnosis of the doctors years before: replacement. I was too young and a replacement now would require another replacement eventually. Even titanium and Teflon parts wore down like bone. They wondered how my knees had come to such ruin so early. I wondered how anyone else's knees were any better. Hadn't they also gone forth to wear themselves against the world? Was I one of only a few who had been injured and reconstructed? Was I the only one who was already worried about the deep system?

I had a "loose body" removed and frayed cartilage shaved. Loose bodies had been taken out before, small pieces of cartilage broken away from the bones and adrift in the joint. They needed to inspect the swelling a few days later. I limped to the registration desk and signed in. Everyone came in either leaning on crutches or walking unnaturally, cautiously. The space was almost still with the slow movement of injuries, the burnt smell of new rubber from the welcome mat, and the rug woven with the colors of desert sand. There was nowhere to rest my swollen leg in the waiting room, and I walked like everyone else to a shiny burgundy seat. In the space where chairs wouldn't fit stood a plant. It was made from the dead limbs of a real tree, holes drilled in them for the molded plastic branches that held pressed nylon leaves, dark green, to catch the fluorescent light. Someone had taken every precaution so that the lifeless stalks would not look artificial in their bucket filled with blackened styrofoam earth, like a miniature tree in a dollhouse made from a dyed green sponge, there to comfort the plastic people who cannot blink or bend their knees as they wait to be seen.

I was finally ushered into a room where I was to be examined by the surgeon. In the corner of the room was a life-sized human skeleton. A sign was taped to the ribs in front. It said, DO NOT PLAY WITH SKELETON. I looked at the knees. No cartilage.

I kept the knees. I'll wait until I can't stand or walk, but I know that I will not have these original joints when I am buried. I still have a ringed scar from putting my finger into a kaleidoscope as a baby, the stitched line on my hand from an accident stacking fire-wood, the lines from a saw on my left knuckles from a Boy Scout camping trip, the scars on my knee from football, the staple still there, markings on my legs from vein removal, and the branding on my elbow from an IED in Iraq. These all mingle with the fresh scratches I acquire doing construction now. There are other scars too that don't blemish the skin. Heart attacks and brain tumors, lunacy and losses. The unmarked graves of mistakes and injuries that have no surface. No monuments but the changing bends of the brow. We allow ourselves our childhoods to explore injury by accident. What comes next is a knowing sense of risk and the strange urge to find out again what we have already learned.

CHAPTER 9

ASH

ASH IS A SUBSTANCE WITHOUT A REAL ATTACHMENT
to air or firmament. It is not part of the fundament, or earth. It
exists only as aftermath, a product of fire and tragedy, a stain on
the ground and in the wind. It is made by the particular destruction of life down to its elemental carbon, our black core. Something has to die absolutely to become ash.

Pompeii was buried in hot ash, hot enough to seal people in
its mass and then burn them so completely that only the empty
volume of their bodies remained, hollow spaces in the settled em-
bers. Plaster has been poured into these molds by archaeologists,
restoring the last form that the dead had assumed before disap-
pearance. We know the most about Roman life because of this city.
The substance of absolute destruction preserved it.

➜ ❧

IT WAS MY CHORE to take out the metal bucket of ash that my
father carefully dug from our cast-iron woodstove with a small
shovel once a week. The ash had its own pile beside the compost,
but both decreased in size as we added to them. I didn't think
much about the ash as I carried it out into the snow. It looked
like a crushed wasp's nest in the galvanized pail. I would dump
it on the snow and watch as it melted its way to the older ash
underneath.

In the summer, I spent long days digging in the abandoned ash
dumps that still held treasures around Poolville. Pieces of china
dolls, glass medicine bottles, and the brittle lids from canning
jars would emerge as I carefully excavated the household garbage
pits. Most of them had already been discovered and dug hastily
by two brothers. They had made a name for looting and for selling the antique bottles that they found, but they were sloppy and
broke as much as they carried off. I was usually left to sift through
what they had missed. The ash left iridescent tarnish on the bottles
but protected them in soft, damp piles. I found marbles, chipped
teacups, rusty razors, and porcelain doorknobs. I didn't consider
what else was in the ash. The fires in stoves and hearths of the
town had burned everything down. The forests that were now
fields had emptied into the endless burning. Love letters, journals,
books, underwear, and the secrets of families went into the fires
along with newspapers, broken plates, and animal bones. They
were all there in the ash that fell through my fingers as I searched

for the objects that were still recognizable. I rarely found what I truly sought.

I remember making the trip with my father to the nearby college town of Hamilton for the newspapers. It was an adventure to see the landscape every time. In the winter I wondered what lay covered under bumps in the snow. I imagined them to be the ash dumps of vanished homesteads. Almost all the remaining houses along the road had firewood stacked on their porches and a trail of smoke from their chimneys. I could smell the wood burn through the vents of our car as we passed. I remember it clearly. The shadow of our car rippled as we moved, changing with the ground, flickering on the stalks of saplings, telephone poles, and fences. We were like soot on the snow, deformed but recognizable. A child's charcoal drawing of a station wagon. I can see myself, small, in the lit frame of the rear window as it expanded and shrank on the slopes with impossible suddenness, and my father in front, driving, changing size, both of us something enough to block the sun as we passed over the countryside late in the afternoon like a cloud of smoke that was known to us.

IN THE SOUTHERN TRAINING AREA of Camp Lejeune, we dug defensive positions, dug until the dry sand and roots turned cool and moist. We dug four feet down, to where the ground bled dark water. Only a few miles from the Atlantic coast the soil stayed damp through the humid summers and felt temporary. We laid pine branches in the bottom of our foxhole to keep from getting wet, and burrowed holes into the drowned soil for grenade sumps on either side, holes we could kick incoming grenades into when attacked, the earth absorbing the explosion, leaving us mostly alive in our grave. We were preparing, again, to be attacked by our own people, pretending to play adversaries but with too little at stake to hate like enemies must.

There would be no madness of self-sacrifice, no unexplainable acts, no one wounded who would inexplicably continue to charge as he died, getting just close enough to do an unimaginable thing, our last transmission going out in the hurried voice of disbelief. No, we would survive the night, my radioman and I. I dug our hole myself, ordering my reluctant lance corporal to rest for a long night of radio watch. I packed the soil in a low sloped berm around us, the thickest part facing out into the woods. It was like building a sand castle, but with ancient filth, gray sand left by the expanding coastline and the rot of forests that grew from it over thousands of years. I was surprised to find no shells in this relinquished beach, no bones. The salts had been washed out by centuries of rain, and the sand no longer had the scent of the sea.

The air smelled of smoke all day. We heard that a mortar range had started a fire somewhere, but we had not seen it. We felt far from the world of people in this forest, waiting to be attacked as if by foreigners. It was like an outpost on the unexplored edge of our own country, a vulnerable place made more vulnerable because it was uninhabited. We had come to fill a wild gap in our lands, forced in some ways to capture it in order to defend it. In truth, the area had been bought by the government fairly recently and added

to the Marine base. Most of the trees here were new growth returning to cleared fields. There were still a few houses left standing,
doors swung open as if they had been abandoned in advance of disaster. As I dug our hole, I wondered if this place had been plowed,
trees pulled down and the sand turned and seeded. Had a farmer
looked out over this ground and thought it could never be forest
again? There was little undergrowth, and I could see through the
trees for quite some distance. The fire appeared in the afternoon.

It just seemed like a wall of gray smoke, neither rising nor
blowing, its source invisible in the grass and leaves on the ground.
There was no wind, and the flames were moving by instinct,
spreading from a now distant center and leaving a layer of warm,
fragile ash behind. It was not until the sun went down that we
could see the flames flickering in the dark, made larger by reflection in their own hovering smoke. It was an eerie experience to
watch the fire advance on us as we guarded our hole. Small sticks,
dried by the long summer, cracked and hissed as they burned,
and in the black night the burning line became the only visible
horizon, the entire earth on fire, apocalyptic, and we in our deep
island left to wait for it to pass. We were to hold our positions.

As my radioman slept, I waited for the fire to come. It took
hours to arrive, its constancy keeping my eyes fixed to it. It was
uncompromising, elegant, and the cruellest thing I have ever seen.
As it reached me, I felt, for a moment, inside it. My head was
level with the flames and I could look down its serpentine line
in either direction, the fire wrapping around our foxhole and the
heated smoke rising straight up into the trees. Far off I could hear

a Marine cough. I had ordered everyone to prepare a wet T-shirt to hold over their faces when the smoke got close, to get low in the hole in the pocket of unconsumed air, but to keep one man up, our perimeter alert to what might come through the cinders. I had never examined fire from ground level before, my eyes in that odd membrane between air and earth where the vulnerable paradise of leaves and grass salved by rains can be charred by flame. The leaves burned slowly, the webbed sails between the woody veins revealing the bones of the leaf for just a moment, the powdered skeleton shivering into ash. The arch of a bent blade of grass burned like the flight of a spark slowed down or a bullet fired into the air. Everything was enkindled by contact and similarly doomed. The people who lived in snow and deserts would never know what I knew about fire on the ground, the firelight on my face warm as sunshine.

We were never attacked that night. No dark forms moving through the ash searching for survivors to practice killing. Just us peering out of our pit at the scorched earth, exposed now, waiting. The fire moved far behind us and my uniform smelled of its smoke, the last evidence of a season's growth rendered down.

Stumps smoked and the sand cooled under its thin blanket of soot. In the morning, we could see every footprint, the ash so fine it seemed to disappear under our boots. The world of leaves and grasses, lives spent catching sunlight, was composed more of light than of carbon. Their mass had been given off in the bright flames.

→ ←

ON MARCH 13, 2005, exactly two years after I had packed for my first deployment to Iraq, I awoke to the familiar effluvium of smoldering garbage. Smoke from plastic bags and discarded food from the chow hall burned in a nearby pit and crept over the small concrete building that was to be my home for the next seven months. It had been a dog kennel before the invasion. I was back in Iraq. It was cold. There was no wind. The sky over the Euphrates was pale orange and filled with seagulls and crows slowly circling the scorched trash. I dressed, struggled into my flak vest with its heavy ceramic-plate armor, strapped on my drop holster and pistol, slung my rifle, and adjusted my helmet. I had to meet with the division comptroller about reconstruction funds and see if I could speak with the State Department representative about the politics in Ramadi. They were across the river in an abandoned palace, and I needed to jump a convoy to get there. I had arrived with the advanced party, and my small Civil Affairs team, with its gunners and drivers, was not yet with me. I was left to annoy the remnants of the Second Battalion, Fifth Marines, or the incoming First Battalion, for escorts anywhere off of the forward operating base where I had been marooned. The base was named Hurricane Point by a previous unit, and its name had already become associated with American casualties.

At the staging area I loaded my weapons, racking the bolt back slightly on my M16 to check that there was brass in the chamber. One round ready. A lieutenant gave me a brief.

"It's only one hundred meters from here, but getting there is a problem."

"Doesn't anyone just drive over the bridge?" I asked. "Don't we own it?" Judging by the gray satellite image of Ramadi, the distance seemed simple enough to negotiate, and we had an observation post on top of the bridge on either side.

"There are barely two lanes on the bridge. Cars are just parked in a line waiting to pass through our entry-control point. Have to shut down local traffic on the far side and then push through the congestion. We don't want to move slowly through a crowd in this town, sir."

The lieutenant knew the ground. I had only been in the city for fifteen days and had not yet been to the North Bridge. You should always know when you don't know. We would have to take a convoy over the South Bridge instead, stopping first at the U.S. Army base across the canal, Camp Ramadi, then pushing north to parallel the highway east over the Euphrates River. Then we would turn south to the Marine headquarters, Camp Blue Diamond. I would have to catch another convoy back later that day. No one was sure when it would come or which direction it would go. My interpreter and I climbed into a seven-ton cargo truck and waited to roll out. The bed of this truck was a typical Marine construct. It had its regular quarter-inch metal sides, but there was also a three-foot-high wall of sandbags faced with sheets of plywood inside. The men of the Second Battalion, Fifth Marines had built these mobile trenches along with the famous "Frankensteins"—Humvees with mismatched steel sheets welded to them as armor. As with all armor, they had missed a spot; the bed itself had not been reinforced with much.

As I sat there I read the graffiti left by passengers. 2/5 WAS HERE
was carefully printed with a Sharpie marker, and across from me,
IF YOU LIVED HERE, YOU'D BE HOME BY NOW was lightly written in pen.
2/5 was leaving soon, and the newer messages were bitter farewells and humorless jokes. SUCKS TO BE YOU was carved into the
wood beside my head by a Leatherman tool or a bayonet.

1/5 was still learning the route and the procedures from 2/5,
and the convoy left late. We swayed in unison as the truck shifted
and slammed over ruts we could not see. We were told to keep our
heads below the sandbags to avoid the infamous snipers in Tameem,
south of the canal. On the other side of the road stood the abandoned glass factory, immense and desolate. We could see its smoke-
stacks as we passed. Suddenly we were coughing dust. The army
unit based at Camp Ramadi used Paladin mobile-artillery vehicles
with heavy armor and tracks, and they had ground the packed earth
near the base entrance into a foam of powder six inches deep. We
stirred it into billows the height of the trucks as we passed through;
it was like being launched into another planet's atmosphere.

Camp Ramadi was dirty. Two years of American occupation
there had left almost no impression at all. Staff members filled
former Iraqi military offices that were cold with air-conditioning
and littered with small comforts, but few improvements had been
made outside. There was a PX, which caused great excitement,
but it sold almost nothing of any use. A large plastic banner hung
outside of the PX read COMPARE OUR PRICES! It was the only place we
were able to shop for seven months.

The convoy finally moved again. My interpreter, Ameen, was

Sudanese, almost fifty years old, and tough. He carried a captured Iraqi 9-millimeter pistol and was good at his job. He was known for saying "This guy's story is lies. He is fucking muj!" He sat across from me in the rear of the truck, and we talked about the river that shrank back toward his village in Sudan. Beside us were two Marine combat cameramen, along for the ride like we were. There was a navy chief and a few more Marines in back with us, as well as a helicopter pilot traveling in the cab with the driver. The route was short, routine, and considered "permissive." We were not to expect any threat.

We moved out of the rear gate and saw lines of Iraqi tractor-trailers that had been contracted to deliver lumber and air conditioners to the base. Many of the drivers had been smugglers running intrigue from Syria and Jordan to Baghdad during Saddam's reign. It was widely whispered by army personnel that they could bring you anything you wanted, and that they always had liquor. I would steal a look from time to time to get my bearings, and the colors along the route were transformed almost as if by my imagination. The dry compacted dirt around Camp Ramadi gave way to rich greens of well-irrigated land beside the Euphrates River. Women cut grasses and arranged them in piles as children played with soccer balls given out by army and Marine units in the area.

As we crossed the Euphrates on a low bridge and passed the army security post, there was a sound and the truck shuddered.

The air was instantly gray and full of objects moving at different speeds, some rising and others falling. Pieces of things. I hadn't trusted the highway bridge above us, so I was facing it with my rifle, luckily, with my back to the blast. My arm suddenly hurt. Time slowed. I looked at the men in the truck bed with me and saw mostly blank expressions. Disbelief. It wasn't until they saw their own blood everywhere that they responded. One Marine was missing some fingers and part of his nose, the navy chief had a wound near his waist, and the Marine beside me was still. I moved in front of him and looked into his eyes. He was conscious but unresponsive. I thought for a moment about nerve agents. We no longer carried our gas masks. I asked him if he could hear me and gestured with my hands in case he could only see. His hand clenched his rifle and could not be pried free. His muscles were locked in the sitting position, and we lifted him out of the back of the seven-ton as if he were strapped to an invisible chair. What we did not know then was that a small piece of metal had slipped beneath his neck guard in the explosion and was lodged near an artery. His body had involuntarily locked itself to avoid move-ment. The slight trickle of blood was imperceptible beneath his body armor, and I was treating him for shock instead, which he was going into. A Marine was searching for pieces of the wounded Marine's fingers as I established security. There was no radio on the truck, a common deficiency with motor transportation, but other vehicles from the convoy were relaying their urgent trans-missions.

I wanted at that moment to locate the triggerman and kill him, but there was no one standing nearby waiting to confess to fighting us. Nothing but Iraq falling away in every direction, sur-rounding us. I noticed that the woman in the field we had passed had resumed cutting grass and laying it in a pile, if she had ever stopped.

I scanned the bridge and buildings in the near distance. No cars close enough to indict. Everyone equally suspicious. All of them equally terrified of our expected unspecific retribution. Ameen had grabbed a rifle from a wounded Marine, and I placed him on the other side of the road from me to turn away cars. He shouted commands in Arabic, and Iraqi drivers retreated in a disorder of inadequate comprehension. Four army soldiers emerged from the bunker on the corner, and I ordered them into security positions facing the bridge. The bomb had somehow been set directly on the corner that they were guarding, probably dropped from a passing car on the street side of their barriers. An empty seven-ton from the convoy was brought up as a medevac, and I pulled Ameen back to help load the wounded. We noticed another 155-millimeter artillery round still lying in the road next to us. It had not detonated. If it had, during the time Ameen and I stood at the corner protecting our wreckage, we would have died there.

As we moved the wounded and looked for ghosts in the dissipating traffic, the smoke from the artillery round moved away from us with the dust from the hole it had made. The scent of explosive residue blew off and was replaced by that of diesel fuel, which emptied without sound from the punctured fuel tanks of our truck. It was only then that I realized that the fuel had not ignited in the blast. Even now, as I think back on the moment, I can remember no flash or flame. It was as if the explosion had been made entirely of dust and sound. Just the shock of the concussion and the color of the air. The peculiar stutter of time. The truck slowing to a stop and the impossibility of retaliation. Cordite and dirt. It was not the smell of smoke from training-range fires blowing gently past the barracks. Not the smell of pine needles and grass burning somewhere at Camp Lejeune or Quantico. It was a smell particular to war and without any pleasant familiarity. Not a shot was fired.

We rushed back to Camp Ramadi, though not by the way we had come. We pushed east and then south, bludgeoning our way through Iraqi traffic waiting to cross the North Bridge, then past Hurricane Point and over the South Bridge again to complete a large pointless circle of the western Ramadi military bases. Then back, finally, into the dust of the army base entrance and on to the casualty facility. Once the wounded were being cared for, I turned to leave. You don't want to stay in a combat emergency room unless you can offer a medical opinion or are bleeding out. I slipped out the door into the quiet of unencumbered space. Soldiers and Marines walked past, unaware of the distress and urgent motion inside. Just across a rutted dirt road was the army mess hall, where contractors and service members laughed and relaxed during catered meals while casualties rushed in from patrols bled to death twenty meters away. This was the first of several times that I would walk out of that building, leaving behind me a crowd of medics circling the panic of wounded men. The bright and claustrophobic room. The smell of pure alcohol and pungent plastics. The low tone of diagnosis and the high pitch of pain.

I thought I should jump another convoy out and go ice my arm, but a Marine looked through the holes in my sleeve and saw blood. I had to look to be sure it was my own. I turned back toward the medical building to have the arm quickly examined, and he escorted me. I felt ridiculous having a Marine walk a hundred feet with me, but he was right to insist. Shock or other effects of an injury can bring someone down in a matter of steps. The body can collapse without permission.

A calm doctor directed me into a back room, away from all the pain and blood of the serious casualties. I had been hit with a fragment the size of a musket ball, but it had been rejected by my bone and there was nothing but a deep hole. The heat and impact of the metal had kept the wound from bleeding, and only smaller fragment punctures above my elbow had blood creeping from them. It looked like my uniform had been shredded near the elbow without producing the expected injury beyond the cloth. I was carried on adrenaline and felt nothing more than a dull sustained pain and limited movement. I was tired. I just wanted to get back to Hurricane Point and my empty concrete room. Ameen was having his ears examined. None of us could hear very well. "Mild concussions," said the doctor. "Typical." I remember a low audible static in my head. It seemed like it wasn't in my ears but rather somewhere inside my mind. I tried to remember what the mission was.

Back at Hurricane Point, I stood at the sand-filled weapon-clearing barrels to empty my rifle. I removed the magazine and placed it in my flak vest to free my hands. I could barely move my elbow, so the intuitive task of pulling the charging handle to the rear was strangely difficult. After two humbling attempts, I racked the bolt back, ejecting the bullet I had checked in the chamber that morning. It fell and was consumed by the fine dust at my feet, disappearing like an icicle into deep snow. I found it with my fingers, wiped it clean, and returned it to the top of my magazine. It would remain the first bullet loaded every day until finally it was fired out into Ramadi. By June, it had been on every street in western Ramadi and had been aimed at almost every window at one point or another. A perpetual golden bullet.

DURING MY FIRST TOUR I had convinced myself that I was invulnerable. I was not careless, but I was unafraid in part because fearlessness was required of me. My Marines assumed that an acceptance of risk was ordinary. We became accustomed to our endangerment. When we took our casualty, we were at a loss to completely believe it and went right back into our ritual of patrols as if nothing had happened. While I was deployed my family worried, all of them keeping their worry from me as much as they could.

My second tour was different. I expected to be killed in Ramadi. After I was wounded it was worse for my wife and parents, the mystery of my situation expanding my peril in their imaginations, my vulnerability exposed. But the belief in immortality and the certainty of doom produced almost the same lack of anxiety in me.

On June 16 we were going south to cross the railroad tracks. It was a routine operation in conjunction with combat engineers conducting a search-and-detonation mission on a tip that there was a cache of explosives hidden near the canal running to the south of Ramadi. The village there was always bizarre, inhabited mostly by fishermen, nets spread out in their yards to be cleaned and repaired by their families. The people didn't seem to mix with the rest of the city that lay a mere two hundred meters away on the other side of the tracks. We never knew who we would find there, the entire settlement sometimes abandoned to children and dogs, sometimes flush with men. We called it Springfield because we thought it had a population of characters to rival that of *The Simpsons*. I accompanied the infantry company led by a captain who had become a friend during the deployment. It was to be a security patrol to do a local census and questionnaire, while engineers located artillery rounds delivered by insurgents to be used against us later in Ramadi. While we patrolled through town, we found it almost empty again, the streets vacant, dogs quiet. To take the edge off, the Captain and I exchanged lines from *Monty Python and the Holy Grail*. One of us would begin:

"You were in great peril."

"I don't think I was."

"Yes, you were. You were in terrible peril."

"Look, let me go back and face the peril."

"No, it's too perilous."

We had a similar sense of humor and were also like-minded about how to approach the embattled city. The day felt long, and we finally got word that the ammunition had been found, and charges set. We took cover and two pitched rumbles sent a shudder through the town. Trucks were inbound, and as we rallied near the edge of the tracks on the south side, we began to receive small-arms fire from somewhere on the north, where we were heading. We boarded vehicles and crossed the tracks, relieved to finally be heading back to base after so much sweating. Mortars came in, and an IED erupted ahead of us on the road, with no effect. Enough trouble, though, to steer us onto another road. The convoy changed direction, turning east on a dirt path through a jumble of houses. Moving under sporadic fire, we knew something bad was imminent, and the enemy picked the first vehicle in the convoy, detonating several artillery rounds daisy-chained together around a fuel tank. The blast was so powerful that it blew the up-armored vehicle off the ground. The road ahead went black with smoke, and the company frequency went silent for a moment. The Captain was dead and his gunner missing, crushed beneath the burning vehicle. I would spend the night protecting my friend's smoldering wreckage while we waited for a recovery vehicle to come.

I wrote home:

. . . *There were too many memorial ceremonies this month and I attended them all. Was in attendance. Present.*

It is early in the night on the holy day and I can hear the broadcasts from three nearby mosques. Praise with the tone of lament. Voice spread out through an extended exhale of language that I can not interpret but feel that I may understand. Bats fly with a random deliberateness in the gray of incomplete darkness. Blind to the world as we see it but somehow not colliding with it, both of us recognizing what is solid and what is not. It is, then, the same world to men and to bats. They hunt insects that hunt us and hunt each other. Everything is similar. Everyone is hunting. I have moved through the dark, defining the space in the grainy green glow of night-vision goggles. I have been out all day patrolling and sweating and thinking that I wouldn't need them. You always bring all of your gear because you never know how a day will end. You have them strapped to the front of your helmet and their awkward weight pulls your head forward. There is no depth perception and objects appear like energy huddled into familiar forms . . . which they are. You can't see the dust but you know that it is there. Something explodes. Try running through a city like that. The phosphorus burn of tracers flashing too bright for your eyes to adjust to. Gone as fast as they pass. You don't know how long you will have to stay on the roof that you have found yourself on. You have ordered the family of the home into a room beneath you. You are out of water. You hope that the rest of the bats in your unit know that it is you on the roof as they hurl themselves into the area to reinforce. Someone is shooting. Watch the tracers. Keep low. You may be there all night. You may be there for the rest of your life. You watch the alleys and the windows for anyone you don't know. You don't know anyone. Think through the Rules of Engagement. Positive identification of a threat is required before you can fire. Reasonable certainty. You are in the middle of an urban sprawl. Your friend's shattered vehicle is upside down by *the road ahead with its tires burning. Extinguishers are all expended and Marines are throwing sand on the wreckage. The tires cannot be smothered. You can smell the smoke. All the while, it isn't your house that you have invaded or guard. The family in the room beneath you is just waiting for you to leave. Someone is still shooting. You are not sure, in the shimmering imagination of night-vision equipment, if you see something moving. It can't be positively identified. You are holding your fire. You are holding your position. Holding your position can be a profession. Three months remain. You don't want to let anyone down.*

My golden bullet was gone. Its empty shell casing lay behind a wall in someone's yard. You build a fort . . . and you defend it. But the fort was not ours. We were not defending its occupants. Leaning against the wall behind a Marine was the single AK-47 assault rifle the Iraqi family was allowed to keep for self-defense. We had emptied it and made it safe as we collected these people in their kitchen and guarded them from us, using their house to fight back against their neighborhood. I had found this danger because I had sought it. I had no one but myself to blame for discovering it to be ugly.

The purity of service had been corrupted by the moral ambiguity of political language. Language had been the first casualty of the war. It was not the dirt or the smoke or the smell or the blood. My days were not condemned by the things I had expected. It was the pointlessness and the faces of people who were left to live in the violence we had brought with us or had drawn to us. Our bullets had gone out into other people's lives. We gathered our wreckage and our dead, and someone, who lived there, filled in the holes in the road made by the bombs left for us.

For 215 days, we threw ourselves at the city and washed back into Hurricane Point. At headquarters, one hundred meters away, other Marines read our reports, and the Euphrates passed between without noticing any of us.

In an essay for *Harper's*, finished while I was still in Iraq, my father wrote, "We do not talk about what could happen to Ben. We cannot. . . . We are in our mid-sixties, and every day is precious to us, but we have talked away a chunk of a year of our lives by ticking off each day of his second tour as one more that hastens him home . . . Perhaps we feel that by slicing another day off our lives, as we wish it away to bring him home, we are spending our lives to buy his."

I returned at the end of September on the day of my daughter's first birthday. She hid behind my wife's legs and sneaked smiles at me. I guessed that she had no idea who I was. I almost forgot why she wouldn't. I had known fathers who were never coming back to their children. I cleaned my rifle and pistol one last time, again, and turned them in to the armory.

ON FEBRUARY 23, 2006, fifteen years to the day after the invasion of Iraq in 1991, 150 days after I returned from Ramadi, my father died of a heart attack on East Thirty-seventh Street in New York City. He was standing beside my mother, reached for her, and fell. I did not know because I was filming *The Wire* in Baltimore. I came home to my wife holding the phone in the doorway. My mother said that he was fighting, but I drove to New York knowing that he was gone. I was not prepared, after so much death, to see him dead that night. The bright white sheet and my father beneath it. He was mortal, I discovered. I returned with my mother to their home in Sherburne the next day and sat with what he had left behind.

My father was always preparing for disaster. To him, life was a series of impending emergencies. In the exterior container of his pickup truck, we found his emergency kit. It had never been waterproofed, and the collection of flashlights, tools, flares, tire jacks, and jumper cables was frozen together in a solid block of ice. It sat like a brick of worry—an ironic memorial to survival. All of the objects of rescue were preserved, suspended, and I considered keeping it in the freezer as an idol. I recognized the flashlight. I had given him a flashlight for Christmas every year as a joke, but I also knew that he placed every one of them somewhere carefully.

My father had chosen words over war. He created families that were under assault and then defended them with language. He wrote of destruction without allowing it to take place. He fought his art on a manual typewriter, and when I was little I could hear the keys banging as he forced letters onto paper. There were pauses, of course, and sometimes I would try to imagine the cause for the break in intervals of tapped code. Was he thinking or had he made a mistake? A writer could erase mistakes. Another difference between art and war. The irregular chatter of keys striking pages was like distant machine-gun fire. Like communication by bullets shot into the sky. He wrote his fears and called them fiction, but the wish that he wrote was for my preservation. He wrote his fear of losing me, but not about how I was to lose him. The one thing that he had never told me was, "Someday I'll be dead, and you won't be able to bring me back." I would stand at his memorial in my dress blue uniform, and along my left leg would hang my empty hand and my decorative sword.

A MONTH AFTER my father had fallen away from us, I returned to our farmhouse in Michigan with the rifle I had bought fifteen years earlier. It had been with him for the last fourteen years, during which it had been fired only twice. I wrapped it in an old down-filled comforter and put it in a place where our daughter could not somehow discover it. It was still loaded, but I did not empty it to count the rounds. I did not empty it to make it safe. It was my rifle, and it had returned to me to protect my home. That was what it was for. It was my own. I knew that it had at least one bullet in its chamber, and knowing that much was knowing enough.

On a cold night, I heard the yelp and bark of a pack of coyotes in the darkness of land behind our house. My wife had fallen asleep reading, and our little girl was bundled under a blanket in her crib as the sounds of the pack grew close. I put on boots and a jacket, unwrapped the rifle, and went outside. I walked away from the thin light falling from the upstairs windows and into the

frosted grass and frozen patches of old snow, toward the fields. My
hands were bare and tight on the rifle, and I realized as I walked
that I was holding it like I had carried my rifle in Iraq. Finger
straight and off the trigger, as if I was expecting an ambush. As
if there was the imminent necessity to raise it to my shoulder
and fire. The fragile hay broke with an irregular hiss beneath my
boots, and the calls of the coyotes were in the wind now, their distance disguised by the density of the chilled air and open space. I
was silhouetted by the dim glow of the house behind me, and the
coyotes could surely see me standing in the emptiness of the uncut
field. I could not see them, but we had an understanding of who
was where. The sky above was in turmoil, and the ground was
gray with the frozen fur of disheveled hay. Wooden posts and the
barbed wire of old fences were declining without elegance into
the dirt they had been raised to enclose. It seemed a lost battlefield
with only the memory of loss. I thought of aiming a rifle at dust
in Iraq. I thought of my father guarding his home with my rifle in
Upstate New York, and my mother's allowance for one to be used
against snakes. I remembered them raising me not to carry a gun.
I remembered them as my father had, in his art, remembered me:

> She remembered them standing side by side and looking up at
> Patrick as he leaned over a rifle that he aimed at them. They were in
> the side yard of their first place, a tall Victorian farmhouse on a half
> acre of land in a little hamlet that wasn't very far from Earlville. It
> was summer, and Patrick had been working for weeks on his fort. As
> an eleventh birthday gift, they had opened an account in his name

at the lumberyard, and Patrick had purchased small lots of planking
and studs, an expensive framing hammer, galvanized nails. He had
built himself a fort in the crotch of a young sugar maple outside the
dining room, and he was up in his safe place after dinner in June, she
thought, or early July—the sun was still high, and no one ever talked
about autumn coming on—and she and Bernard looked up at their
son. He looked down over the sights of his wooden scale-model Garand
M1 rifle.

"You didn't see the ambush," he'd said.

"No, we didn't," Bernard had answered.

"You don't need to worry, though, on account of I won't shoot."

"You know, I knew you wouldn't," she remembered telling him.
She remembered, now, in the old feed mill, looking at her grown and
damaged, dangerous son, how disappointing to the boy her confidence
had been.

"You knew?" he'd said.

"I mean I was hoping," she'd told him.

"We hoped you wouldn't shoot," Bernard had said.

"Please don't shoot," she'd called to him in the shadows of his
fort.

"No," he'd said, "I won't."

I heard the voices of predators again through the wind. And for
loss, for vengeance, for sorrow, I fired the last three rounds that
my father had left in my rifle into the dark of the field behind the
barn. I was responsible for the bullets and knew, as I sent them,
that they would have to fall somewhere.

→ ←

I **WENT BACK** to Sherburne to surprise my mother on Thanksgiving, and she was not herself. A friend had warned me that I should go see her, that her depression over the loss of my father had developed odd physical manifestations. When I came into the kitchen she paused and then said, "Oh . . . Ben," as if my name had finally reached her memory. She was moving as if through water but without buoyancy, and there was measured incomprehension in her eyes. I had brought soups from Fairway in New York City, where I was editing a film, and I watched across the table as she forgot to eat it, spoon in her hand.

Her doctor had put her on mood-enhancement drugs and convinced her that she was depressed. What he hadn't done was note that she had lost her peripheral vision on one side and most control of her right arm and leg. She was having difficulty focusing, trouble with direction, and I didn't know what to think. I left to see my family in Michigan and started calling doctors. I called psychiatrists who could not see her quickly enough, and I called her doctor who was annoyed by my alarm. I wanted her to be given an MRI, but a doctor would have to order it. It would be expensive. I continued to make phone calls to people who spoke with the deflective assumption that I was merely an anxious child worried for his mother.

While I tried to convince her doctor of more than he had found, our friend Patricia Kramer found my mother on the floor of her bedroom unable to stand again. An ambulance took her to

Cooperstown, New York, where she was admitted into the emergency room, an MRI was done, and an immense tumor was discovered. Surgery was required immediately or she would likely go into an unrecoverable coma within days. Arrangements were made to transport her to Sloan-Kettering in New York City, and Patricia and I stayed by her bed awaiting surgery. Steroids reduced the swelling, and she returned, briefly, to herself. She was funny and I did not take the moment to tell her how important she had been, or how wonderful. I didn't ask her for our stories, one more time. The CAT scan was done and the doctor gave us the name of the enemy. Glioblastoma. Incurable. Surgery would prolong her life by as much as a year with chemotherapy, maybe more with a good remission, but it would recur and would not be operable a second time. Back in her room, I believed that she would not yet be lost. There would be time to tell her things. There would be time to record the stories that we relied on her to recount. Our history was in her head. I thought that we were buying her a year to remain my mother, to be a grandmother. There would be time and we could move in with her to spend it well.

A week after the surgery her cancer returned. Its ruthless speed was unexpected. Doctors were sober and spoke of comfort instead of treatment. No one gave me fair warning. It was too late, already, to be so sorry. In Utica, New York, it had been raining since New Year's Day. Two days into the new year. Three hundred ten days since my father had passed away. I watched it strike the windows on the other side of my mother as she slept. It was night, and the glass held up a dense pattern of glowing drops lit from somewhere below our third floor. Often a drop would form and move downward, gaining speed as it consumed other drops in its path, taking part of them and leaving part behind, rearranging the order of drops, still water but not the same water. Random, you would think, and without rest. Life on earth depended on the motion of water. But it was the world outside of our room. The sky falling as she began to die, and the window keeping the vitality of the rain from her. Her labored breath was all that I heard. Its struggle was no longer representative of any defiance but was now a cadence for the inevitable. A rasping marking of time. I was talking to her when I suddenly realized that my voice was the only sound.

I held my breath. Across from me, Patricia did the same. None of us were breathing. Her heart would stop next, and I waited, holding her hand and talking softly to her mind. Time stretched in my hand, holding hers as she passed away. I was told that hearing was the last sense to go. Could you hear being told that you were dead? Her mind invaded, she continued to think, dream, and I imagined all the images and voices of a life hurrying to be remembered one last time. What was last? What was the last impression? I could remember her last words from hours before the deep of coma. She was awakened by a nurse who rubbed her throat and brought her up gasping as if from underwater. She saw me and said: "Oh my baby boy." Then she went back into sleep. She never spoke again.

The cancer was a darkening knot, a madness of living tissue growing into her memories and confusing the order of events. As I sat beside her I recounted places that we had been. I wanted to give her images of oceans and forests. I didn't know if they had been lost to her, taken from her, consumed. Mice making nests of old letters, and trees growing back into the field. I wanted her to see, knowing that her eyes would never open again. If she could only hear, then it would have to be words for pictures. I was not able to speak with the things I understood. The stones, streams, and wood were without speech here in this room. I was in the interior, where my father had lived, and trying for language that could reach into her trapped and expanding mind. She had been a librarian. All of the books and conversations about the importance of written words swelling inside her head like a star undergoing gravitational collapse into a black mass, its light still traveling out into space but its fire already burned out. Nothing left but ash. Her heart stopped. I was telling her that it was all right to go, as if I had any permission to grant. She was gone with no more than a small scar hidden in her hair, and all of her life in her head. I wanted to go into the forest and come back out to her years earlier. I wanted to take rings back off of the trees.

Less than a year after my father's ashes had been brought home to my mother, the courier said, pleasantly, that "it was still a little warm" as he handed me the box that contained my mother's "cremains." I carried her through her house touching chairs and countertops for her and feeling, again, her warmth, trying to keep it. I remembered her body cooling days before as I held her hand in the hospital. Finally, I sat in the back of the house, a room built around its windows, designed by my mother, and realized that there was no sound. It had been a long time since I had listened for the silences that can exist in the world. I did not take her outside. I wanted to keep her in her home. To keep the house from being as cold as it was. It had rained hard through the night before, a frozen rain that smacked into the windows on one side of the room. There had been sound. As I sat with the box, the sun was bright through the windows and the ground was dark with moisture. By afternoon, clouds had returned with wind and the landscape outside was gray and brown. The day changed as I looked out. Vibrant with blue skies and winter sunlight on green pines, then subdued with dead grasses, stark branches, and slate-colored clouds. Her body gave up the last of its heat, and the box felt heavier without its warmth. It was cold and winter, and I did not know what to do next. The wind pushed on the house throughout the night and I could not sleep. The world was dark and unsettled. It was about the movement of sky over the land and the ashes in their boxes waiting to join the soils. I remembered, before invading Iraq, that I was told to hope for winds. I remembered carrying the buckets of ash out into the snow. I was not at home, eleven months earlier, when the funeral director brought my father's ashes to my mother, but I remember what she said to me when he did. "Now he truly won't come back to me. I don't know why I thought he could."

IN WHAT IS CALLED the Poolville Rural Cemetery, there are many markers missing near the front, consumed and sunk into the world, broken, carted off. The graves are not missing, just the stones. All the names etched carefully and removed slowly. No one alive to remember them now. Nothing in the ground but bones, wedding rings, and coffin nails. The new coffins are all clad in metal, hermetic, but most of the coffins buried here were pine, nailed closed and left to rot. I went back to Poolville, stood on the bridge over the river, then walked the path around the cemetery. In the rear are all the people I knew when I left town to move to Sherburne. It was sad to see them all here, wives beside their husbands. Their parents often in older rows. Children, sometimes, nearby. They were the older generation that had known the village, its earlier years and its stories, had grown up and grown old here, stayed here still. Even those who had moved away were brought back to be buried. Macgregors, Tackaberrys, Tuttles. I knew these people.

I tried to picture their faces as they had smiled and waved to me in my endless pacing of the town, passing them on my bike with a fishing rod. It was strange how my memory of them was composed. No sharp details, their faces in an odd constant motion, blurred portraits of their spirit and manner. Mrs. Tackaberry and I gutting peas from their pods on the steps of her porch next to her dead son, Cyle. Mr. and Mrs. Tuttle guessing our names as we walked to their door in our Halloween costumes. Mr. Macgregor, rarely seen out of the seat of his riding mower. They were all here, as if they had been killed in 1982 moments after we drove away with our last load of furniture. There were only two couples who were still in the houses I had known them in when I lived here. It was as if a plague had come through, everyone dying in their beds and buried in the cemetery at the edge of the village, their homes falling vacant and then filling again with people who had heard nothing of the tragedy that had left the houses empty.

I had not walked through town once in the three decades since my departure, and all that time collapsed into a short moment, the villagers vanished into this mass grave site. My parents had bought grave plots here when they arrived. At some point after we moved away, they sold them, deciding instead to be cremated. No graves. No gravestones. I have no idea where their space had been reserved, who was buried in their place. I don't know where they would have been laid, the cemetery now almost full, what would have been cut into their stones. My mother would have designed the stone for my father, and I would have had hers carved. What final words would I have placed on them? Perhaps nothing more than names and dates on a stone set on the dirt over the wooden box holding their bones.

The manual pump was missing. We always cranked the cast-metal handle when we walked through the cemetery to fish in the Tackaberrys' pasture beyond. Now, not far from the fence lining the back of the cemetery, was their headstone. A water bucket once sat beneath the spout, and the pump needed a full cup poured into the pipe to prime it. It made a rapid deep breathing sound as we worked the handle, sucking water from below the dead to arrive cold and clear.

In the fall, on the other side of the river, the wrecked cars in Jim Pound's junkyard were visible through the bare trees, the colored leaves and the painted metal all glossy with the cool moisture of a world going to sleep. We didn't come to the graveyard in the winter, and the pump stayed frozen until May. The junkyard had been sold, the cars all towed away, and the pump had been dismantled, a naked pipe left extending from the ground.

➜ ⬅

MY MOTHER HAD TAKEN a handful of my father's ashes to a tidal pool in Maine where they used to sit and watch the water come in. She mixed ash and ocean with her hands, joining his dry body with salt water. Then the tide came in. He is now with the whale and the silt of rivers, missing but not entirely absent. I took my mother there to join him, she told me where, the gray powder forming a falling cloud spreading into the tangle of green strands.

My parents wanted to be poured on the hill above their house and into the sea on the coast of Maine. Together. I promised and went to Great Wass Island to empty the tins at low tide. The ash, like the silt of old breath, fell slowly, as if smoke could sink instead of rise, becoming heavy, the ocean honoring the weight of what had been burned, two lives, coloring the green, restive seaweed with gray. In the push and swirl of water returning, it slipped farther down, settling into the fragments, the crushed shells of living things that had examined this very place, sifting the tidal floor for tragedy. They had all become destroyed like everything else. Shell, bone, and stone all ground down here, unconcerned with damnation or memory. Hundreds of years blended, churned by swells of storm waves and left to diminish continually, but unable to ever be nothing in death.

EPILOGUE

I HAVE SEEN CITIES DESTROYED IN MY LIFE, PEOPLE buried, graves dug up. I have lived outside in the elements. I know that everything is recomposed from preexisting matter, that we are all fragments from earth and life blown apart and gathered up. Pieces of us are from stars and meteors, the ocean, dirt, and the dead. We will not be able to keep these pieces either, our bodies doomed to be given back to the ground. On the hill above Sherburne, the bone ash of my parents is rising in the saplings, alive again, the wind through them making the sound of oceans, their journey down the hill to the stream beginning. On the coast of Maine, they are passing into the shells of snails, the bones of fish and birds, seagulls and eider ducks laughing my mother's voice over the sea as my father makes his way into whales. I have been

presented all the evidence of every particle's part in universal tran-
sience, and I have decided to believe none of it.

I WENT HOME to Sherburne, and the wall that I had built beside
the driveway was in disrepair and widening with collapse. Years
of plows hitting it beneath the snow and the freeze and thaw of
water inside it was sloping its edges and curving its lines. It had
been straight and sharp when I had finished it in middle school,
but it had been dry laid and had nothing more than balance as
mortar. The rocks had been put into a particular order but not
bonded together. They were not indivisible. Its impermanence
disappointed me. I looked at it, trying to remember its construction. It had been twenty-five years, and the stones were all unfamiliar except for one. At the end of the wall, where I had made the
opening to the garden, was the cornerstone that I had dislodged
from the darkness of dirt. The rocks above it had slid, and the
formality of the wall's end had deteriorated, but the cornerstone
maintained its discipline. Its straight edges defined the corner by
which the rest of the falling wall had been measured. It was exactly where I had placed it.

I walked the land. My father had been gone for two years, his
path filled in with the dry stalks of goldenrod, Queen Anne's lace,
and the rotting trunks of quaking aspen that lay across it where
the vanished beavers had felled them.

In the swamp, there were a number of dead trees drowned
when beaver had dammed the stream by stacking wood. The

swamp looked like a land laid waste by flood: blanched branches spilled everywhere like bones trapped in a glassy pool of tar. A pileated woodpecker pounded into the gray wood of the standing trunks, taking pauses but proceeding, cutting through the wrapped layers. It chipped toward sounds within the tree, listening sometimes as if for a word. It opened up the wood with deep oval wounds as if searching for the language between the rings or trying to cut out a cancer. Either way, the tree could not be saved. There is nothing but past in a dead tree.

The tracing of time is never made so clear to me as in the counting of the growth rings on a stump. The years of ample water are thick, the years of drought thin. The wood is harder when conditions have been the worst. It seemed like that with some people, too. But our skin grows and falls off, the rings are lost, and there is no way to easily track our age or how we make it so far. Our mind holds our journey in its folds, invisible.

For years the property had been left largely unguarded, my forts unmanned, and trash had been thrown from passing cars. The beavers had finally been trapped out after doing the most damage, and there were no new sightings. So much had been destroyed that new beavers had found no reason to reoccupy the area. Grass now grew on the wooden islands they built, and geese had settled on them, nesting in the safety of their moated distance from the shore, arranging baskets of grass and feathers for their eggs, never wondering at the occurrence producing the carefully piled sticks, never guessing that the space below their nest was hollow with the strange vacancy of an empty home, its family killed off. I arrived at the pond to the alarm of four pairs of Canada geese, their odd honking and wing flapping keeping me terrestrial, tracing the shoreline, as they paced in the water, alert with suspicion, as if I might enter the flooded world as an equal. I had the look of a predator, and that is what I am.

I can look out at the swamp and these old fields, land long labored over and filling in with nature testing itself against our vigilance. I can pretend that I have never been anywhere else but here. Not in mountains, in deserts, or on oceans. Not in streets angry with cars and bombs or sidewalks awkward with people or alleys reefed with trash. If I am very careful, I can just be here looking at the land that is already not as I remembered it, everything changed despite my never having gone away. Here, my mother is weeding in her garden, my father writing in his workroom, a hatchet in my hand and I have cut nothing with it.

NATURE USUALLY FINDS the point of least resistance. Most things break where they are weak or are attacked where they are vulnerable, but it was not so with either of my parents. They were struck at their points of strength, my father, his heart, and my mother, her mind. They were granted no quarter. My wife said that with the passing of my father, my mother lived for them both. She carried him and kept his presence with us. He was still alive in her head, his stories preserved with hers. Parents are immortal to their children. They are inviolate beings and for the duration of their lives you are awarded the comfort of living under their fierce protection. All of my memories of youth revolved, in some way, around their vigilance. With my mother's death went both of them and came the true end of my childhood. I am, finally, no longer anyone's child. This time comes for us all of course, but like all children, even of my age, I was conditioned by their constancy to believe that they would never be gone. There is, for the first time, no home but that which I make for myself. I have two little girls now, and I am already so sorry to know how it ends. My parents never warned me, and I cannot warn them.

My parents' home is now a museum to my memory of them in it. No one to greet me at the door. No warmth inside. Nothing cooking. Just the things that they had collected in a life together and a history of things that I had given them all preserved within a tomb that holds no remains but what remains. Full of them and empty both. Paintbrushes arranged in a jar by an unfinished watercolor still taped to an easel in my mother's cellar studio. My father will never come in from his workroom to sigh disappointments about the difficulties of his writing or his worries over the unfairness in the world, and my mother will never be there to greet him after a morning in her garden with a pleasant dispatch for his ills. He cannot talk and she cannot listen. Christmas will never have the magic of them waiting for us downstairs in the morning, the smell of coffee coming up, and my father standing out of sight saying "Ho, ho, ho." My mother's daffodils are blooming, but I am an orphan now.

I went back into the house through the kitchen around which their lives had revolved. It was here that they danced to Gerry

Mulligan while they washed the dishes after dinner. All of the pots and plates were there, the cookbooks, and the table with our four chairs. The rooms had the colors my mother had painted them— slates and mosses. It was like a house cut from the earth. I went upstairs to their bedroom. In my father's top drawer were his treasures. There was an old watch—his father's—reading glasses, my Purple Heart medal, some coins from England and France, wallet photographs of my brother and me as children, and, in the corner, covered with a layer of lint, a gray bullet made from a crayon.

I delayed the exploration of my father's workroom for as long as I could. I had only been inside a few times during the twenty-four years they had been there. I opened the door with his key, the worn coin from Morocco still beside it on the ring. It was morning, his writing time, but I could not interrupt him anymore.

Inside lay his dust, the last of him, rubbed off during years of thought and spread thin on his shelves and tables. Beside his desk and planted around the room were lined pads of paper marked with notes. Ideas for stories, pieces of conversations he had heard or imagined, partial sentences, lists. Every tablet had something written on it—except the one on his desk. There was, when I held it close, a slight impression, almost floral, in the paper between the lines. Something had been written, the page torn off. I tried to decipher the trace as if it were of more importance than the notes left in plain sight, struggling to read the last word pressed into the notebook by his pen.

His wastebasket had been emptied, and I didn't see the page in the piles on his desk. I wondered how many books and manuscripts, notes and letters, were macerated, recycled, and flattened into new paper. So much language erased, and new language coated onto the bleached threads. So much burned. In this endless circulation of dead matter, where is the first language? Were all of the first thoughts and last words there? The last impressions stamped into the pulp of trees? I stood in his room, surrounded by his wall of books. It was silent, neither of us talking. For once, no flies in the windows. The room felt truly empty, even with me in it.

Beyond the barn where my father wrote was the old hayfield. He had always wanted to dig a pond between the barn and the field so that he could look out over water. But it had remained a depression filled with brambles. The field was dark green in the gray of spring rain. I carried boxes of books from shelves in the house into the barn. In the late summers, the grasses in the fields stopped growing and began to feel like paper. Tan began descending the stems, and the blades made more sound as the air moved, their words spoken in a hush, language pressed by wind in waves passing over the field and into the trees to the east.

Once, fall had brought the last swaying of grass as tractors circled the fields pulling their spinning blades and cutting close to the ground in swaths. After the harvest, the field was a bald wasteland of chaff and hardened stubble. The mice were exposed to the gyre of hawks, and the sun dried the shadowless ground between the stumps of grasses. Powder from the beaten seed and splintered stems would blow into the air in clouds. I would follow the wagon, throwing bales up onto it. Prickly ends of tightly bound stalks tore at the skin on my hands, cutting into the soft insides of my fingers where I caught the taut twine, pulling and lifting the bales from where they lay in the field. I could feel the thickening of my lungs with their dust, breathing it in but not out. I felt it gather in me like smoke, its death a message to me of mine.

My father's workroom still looked out over the hayfield, though it hadn't been mowed in fifteen years. I looked out his window. Trees were beginning to erode the sharp edges of the rectangle draped over the hill, consuming the fence line. The saplings were just pith and pulp rising again from the space where forest had been cleared. My father never carried a bale of hay, but he had watched it done and, from within his room, could guess at the effort enough to weigh the right words for its description. Beside the window hung a framed poster of Ernest Hemingway. It said: "All you have to do is write one true sentence."

In the house and workroom were all of their books, the distilled collection of a lifetime of reading. I had read almost none of them, but I knew that the placement of these books around my parents had indicated their importance. Many were signed by their authors; some had been carried from their apartments to houses since college or childhood. My father kept a number of old leather-bound books on a shelf in his workroom. He had found them at library sales and had declared them priceless. A fragile copy of *Oliver Twist*, an 1834 pair of the works of Lord Byron, a tattered 1852 first edition of *Uncle Tom's Cabin* that had been rebound in leather and tunneled by insects. Few had titles surviving on their exterior flesh, and they had to be opened to discover their

contents. I hadn't thought of their being wrapped in hide, sometimes printed on vellum or parchment pages made of stretched
skin, inks staining words onto them like tattoos. I had never examined these books in all the years that they had stood in their
row, but as I looked at them now, I noticed that one was not there.
I searched around the room, now mostly covered in sheets I had
brought from their bedroom. I had drawn sheets over both my
father and mother in hospitals, and I felt the urge to cover all their
things—to preserve the moment of their departure as if it were
only sleep. I had not covered my father's desk, and the book was
there. It had been under the pad with the missing note. There was
nothing on the cover and little remaining on the spine. I opened
the book carefully, afraid that it held a last breath, and found it to
be a copy of *Paradise Lost* printed in 1727. I wondered why he had
taken that book down and placed it beside him as he began to type
the novel he would never finish. I turned to the last page of the
twelve books of verse.

In either hand the hast'ning Angel caught
Our lingering Parents; and to th'eastern gate
Led them direct; and down the cliff as fast,
To the subjected plain; then disappeared.
They looking back, all th'eastern side beheld
Of Paradise; so late their happy seat!
Wav'd over by that flaming brand; the gate
With dreadful faces throng'd, and fiery arms.
Some natural tears they drop'd, but wip'd them soon:

> The world was all before them, where to choose
> Their place of rest, and Providence their guide.
> They, hand in hand, with wand'ring steps, and slow,
> Through EDEN took their solitary way.

Outside my father's workroom were wooden closets with shelves for boxed books and personal records. I opened them and was sad to discover their long neglect. Inside were boxes of my father's remaindered books, tax documents, old family photographs, and years of Christmas cards saved by my mother. The bodies of mice, skeletal now from years of lying in their traps, had clouds of fur around them. I began to excavate the crammed shelves. Powdered blue rodent poison, mouse-gathered fiberglass insulation, masticated paper, and the segmented remains of cluster flies fell from every box. Mice had made nests of the chewed corners of letters, books, and maps of the places my parents had been. One shoe box had contained only maps, and mice had gnawed them all into flecks. The nest was speckled with the blue of lakes and oceans, green of forests, gray of cities, and red of roads. The way back destroyed. The mice, like the woodpeckers and the paper mills, had been chewing the sentences back into letters, reducing the archives to the pulp from which they had come, preparing the documents to be dirt again. But on his desk the lost book was there, covered in the skin of its birth, the trees pressed thin and stamped with words inside.

I rubbed a pencil carefully across my father's pad to reveal the words. There was only one word: *Pileated*. I remembered that my father was always forgetting the name of the woodpecker that pounded into the trees in the swamp as he typed.

My father feared both the insignificance of his prose and death. One not more than the other. It is the living task of every artist to suffer the constant premonition of death while drawing plans for immortality. In his first letter to me as a freshman at Vassar, and the first time that he had needed to write me a letter, he wrote of the passing of a friend of his. A writer. His letter ends: "Time gets so precious. Death is a bastard of an enemy. Fuck it, kid. Let's live forever."

ACKNOWLEDGMENTS

I'm grateful for the love and munificent support of my wife, Tracy Susan Nichols Busch, and the laughter of our fantastic daughters, Alexandra Hoefflinger Busch and Kyrah Nichols Burroughs Busch. So wonderful.

Dear friends Harry Roseman and Catherine Murphy. I thank them both for their love, inspiration, wisdom, and art. Perfection.

I wish to thank my agent Elaine Markson, who for over twenty-five years so lovingly carried my father's work into print, Geri Thoma, and Gary Johnson, who gracefully kept me in orbit at the Markson Thoma Literary Agency. Thanks to Jonathan Freedman and Vicki Lawrence at *Michigan Quarterly Review*, and Ben Metcalf at *Harper's*, who deftly delivered my first essays onto pages.

I thank the teachers and staff at the Sherburne-Earlville public schools and Vassar College. I was paying attention.

I salute the Marines and Navy Corpsmen of the Second Battalion, Eighth Marines; of Delta Company, Fourth Light Armored Reconnaissance Battalion; of the Fifth Civil Affairs Group; and of the First Battalion, Fifth Marines, for their profound courage and professionalism. It was my honor to have served with them. Semper fidelis.

I am forever grateful to Ed Burns, David Simon, Nina Noble, Pat Moran, and Alexa Fogel of HBO's *The Wire* and *Generation Kill*, for allowing me to be a small part of their magnificent works of art. My thanks also to friends John and Nancy Romano, and Ray and Helen Hartung in Los Angeles, for supporting my trespasses into Hollywood.

For their love and absolute belief in me, I am indebted to Patricia, Jeff, Sasha, and Tara Kramer, and Dan and Ellen Silver. Dear friends.

For their great friendship and generous encouragement, it is a pleasure to thank Richard, Carole, Randy, and Michelle Boice; Dave and Donna Avery; Melissa Reider; Dr. Seiji Hayashi and Dr. Joan Myles; Partha Mazumdar; John Murray; Doug Bell; John Trotta; Dr. Alex and Monica Kladakis; Norma, Jeremy, Richard, and Robin Allnutt; Jim and Sharla Desy; John and Tonia Schafer; Domenick Lombardozzi; Joe McManus and Lara Elin; Benji and Mandy Rogers; Wes Muller; Ryan Sands; Doug and Anne Stanton; Ward Just; Paul Nelson; Donald Anderson; Sara Corbett; John Mauk; Tim Bazzett; and Adrienne Rush. Thanks also to Neill, Mary, Edmund, and Teo Joy; Travis and Beth Dubois; and Dana Petersen from my home town. All roads lead back to Poolville.

Love to all Hosbachs, Connells, Burroughs, Hoefflingers, Nichols, and my brother, Nick.

I am grateful to Daniel Halpern and the staff at Ecco for believing in this book and for wrapping it so well.

It is with respect beyond measure that I thank my editor, Matt Weiland, who found this book in pieces, championed it, and brilliantly advised its final craft.

In memory of my parents
Frederick Matthew Busch
1941–2006
Judith Ann Burroughs Busch
1941–2007